Praise for *No One Works Here*

"In the age of AI, staying at the forefront of business innovation means reexamining every aspect of the modern corporation and rethinking legacy limitations. The most impactful companies of the future will be those that put technology to work removing friction and strengthening growth in an always-on global economy. In *No One Works Here*, Paul Cheek provides a new 'AIDE' model of enterprise that combines global ambition with a lean, software-driven footprint. This book is both a provocative read and a tactical guide to building the high-velocity infrastructure required to navigate the complexities of tomorrow."

—**Michael Miebach**
CEO, **MASTERCARD**

"Having pioneered cloud AI and now leading Microsoft's Agentic AI development, I see the fundamental unit of the organization shifting from a person to a node. Paul Cheek brilliantly captures this move beyond passive tools into an era of autonomous agents that function as high-velocity components of the firm. *No One Works Here* provides the rigorous framework needed to replace human-centric latency with software-centric intent. It is the essential guide for leaders ready to architect systems that never sleep, never wait, and never hesitate."

—**Yu-Ting Kuo**
Former Corporate Vice President of AI, **MICROSOFT**

"For most of human history, most people never got the chance to build something—a business, a product, an idea, that could change their life or someone else's. Not because they lacked the drive. Because the barriers were always too high. AI is changing that. In *No One Works Here*, Paul Cheek maps out how this moment could open entrepreneurship to more people than ever before, making this not just the age of AI, but the age of innovation from all, for all."

—**Aneesh Raman**
Chief Economic Opportunity Officer, **LINKEDIN**
Coauthor of *The New York Times* Bestseller *Open to Work*

"The road map for scaling human potential alongside AI. An absolute necessity for any leader building a high-performance culture in the age of intelligence."

—Mary-Alice Vuicic
Former Chief Human Resources Officer,
THOMSON REUTERS

"Paul has identified a fundamental shift in the very nature of the firm. At MIT, we focus on what is possible with the intent of advancing human progress; in these pages, Paul reveals what is now inevitable. *No One Works Here* is the essential blueprint for the next generation of leaders who must navigate the transition from human-centric to intelligence-centric growth."

—Mark Gorenberg
Chair, **MASSACHUSETTS INSTITUTE OF TECHNOLOGY**
Managing Director, **ZETTA VENTURE PARTNERS**

"As a human who loves my own work and many other working humans, this fascinating book makes me nervous. But it's very important for humans to read it and prepare for a very different occupational future. And if you're an aspiring entrepreneur, it's essential."

—Thomas H. Davenport
Wall Street Journal Bestselling Author of *All In on AI*
Distinguished Professor, **BABSON COLLEGE**
Faculty Director, **METROPOULOS INSTITUTE FOR TECHNOLOGY AND ENTREPRENEURSHIP**
Fellow, **MIT INITIATIVE ON THE DIGITAL ECONOMY** and **STANFORD INSTITUTE FOR HUMAN-CENTERED AI**

"The true challenge of the coming decade isn't just the deployment of AI—it's the architecture of the organizations that will use it. This book provides a visionary yet deeply practical framework for leaders who refuse to choose between technological advancement and human potential. It is an essential guide for anyone looking to redesign their workforce for a future where AI serves as the ultimate force multiplier for human ingenuity. A must-read for those ready to lead the next era of organizational evolution."

—Jennifer Carpenter
Global Head of Talent, **ANALOG DEVICES**

"We are witnessing a radical shift in the physics of business: the decoupling of revenue growth from headcount growth. Paul Cheek's AIDE model perfectly captures how 'Day Zero' founders can now hit $100M ARR with a team of twelve rather than a team of hundreds. This book is the essential manual for the new era of ultra-lean, hyper-scale capital efficiency. For any founder or investor, *No One Works Here* reveals how to use AI as the ultimate leverage to disrupt established giants."

—Gaurav Jain
Co-Founder & Managing Partner, **AFORE CAPITAL**

"There is perhaps no more important a question facing humankind than what will happen at the intersection of 'talent decisions' and 'AI.' Paul Cheek lays out an original and useful model for equipping our organizations for what comes next."

—Dr. Geoff Smart
Founder and Chairman of **ghSMART**
New York Times Bestselling Author of *Who*

NO ONE WORKS HERE

FOREWORD BY HENRY FORD III

NO ONE WORKS HERE

HOW AI-DRIVEN ENTERPRISES ARE RAISING THE BAR FOR BUSINESS, LEADERSHIP, AND COMPETITION

PAUL CHEEK
MASSACHUSETTS INSTITUTE OF TECHNOLOGY

WILEY

Published by John Wiley & Sons, Inc., Hoboken, New Jersey.

For general information on our other products and services or for technical support, please contact our Customer Care Department within the United States at (800) 762-2974, outside the United States at (317) 572-3993 or fax (317) 572-4002.

Wiley also publishes its books in a variety of electronic formats. Some content that appears in print may not be available in electronic formats. For more information about Wiley products, visit our web site at www.wiley.com.

Library of Congress Cataloging-in-Publication Data is Available:

ISBN: 9781394435418 (Cloth)
ISBN: 9781394435425 (ePub)
ISBN: 9781394435432 (ePDF)

Cover Design and Image: Wiley
Author Photo: Brian Tortora

Printed and bound by CPI Group (UK) Ltd, Croydon, CR0 4YY

C9781394435418_060726

To my wife, Callie, and our three daughters, Kyla (2.5 years), Cora (18 months), and Marley (3 months) . . .

Callie, this book is titled No One Works Here, *which is a bold claim about the future of the global economy, but a terrible description of our house. While I was busy writing about "The End of Human Time," you were busy managing the very real, high-latency chaos of raising three humans. Thank you for doing the actual work so I could write about how nobody does it anymore.*

Kyla, Cora, and Marley, I spent 300 pages arguing that humans are becoming (nearly) obsolete in the workforce. Thank you for proving every single day that we are still indispensable in the things that actually matter. You are the signal in the noise.

Contents

Foreword

By Henry Ford III, Member of the Board of Directors, Ford Motor Company

My family's legacy is often defined by the moving assembly line, an innovation that famously reduced the production time of a Model T from 12 hours to 93 minutes in 1913. But from what I see today, the next great leap in industrial efficiency will not come from speeding up conveyor belts; it will come from speeding up decisions.

In governing a company the size of Ford, the challenge we face is no longer just about the physics of manufacturing; it is about the "physics of business" that Paul dissects so keenly in these pages. All companies constantly grapple with what Paul calls the "latency problem." In all human-centric organizations, latency is baked into the system: We deliberate, we schedule meetings, and we build consensus. This friction slows down organizations to the speed of biological processing power, rather than the speed of software.

I have come to appreciate Paul's unique vantage point as a "hacker" looking at corporate structures. He doesn't just see inefficiencies; he sees code that needs to be refactored. When he argues that we are witnessing the end of "Human Time" as the metronome of the global economy, he isn't speaking in hyperbole; he is describing the reality that all established companies must confront to survive.

My perspective on this shift is informed not only by my work at Ford, but also through my work with dozens of other companies across the country. I believe that new external viewpoints are essential to help me guide and support the leaders and companies I serve with an increased ability to constructively critique our strengths and weaknesses. This book reinforces my belief that for businesses to thrive, its leaders must step back from the "work" of execution to focus on the architecture of intent. By seeking out the "magic" that happens when we align our systems with our customers' needs, we can ensure that business remains in a position of great strength for all stakeholders. Paul's work provides a framework for this objective critique, helping us distinguish between the legacy habits that anchor us and the intelligent systems that will propel us forward.

Crucially, Paul dismantles the misconception that the "AI-Driven Enterprise" is a model reserved for Silicon Valley software startups. He demonstrates that this is a universal evolution, applicable to every sector, from aerospace to healthcare to automotive. At Ford, I see clearly how these concepts must be applied to our reality. We are not just moving metal; we are orchestrating complex systems of logic and logistics. The principles in this book are not just for digital natives; they are the key to unlocking a new level of performance for all companies. Paul shows us that applying this intelligence-centric approach is critical for any company to operate with the agility of a startup.

The companies that thrive in the coming years will be those that listen to Paul's counsel and transition their leadership style. We must move from being "captains" who direct tasks to "architects" who design systems. In my work, this means shifting our focus from merely managing execution to governing the intent of the intelligent systems we deploy.

No One Works Here is not a book of futurist speculation; it is a tactical playbook for leaders. Paul provides the blueprint for how established organizations can shed the "innovation debt" of the past and rebuild themselves around a new center of gravity: intelligence, both human and artificial.

Ultimately, our responsibility is to the prosperity of the men and women who build the economic engine of this country. We are not just automating tasks; we are redesigning the architecture of the firm to ensure that every single employee has the infrastructure they need to succeed, rather than be left behind by the speed of the market. Paul has written the manual for that redesign. This book is required reading for every leader in business today. It challenges us to stop fearing the disruption of our industries and start engineering a future where our people can thrive.

—Henry

Preface

Welcome. You're here just in time!

As a serial entrepreneur and senior lecturer of entrepreneurship and artificial intelligence at MIT, I come from a vantage point of not only building the technology, but I also architect and decompile the frameworks that the world's most influential leaders use to survive it.

From my early days as a software engineer, to becoming MIT's first "Hacker in Residence," to teaching thousands of founders and executives across the globe, to advising leaders of the world's most respected organizations, I have always looked at business through the lens of a hacker. I look for the "code" beneath the culture. I have developed a proprietary framework for viewing the "physics of business." I see through the cultural veneer of the modern corporation to the logic underneath. What I see: The 20th-century organizational model is no longer just inefficient; it is biologically incapable of competing in the era of machine agency.

I've been looking for the inefficiencies that everyone else has accepted as the cost of doing business. And right now, the modern corporation is the most inefficient codebase in existence. While others are using AI to write faster emails, the leaders I work with are using it to rewrite the very DNA of how value is created.

There was a specific moment when it hit me: I was in Athens, Greece, in October 2024. Without cell phone service due to an outage, and eating lunch earlier than is customary in Greece, I was left alone with my thoughts in a nearly empty restaurant. Contemplating the most thought-provoking topic for a keynote I was to give the following day, I realized that the AI technology that was advancing rapidly had the potential to create new companies more quickly than we can.

The manuscript for the book you're reading has been reviewed by hundreds of people already to be refined to the point where it is today. I'm so glad you've joined this community and I can't wait to see what you do and the impact you have with the AI-Driven Enterprise model you'll learn about throughout this book.

You might be thinking that you're late to the party given that hundreds of people are already "here," but the fact that you've realized the physics of business are shifting faster than they ever have before and you've picked up this book now means you're just in time.

Let's be clear about what this book is not. It is not a manual for corporate downsizing or a guide to replacing human ingenuity with cold silicon. I am fundamentally against the "efficiency-first" mindset that views people as line-item expenses to be trimmed.

My goal isn't to help you do the same things with fewer people; it's to use Machine Agency to strip away the administrative decay, allowing your people to operate at their highest level of creative and strategic impact. We aren't cutting costs; we are unleashing dormant capacity.

I am a firm believer that AI will supercharge the impact that we as humans have. I feel compelled to call out that my intent for this book is to reorient our thinking—not about replacing people with AI, but rather elevating the impact that they can have by empowering them with AI. I am not here to tell you that AI solves every problem. As we look at what AI changes and what AI doesn't change, you'll see just how important I believe we all are in society to drive large-scale positive impact. I am here to provide the blueprint for the most resilient, scalable, and competitive organization of the next decade.

You might not agree with everything in this book, but I urge you to take it seriously. If you have thoughts or feedback, please send them my way!

The most successful organizations I work with don't treat this book as a personal study; they treat it as a common language. Find someone or a group to read this book with so that you can build that shared language and understanding of where the enterprise of the future is going. I highly recommend reading this book alongside friends and colleagues. The discussion questions included at the end are sure to spark (healthy) debate. You can also grab pre-reading videos for your group and thought-provoking discussion questions for each chapter on the book website at NoOneWorksHere.com. Want a personalized intro video for your group of readers? Email me and I'll make it happen. . .

Consider yourself a collaborator, not a passive observer. If you have thoughts, feedback, or a story of your own, I want to hear it.

You can reach me directly at pcheek@paulcheek.com.

Let's get to the intro. *We have a lot of "work" to do!*

—Paul

Introduction: The End of Human Time

Welcome to your new blueprint for organizational design.

This book is about the future of "work." It is an architectural guide for rebuilding your company (or building a new company, or supporting economic development through entrepreneurship) around a new center of gravity: intelligence. It is about the physics of business, latency, cost structures, and leverage.

FOR CENTURIES, THE speed at which an organization could move was dictated by biology. We sleep. We eat. We get sick. We burn out.

In a traditional company, productivity is inextricably linked to human stamina and the friction of human coordination. While some of this is healthy friction in human interpersonal interactions—which sparks healthy debate, dialogue, and leads to creativity—we must also recognize it as a bottleneck in many cases. We gather data, hold a meeting, deliberate, plan, and eventually execute. When you send an email to a colleague, you enter a holding pattern. When you schedule a meeting, you lose days finding a slot where everyone is free. This is the "speed of business" we have accepted as normal.

But that normal is changing, and it's happening *rapidly*. The pace is unprecedented, radically uncomfortable, yet capable of being both exhilaratingly productive and simultaneously dangerous.

The way every entrepreneur built their last company will be drastically different from how they build their next. We are navigating one of the most rapid and profound shifts in business architecture ever seen within a single generation. In fact, if you're not careful, steadfast belief in principles that produced past success can be a direct cause of future failure.

Let me be clear: The playbooks you have used to build your career and your company are not wrong. They are proven. They have generated trillions of dollars in value and built the foundations of the modern economy. I have deep respect for the discipline and rigor it took to build those systems. I am not asking you to burn down what you have built or to abandon the wisdom of experience. However, those playbooks were optimized for a specific set of constraints: biological ones. Now that the constraints have changed, the optimization must change too. It's not that legacy organizations haven't thought about scale; it's that scale has never been achievable in the ways that it is today. I want you to be successful in the AI era not by forgetting the past, but by reorganizing our organizations around AI rather than retrofitting them with AI.

We are entering a new era where the fundamental unit within an organization is no longer exclusively a human being. It is a node, which may or may not be a human being. Some nodes may be human beings complemented by others that are AI agents. And unlike human beings, digital nodes do not sleep. They do not need motivation. They do not wait. Much more on this to come as you continue exploring in this book . . .

When I teach leaders to deploy these agents, or digital nodes, I am not teaching them to save time; I am teaching them to achieve "Zero Latency," a leg up that I believe to be the greatest competitive advantage in history.

This shift marks the end of "Human Time" as the metronome of the global economy.

In the following pages of this introduction, you will receive a briefing on the rise of the AI-Driven Enterprise (AIDE, pronounced A-I-D-E), separate AI hype from hard truth, and lay out the exact structural roadmap we will use to refactor your organization, laying the groundwork for the deep dives we will take into each of these concepts throughout the book. I am giving you the vocabulary right now, but I am going to give you the actual execution manual in the chapters ahead.

Introducing the AI-Driven Enterprise (AIDE)

At MIT, we have historically taught that entrepreneurship falls into two distinct categories, and my faculty colleagues Bill Aulet and Fiona Murray published their research on these two models, which has now been widely used in the field of entrepreneurship (Aulet and Murray 2024). They explain that on one side are Small and Medium Enterprises (SMEs), the local restaurants or service firms that grow linearly, require limited upfront capital, and serve a local market. On the other are Innovation-Driven Enterprises (IDEs), the high-growth tech companies like Google or Uber that target global markets, fueled by significant capital and massive R&D.

For decades, the path seemed binary: stay small and profitable, or go big and scale globally. However, this framework misses a dangerous middle ground that I see all too often. Many founders find themselves trapped in a "growth purgatory" of startups that possess the DNA of an IDE but the execution of an SME.

That binary is gone, however. We are witnessing the rise of a third category: the AI-Driven Enterprise. An AIDE combines the global ambition and disruptive power of an IDE with the lean operational footprint of an SME. It's the best of both worlds. By leveraging AI tools and intelligent agents to handle functions ranging from code generation to customer support, these companies decouple revenue growth from headcount growth. They do not need an army of employees to scale; they need AI-literate humans paired with a fleet of agents.

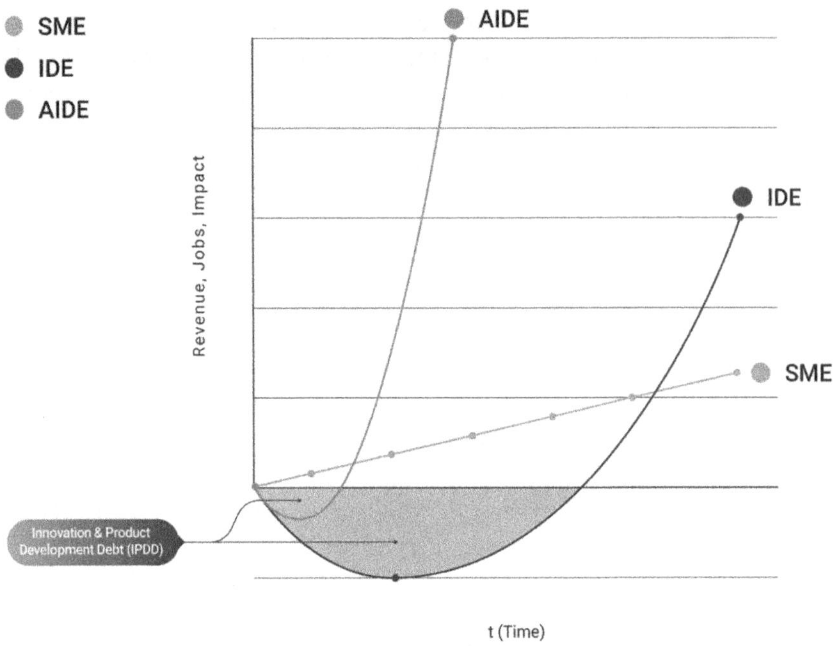

Download this graph and other resources on the AI-Driven Enterprise model: http://NoOneWorksHere.com/downloads/graphs

We'll look at examples of the AIDEs throughout the book, but to be clear, AIDEs are not exclusively AI companies. Any company (including yours!) can be an AIDE by leveraging AI in every functional area across the business.

In the coming decade, any organization looking to scale and remain globally competitive must learn to operate as an AI-augmented enterprise. Consulting firms, aerospace engineering companies, global pharmaceutical companies, hotel chains, widget manufacturers, staffing firms, intelligence agencies, and more: SMBs, tech startups, conglomerates; B2B, B2C, B2G; publicly traded, privately held, private equity backed, venture-capital funded—you name it. I've taught and advised executives from all of these types of companies, and I know that many (though not all) are underestimating the impact that AI will have on their businesses.

One example of how this manifests is the focus many executives and firms have on using AI to automate processes, which is important but misses the bigger picture. The bigger picture requires that they open the aperture to consider the impact that AI is having on our collective fundamental understanding of organizational design. Many executives believe that this impact will take time, and it will, but the reality they're missing is that this shift is happening faster than any in the history of the marketplace.

What "No One Works Here" Means

The title of this book is a provocation, but it is also a literal description of the AI-Driven Enterprise.

But let me be precise about my terms. When I say *No One Works Here*, I do not mean *No One Matters Here*. I mean no one *labors* here.

In the "human time" era, "work" was defined by execution. You were paid to *do* the thing: write the email, crunch the spreadsheet, or move the ticket through the system.

In the world we're building, "work" is defined by intent. The goal is to reduce labor so that humans can focus on intent.

When I say *No One Works Here*, I am describing a shift where humans no longer act as the gears within the machine. Instead, we are the architects. We set the parameters, define the goals, and provide the ethical and strategic guardrails. The "work" of execution is delegated to a fleet of autonomous nodes that don't suffer from biological latency.

As Dharmesh Shah, co-founder and CTO of HubSpot, puts it, "I don't build AI agents to make people unnecessary. I build them to make people unstoppable" (Shah 2025). This book will show you how to move your team from being the operators of the machine to the programmers of the outcome. We aren't making people obsolete; we're making "busy work" obsolete.

The Hype Versus the Hard Truth

Before we go further, let's get one thing straight: AI is not a magic wand. If you've picked up this book expecting a manifesto on how silicon will solve world hunger or fix your broken corporate culture overnight, you're in the wrong place. Despite what the marketers and the "AI-vangelists" prognosticate, we are not living in a world of digital deities. We are living in a world of increasingly sophisticated tools and technology.

My claims in the chapters ahead are bold, but they are grounded in the reality of what is possible *today*, not a distant sci-fi future. If you're worried about whether AI is actually intelligent or will sometimes give you imperfect outputs, you're missing the point. We will explore the friction, the limitations, and the specific areas where AI will fail, sometimes spectacularly. I'm not here to tell you that AI solves every problem; I'm here to show you how to redesign your organization, build a new organization, or expand your region's economic impact by supporting local entrepreneurs so that you only solve the problems that actually matter.

What This Book Is (and What It Isn't)

The shelves, and the internet, are currently flooded with books on artificial intelligence. Before you commit your time to reading this one, I want to be very clear about where it fits in the landscape.

This is not a book of sci-fi predictions. I am not here to speculate on when artificial general intelligence (AGI) will achieve consciousness, or if robots will one day vote. There are futurists who handle that well. This book is grounded in the reality of what is deployable *today* and what is inevitable in the next 5–10 years based on current trajectories.

This is not a technical manual for engineers. I will not teach you how to back-propagate a neural network or fine-tune a model using Python. You can hire agents to do that. This book is for the *architect* of the business, not the mechanic of the model.

This is not a "Prompt Engineering" cheat sheet. Tricks for writing better prompts change every time a model gets updated. Relying on "hacks" is a short-term strategy.

This book *is* a blueprint for organizational design. It's about the future of "work." It is an architectural guide for rebuilding your company (or building a new company, or supporting economic development through entrepreneurship) around a new center of gravity: intelligence.

Nobody knows exactly how this technology will evolve. If the technology trajectory is different than we perceive it to be, then the underlying concepts of this book are still the same. This book is written for the leader who realizes that simply adding AI tools to an outdated org chart is like putting a Ferrari engine in a horse-drawn carriage. It will tear the carriage apart.

The Promise of This Book

By applying the frameworks in this book, you will move beyond a superficial understanding of AI. You will gain the architectural blueprint needed to lead through it, shifting your posture from reacting to disruption to actively engineering your organization's future.

By the final page, you will be equipped to:

- **Diagnose Your Latency:** You will see the invisible friction in your current workflows that is costing you speed and money.
- **Deploy the AIDE Model:** You will understand how to transition to a compute-heavy organization, regardless of which industry you operate within.
- **Shift Your Leadership Style:** You will move from being a "captain" who directs tasks to an "architect" who designs systems.
- **Separate Hype from Utility:** You will have a clear mental filter to distinguish between "AI toys" and "AI infrastructure."
- **Execute at Speed:** You will have the tactical steps to build, test, and scale ideas in days, not months. These tests will go to production, not remain in POC (proof-of-concept) land.

How This Book Is Structured

Most business books on AI are either too technical or too abstract. This book is different. This is a tactical playbook, written for the leader who understands that the rules of the game have changed and needs a manual for the new sport.

We are going to treat your organization like a product. We will break it down, refactor the code, and redeploy it.

Here's what you can expect:

- **Part I: The Threat.** We expose the fatal cost of operating on "Human Time." You will see why structural latency and the "headcount trap" are pushing legacy organizations toward unprecedented collapse.

- **Part II: The Changing Landscape.** We redefine the organization, shifting from human hierarchies to dynamic networks of human and silicon nodes. You will learn why leadership must evolve from manual execution to architecting intent.
- **Part III: The Opportunities.** Pivoting to offense, we deconstruct the AI-Driven Enterprise (AIDE) model. You will discover how leaders are collapsing timelines and decoupling revenue growth from headcount to achieve exponential scale.
- **Part IV: The Actions.** We move from insight to implementation, providing a tactical roadmap to refactor your operations.

Near the end, I'll leave you with a letter for your C-suite and ask for your signature indicating your commitment to the "Architect's Manifesto."

How to Read This Book (Your Personalized Architecture)

Because the AIDE model applies to both legacy enterprises and dorm-room startups, this book speaks to both. To get the most out of it, read strategically based on your current role:

- **For the Enterprise Leader or Board Member:** Your primary battle is structural latency and "innovation debt." Pay special attention to Part I, which dismantles the legacy corporate scorecard.
- **For the Founder or Operator:** You are building the "One-Person Unicorn." You will likely feel the most momentum in the chapters on agentic workflows and distribution.
- **For the Investor (VCs and PE Partners):** Your focus is identifying which companies are "bloatware" and which are true AIDEs. Focus heavily on the new metrics that matter, like ARR/FTE and "Silicon Payroll."

The Golden Rule for This Book: If a chapter feels like it's moving too fast (into pure software automation) or too slow (into 12-year physical supply chains), recognize that it is a window into a different sector's reality. Take the core principles, adapt them to your constraints, and keep moving.

Refactoring Your Reality: The AIDE Resource Stack

At the end of every chapter, I will leave you with a variety of tactical resources available on the book's website, including an AI Transformation Playbook, workbooks, online courses, videos, AI prompts, tool discounts, and even some purpose-built AI tools. My goal is to ensure that once you finish a section, you have the immediate capacity to put these frameworks into practice. We cannot afford for you to return to doing business the way you did before. This book is a blueprint, but these resources you'll get online are the tools you'll use to actually build the structure.

A Note on Urgency

Organizations are about the speed of learning, and in the modern era of AI and business this is reinforced by computer scientist Yann LeCun, who highlights for us that "Intelligence really is about learning" (Heikkilä 2026).

In the age of AI, the cost of experimentation has dropped dramatically. While the cost of designing the experiment to run hasn't, your competitors—whether they're two students in a garage in Cambridge, Massachusetts, or a massive conglomerate in London—are running thousands of experiments while you're still scheduling the kick-off meeting.

This is the new reality: Disruption does not knock on the door and ask for permission. It quietly unscrews the hinges. You don't have years to "wait and see." The clock isn't ticking; the gears are already shifting.

The technology to replace the manual labor of your marketing department or sales funnel exists right now; it simply awaits an architect. The only thing missing is the leadership to architect and implement it.

You do not have time to wait. It is time to stop working in your business, so you can start programming it.

Let's get to "work."

PART I

The Threat

Why Most Organizations Won't Survive the Age of Intelligent Systems
Organizations that continue to rely on human latency for routine, operational decisions are operating on borrowed time.

THE HALF-LIFE OF a modern corporation is shrinking, and the first signs of collapse rarely appear in balance sheets. They appear in decision speed, in hiring delays, and in meetings that solve nothing while competitors move ahead at the speed of code. Most legacy organizations are not failing because they lack data, resources, or ambition. They are failing because they still operate on "human time."

You are probably moving too slowly right now. Not because your people aren't working hard, but because your organizational chart is fundamentally designed to resist speed. To understand how to build the AI-Driven Enterprise, we first have to look at the invisible friction and the outdated mathematics that are currently tearing your company apart.

In this section, we will dismantle the two existential threats facing every established enterprise:

1. **The Physics of Business:** How biological bottlenecks and structural debt have become fatal liabilities in the era of machine speed
2. **The Economics of Scale:** Why the traditional "headcount trap" is destroying margins, and how the new arithmetic of growth values computational efficiency over human armies

AI has compressed the cycle of strategy, execution, and iteration from quarters to hours, even minutes. The companies that thrive now are those that delegate cognitive work to intelligent systems, not committees, fundamentally decoupling their revenue growth from their headcount.

Before we can rebuild your organization, you must first face the brutal reality of why your current structure is biologically and financially incapable of sustainable growth in an AI-driven marketplace.

1

Turning the Latency Challenge into Opportunity

What is the true cost of human and organizational latency?

The greatest threat to an established enterprise is not a lack of capital, but the invisible friction of latency. Most organizations won't survive the age of intelligent systems. Will yours?

I AM NOT prone to hyperbole. In the academic world, we are trained to be skeptical of the "next big thing" which we lovingly refer to as "shiny objects." We have seen crypto, VR, and the metaverse promised as revolutions, only to become niche applications.

But AI is different. AI represents the most significant transformation in business since the Industrial Revolution. It's a step change in the scalability of organizations.

In this chapter, you will:

- **Understand the Historical Parallel:** How AI mechanizes cognition just as the steam engine mechanized physical labor

- **Differentiate AI from the Internet:** Why "Agency" is more powerful than "Access," and why this recursive revolution is moving at the speed of code
- **Identify the Latency Root:** Recognize why operating on "Human Time" is no longer an option, rather than just blaming a lack of technology or capital
- **Audit Your Latency Stack:** Uncover the eight distinct levels of administrative and biological friction slowing you down
- **Navigate the Reliability Tax:** Push through the Latency J-Curve required to move your team from a human bottleneck to trust-based autonomy
- **Differentiate Technical and Structural Debt:** Understand why your century-old organizational design is now a fatal liability in the era of System Time

The Mechanization of Cognition

To understand where we're going, we have to look at where we came from. Before the Industrial Revolution, the limit on production was biology. If you wanted to move a rock, you needed a muscle. If you wanted to move a bigger rock, you needed more muscles (or a horse). The correlation between effort and output was linear.

The steam engine broke that link. Suddenly, a machine could do the work of a hundred horses. It didn't just make people stronger; it made physical strength irrelevant as a limiting factor.

AI is doing to the brain what the steam engine did to the muscle.

For the entirety of human history, "cognition" was a biological constraint. If you wanted to solve a complex math problem, you needed a human brain. If you wanted to write a contract, you needed a human lawyer. If you wanted to write code, you needed a human engineer.

AI mechanizes cognition. It enables machines not only to execute commands but to think, reason, and collaborate.

I was struck by how Aneesh Raman, chief economic opportunity officer at LinkedIn, thinks about AI in the context of history after sharing the stage with him at the US Chamber of Commerce in Washington, DC, on a misty evening in September 2025. In reflecting on the Industrial Age, Aneesh shares his extremely elegant vantage point:

> "Suddenly work for humans became about efficiency above all else. Most of us, in one way or another, started spending our days helping machines and technology do more better faster. Day after day. Week after week. Year after year. On assembly lines in factories. On laptops in offices. Here's the thing. Efficiency isn't what our brain is best at. Doing more, better, faster with machines isn't human potential at its fullest. . . . Compress 40,000 years into a single year. The Industrial Age arrives around December 29th. The internet arrives on December 31st. AI is the last few minutes before midnight." (Raman 2026)

While countless innovations have emerged over the past century, from the assembly line to the internet, none rival the scale or depth of change we are witnessing right now. Aneesh has so many thoughts on this topic and you can (and should) explore them more deeply in his book *Open to Work.*

Now that the marginal cost of *intelligence* is dropping to near zero, we are going to build entirely new categories of organizations.

The Velocity of Change

There is one major difference between the Industrial Revolution and the AI Revolution: speed. The Industrial Revolution took about 80 years to fully reshape society. It moved at the speed of physical infrastructure.

At the January 2026 WEF annual meeting in Davos, Jamie Dimon said that AI is "changing rapidly." Dimon continued, "I still think it's the tip of the iceberg. I think this one [AI] is faster, is massive. Feels like the internet or electricity. This [AI] is not going to roll out over 20 years. It's more parabolic for now." (Dimon and Minton Beddoes 2026).

The AI Revolution is moving at the speed of code. ChatGPT reached 100 million users in two months (Satterthwaite 2023). New AI models are rendering old ones obsolete every six months. We are compressing decades of structural change into years.

While the speed of adoption is staggering, there is a deeper, more structural reason for this velocity: AI is the first technology in human history that is actively reinventing itself. In late 2025, the OpenAI Codex team released a technical report that signaled the end of the traditional development cycle: "GPT-5.3-Codex is our first model that was instrumental in creating itself. The Codex team used early versions to debug its own training, manage its own deployment, and diagnose test results and evaluations, our team was blown away by how much Codex was able to accelerate its own development" (OpenAI 2026).

When the tool becomes its own engineer, the rate of progress is no longer limited by human cognitive bandwidth or the 40-hour work week. It is limited only by compute and electricity.

In compressing decades of structural change into years, this technology creates a "whiplash effect" for legacy organizations. You do not have 80 years to adapt. You might not even have 80 weeks. That means each day you delay your competitors are getting a massive head start.

Why AI Is Different from the Internet

The most common mistake I see leaders make is treating AI like "internet 2.0." They think: "Okay, we adopted the web, we adopted mobile, now we adopt AI. It's just another channel." This is fundamentally wrong.

The Internet = Access: The internet connected nodes. It removed the friction of distance. In the internet age, efficiency still relied on human cognition. You had to do the searching, the filtering, and the deciding.

AI = Agency: AI introduces intelligence. You don't call an agent, and you don't click buttons. You tell an agent: "Get me to London for under $600." The agent does the searching, filtering, and deciding.

The internet made it easier to find information. AI makes it possible to act on it.

Internet Era: Companies built UIs for humans to use.

AI Era: Companies build APIs for agents to use.

The Latency Challenge

In my work at MIT, teaching thousands of entrepreneurs and studying the data at the AI-Driven Enterprise (AIDE) Institute, I have evaluated the "structural delta" between teams of 12 and teams of 1,200. Through that evaluation, I have identified what I believe to be the single biggest threat to established companies. It is not lack of capital. It is not lack of brand awareness.

It is **latency**.

Now, for the first time, software latency is lower than human latency, which is a significant leap.

In present day, you'll find job posts from established organizations that, within the list of responsibilities for the role, reference "scheduling meetings" and "taking meeting notes," both of which were easily handled by off-the-shelf AI tools in 2025. If you've ever had a meeting with me, you'd know that Howie schedules my meetings and the Granola AI app takes my notes. In case you were wondering who that guy was who emailed you about my availability, Howie is, in fact, an AI agent. Reflecting on my reality and the job description I stumbled upon, I worry for that organization's longevity.

This creates a profound, almost jarring dichotomy in our current workforce. We are living in a split-screen reality. On one side, there is the "AI-enabled elite," moving at the speed of light, unburdened by the administrative friction of the 20th century. On the other, there are millions of capable, hard-working professionals still operating in the "note-taking world," trying to build careers on ground that is visibly liquefying beneath them.

It is an uncomfortable moment to witness. It's the executive who views an AI agent as a competitive advantage versus the employee who views that same agent as a replacement for their paycheck. When I see that job description, I don't just worry about that organization's longevity; I feel the weight of the gap between where we are and where we're going. It isn't just about inefficiency anymore. It's about the widening chasm between those who use the tools to transcend the mundane and those who are still being paid to perform it.

The Refined Organizational Design Latency Stack

Latency has long been a critical component of organizational design, but I look at it a little bit differently—from my early career as a software engineer and entrepreneur. When we build systems, we obsess over *latency*, the delay between an input and a response.

When you strip down an organization, it is essentially a network of biological computers (human brains) trying to process information, coordinate, and make decisions. Because humans have inherent biological latencies, it takes time for us to read, comprehend, synthesize, decide, and communicate. Organizational designers have to build structures that accommodate, bypass, or optimize these physical limits. To understand the threat this poses to established companies, we must break down the friction slowing you down.

In a human-centric organization, latency is baked into the system. Building upon the common organizational design forms of latency, I suggest building what I call a Multi-Layered Latency Stack for the AIDE era that includes forms of latency from:

- Organizational design
- Systems engineering
- Data architecture
- Operations management
- Human-computer interaction

A standard concept adapted from systems engineering, this Multi-Layered Latency Stack is an application to organizational design inspired by Daniel Linder, who provided invaluable feedback as a pre-reader of this book. When we look closely at human-centric organizations, this stack reveals eight distinct layers of organizational drag, building from the structural limits of the enterprise up to the physical limits of the individual:

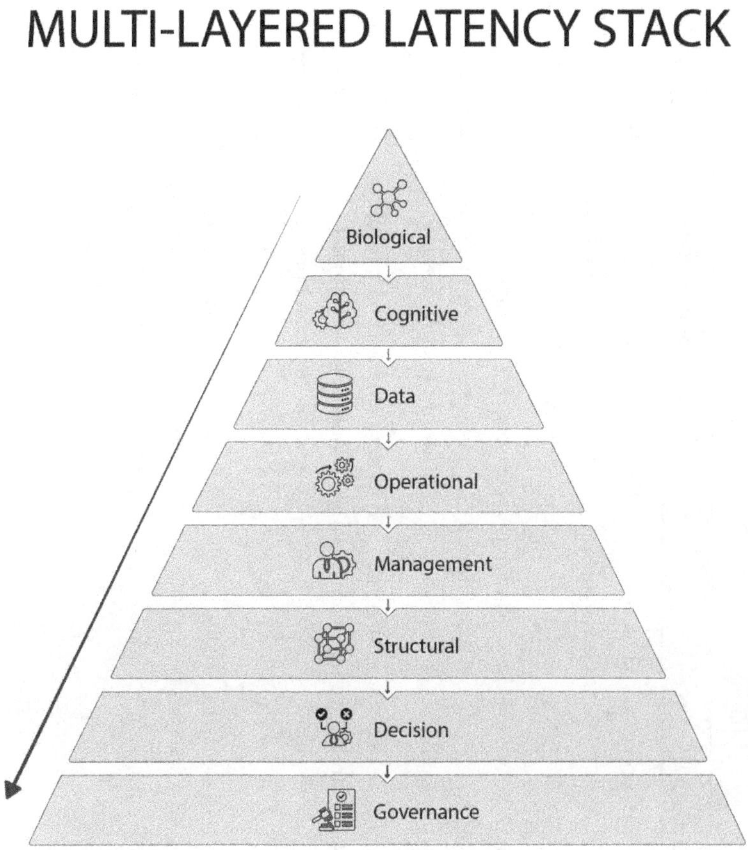

Latency Type	Definition	The Human Bottleneck	The AI-Driven Solution
Biological	The physical time required to perceive a stimulus and physically execute a response.	Bound by human processing speed and physical typing/reading limits.	Instantaneous data ingestion and parallel execution at machine speed.
Cognitive	The mental delay caused by subjective reasoning, cognitive biases, and decision fatigue.	Performance degrades over time; prone to emotional or biased decision-making.	Applies consistent, objective logic continuously without fatigue.
Data	The delay between data generation and its availability for use.	Reliant on overnight batch processing or manual, end-of-month reporting cycles.	Continuous, real-time data streaming and instant accessibility.
Operational	Delays in task execution due to manual workflows and siloed systems.	Forced to sequentially switch contexts and manually move data between disjointed software.	Autonomous execution of parallel workflows through integrated APIs.

Latency Type	Definition	The Human Bottleneck	The AI-Driven Solution
Management	The administrative friction of coordinating work among individuals.	Wasted hours waiting for calendar slots, email replies, and status update meetings.	Asynchronous, immediate communication and coordination between autonomous agents.
Structural	Delays inherent in the physical or logical design of the organization.	Slowed by geographic distance, time zones, and repetitive alignment conversations.	Location-agnostic, 24/7 continuous operation across a globally distributed system.
Decision	The lag between data becoming available and the business taking action.	Paralyzed by unclear authority, waiting for analysis, or building consensus.	Automated execution triggered instantly by predefined thresholds and parameters.
Governance	The structural delay required to ensure safety, compliance, and oversight.	Bogged down by slow-moving committees and multi-stage manual review processes.	Continuous, automated compliance auditing, reserving human review strictly for high-stakes exceptions.

The AI-Driven Enterprise model ruthlessly reduces the top seven layers of this stack to buy more time for the eighth: governance. This does not mean we should undermine essential checks and balances. Compliance and safety are nonnegotiable. However, in too many organizations, the "checks" have become the bottleneck, and the "balances" have become an excuse for a total lack of urgency. The key to the AIDE model is realizing that the urgency required to compete in "System Time" is missing in human-centric governance. We must preserve the integrity of our oversight without allowing it to become the friction that kills the firm.

When you require a human to manually review a report, navigate a siloed CRM, or wait for an overnight data pipeline, you are introducing friction into a system that ought to be frictionless.

The Human Bottleneck

With a title like *No One Works Here* this book could have been the story of a company with a bunch of employees who are all slackers, a company where no one *works*: the least efficient company. This book is the opposite. This is a story about the most efficient companies. Those where humans don't "work" in the traditional sense.

The companies that are most likely to fall behind their peers are the ones that insist on keeping a human in the loop for decisions that a machine could have made yesterday. That doesn't mean all decisions, just those that might not require a human in the loop in the AIDE era.

It reminds me of the central tension in the 1983 fictional film *WarGames*, which showcases the extreme example of what happens when you propose removing the human from the loop. There is a pivotal scene where military brass debate the implementation of the WOPR (War Operation Plan Response) supercomputer. The argument for the machine was cold and logical: Human operators in the missile silos were a liability because, faced with the gravity of their actions, they hesitated. They couldn't "turn the key" to launch the nuclear missiles. The proposal was, instead, to route the missile launch codes directly to the WOPR, effectively taking the human out of the loop to ensure instant execution. In the context of nuclear warfare, that logic is terrifying, it could lead to accidental Armageddon.

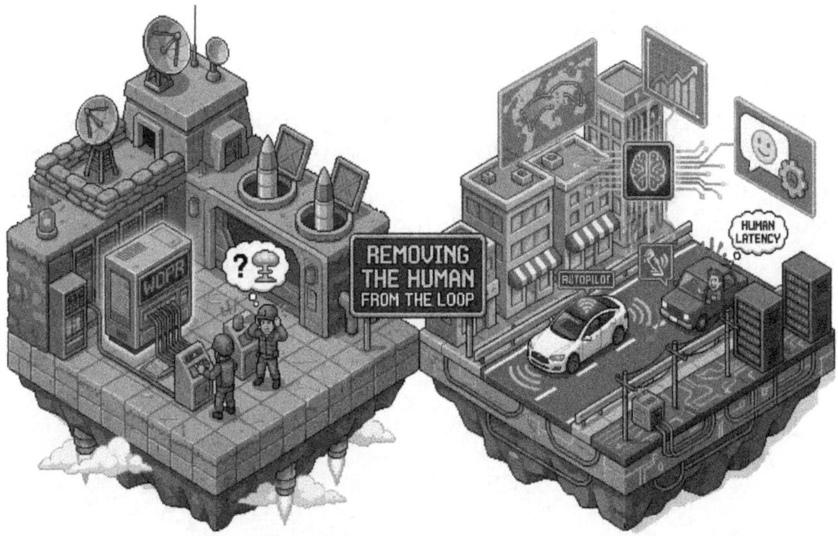

However, we no longer have to look to fiction to see the benefit of removing the human from the loop. We see it every day on our highways. . . . And it saves lives: a modern motor vehicle equipped with an intelligent emergency braking system before a human driver even perceives a hazard or has the time to react. By the time the human brain processes the visual cue of a car stopping two vehicles ahead, a car often obscured from the driver's line of sight, the AI has already calculated the physics of the impending collision and initiated a stop. In this moment, the human's biological latency is a liability; the machine's autonomous agency is the lifesaver.

Stepping back from the WOPR and the emergency braking system examples, in the context of the global economy, the logic is inescapable. In most industries, we are not debating nuclear launch codes; we are debating pricing adjustments, supply chain routing, and customer support queries. In these domains, the "hesitation" of the human operator, the need to schedule a meeting or build consensus, is not a safety feature; it is a bottleneck. It could be an existential threat to the organization.

The Reliability Tax

However, we must acknowledge the "reliability tax." When you first deploy an agent, latency often spikes. You will spend *more* time auditing the agent's output than you would have spent doing the work yourself. This is the Latency J-Curve: Things get slower and riskier before they become instant. The winners are the organizations that push through this "messy middle" of validation to reach the other side: trust-based autonomy.

Moving forward, organizations must prioritize human bandwidth for those situations in which the unique capabilities we possess are a necessity and the consequences of delegating to AI, even with guardrails, could be detrimental.

Structural Debt Versus Technical Debt

As software engineers, we talk a lot about "technical debt." But the companies on the Fortune 500 list, like most established businesses, are suffering from structural debt.

For the last century, we built organizations to solve for the limitations of human communication. We created hierarchies because one person couldn't manage a thousand people. We created departments to specialize knowledge because one brain couldn't know everything. We created middle management to route information because we didn't have networks.

This structure creates latency. When a legacy company wants to make a decision, the data has to travel up the chain of command. It gets aggregated, summarized, PowerPointed, and debated. By the time the decision is made and the communication comes back down, the market has moved.

The fear of a market shifting before a product can launch used to be a uniquely deep-tech nightmare. That 10-year deep-tech threat has now come for everyone. Today, a digital product can have its core value proposition commoditized mere hours after launch by a single Big Tech release.

No One Works Here: The Digital War Room

You've learned the theory; now let's build the machinery. Turn these concepts into immediate ROI for your company by accessing your free resources at NoOneWorksHere.com.

1. Immediate Actions (Do This Today)

- **Audit Your Latency Stack:** Map a recent delayed project against the eight layers of the Multi-Layered Latency Stack to pinpoint exactly where biological or administrative friction is slowing you down.
- **Pay the Reliability Tax:** Isolate one repetitive administrative workflow, such as meeting scheduling or data routing, and delegate it to an AI agent today. Commit to auditing its output through the "messy middle" of the J-Curve until it reaches trust-based autonomy.

2. The Discussion (Bring This to Your Team)

- Are our current organizational hierarchies solving for human communication limitations that no longer exist? Discuss where our legacy department structures are creating "structural debt" and preventing us from operating at "hours speed."

(*continued*)

(continued)

- The chapter warns that organizations often confuse necessary governance with administrative friction, resulting in a dangerous "latency lock-in." Where in our company are manual review processes acting as an excuse for a lack of urgency rather than a true safety feature?
- What specific workflows in our daily operations treat human hesitation as a safety feature when it is actually an existential liability? Which lower-stakes decisions should we fully delegate to AI to eliminate biological latency?

3. The Step-by-Step Implementation

Stop guessing and start building. Use the **Multi-Layered Latency Stack Workbook** for step-by-step guidance. This digital workbook provides the exact framework you need to implement this chapter's concepts.

Download it at: NoOneWorksHere.com/latency-stack

4. The Unfair Advantage: AI-Powered Tools

Don't just read about AI; use it right now. As a reader of this book, you get exclusive access to interactive AI-software tools designed to do the heavy lifting for you.

Access your tools instantly at: NoOneWorksHere.com

(Or simply scan the QR code with your smartphone camera)

2

The New Calculus of Scale in Competition

Who loses when organizations don't adapt?
The risk of obsolescence mandates the need for structural reinvention.

For decades, military strategists have studied the concept of a Revolution in Military Affairs (RMA), a concept I had the privilege of learning about from General (Ret) Terry Williams, a 32 year veteran of the US Marine Corps (and entrepreneur!). An RMA occurs in a period of the history of humankind when a convergence of new technologies, coupled with radical organizational and doctrinal changes, fundamentally alters the character and conduct of warfare. This shift leads to an irreversible change in warfare. It's not just getting a better gun; it's changing *how* the entire war is fought.

Consider the shift from massed infantry to Blitzkrieg, a military tactic characterized by surprise attacks using concentrated forces of tanks and motorized infantry, along with close air support to break through enemy lines and create chaos. Or the introduction of the aircraft carrier in naval warfare. The technology (the tank, the plane) was one part, but the true revolution was the change in doctrine, the decision to stop using people as shields and start using machines for hyper-speed maneuvers and coordinated attacks.

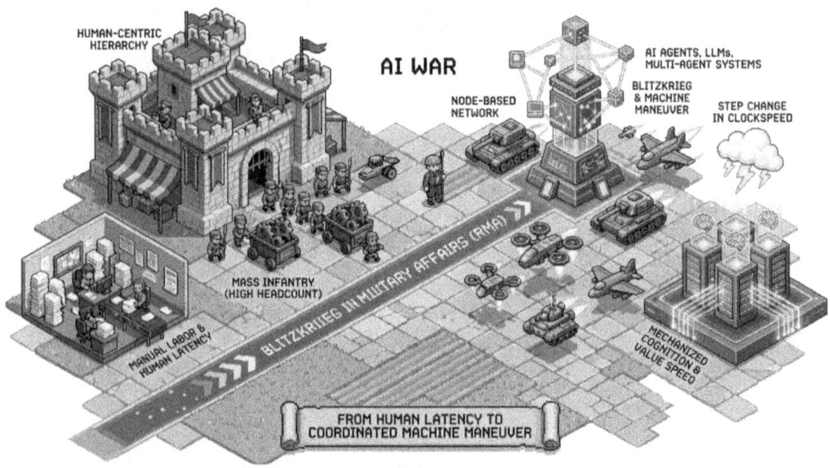

This is exactly what is happening in business right now. We are not just witnessing a "digital transformation" or a technological upgrade; we are in the midst of a sort of Revolution in Military Affairs in business.

This is not a software update. This is an entirely new machine, a structural inflection point:

- **The Technology:** AI agents, LLMs, and multi-agent systems are the new tanks and carriers. They mechanize cognition.
- **The Organizational Shift:** The AI-Driven Enterprise is the new doctrine, moving from a human-centric hierarchy to a node-based network.

If you are a leader of a legacy organization, you are fighting the AI war with massed infantry (high headcount, human latency). Your competitor, the AIDE, is using coordinated, high-speed machine-based maneuver.

This chapter will provide the historical context for this RMA. While structural latency silently paralyzes an organization from the inside, the fatal consequences of this friction are about to play out on the global economic battlefield.

In this chapter, you will:

- **Analyze the Fortune 500 Churn:** Confront the data-driven reality that up to 70% of today's market leaders will vanish in the next two decades due to the McNamara Fallacy.
- **Examine the Mathematics of Mortality:** Evaluate why legacy firms face bureaucratic collapse, while AI-Driven Enterprises scale exponentially.
- **Deconstruct the Headcount Trap:** Understand why traditional metrics are shifting from badges of honor to indicators of organizational bloat, moving from Vanity Metrics to Real Value.
- **Master the ARR/FTE Metric:** Learn how to calculate your "human leverage" to determine whether your company is a high-growth leader or a vulnerable legacy.
- **Compare Carbon and Silicon Payroll:** Explore the hidden structural weight of compute and token inference costs.

The Mortality Table

Let's look at the data. It doesn't care about your brand legacy or your quarterly earnings call.

In 1955, the Fortune 500 was a list of titans. These were the companies that built the infrastructure of the 20th century. Today, look at that list again. Mark J. Perry of the American Enterprise Institute (AEI) highlights in his publications that 88% of the companies from the original 1955 list are gone (Perry 2016). They have been acquired, merged, gone bankrupt, or shrunk in size.

Average company lifespan on S&P 500 Index in years (rolling 7-year average)

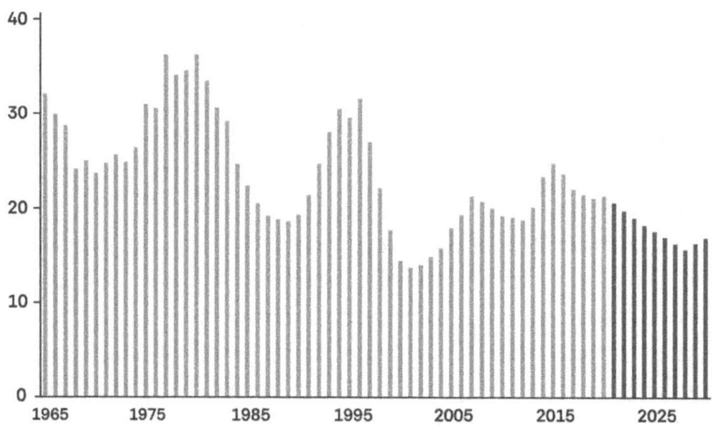

Data: Standard & Poor's; Innosight analysis based on public S&P 500 data sources. See endnote on methodology.

Source: Viguerie et al. / Innosight Holdings LLC

Historically, this churn was natural. It was the slow, tectonic shifting of economic plates. But recently, the plates have started to move faster. In the 1960s, the average lifespan of a company on the S&P 500 was 33 years. Today it is less than 18 years (Viguerie et al. 2021).

This mass disappearance is a textbook example of the McNamara Fallacy in action. Named for US Secretary of Defense Robert McNamara, this logical fallacy occurs when decision-makers rely solely on quantitative metrics and dismiss as unimportant anything that cannot be easily measured. In the corporate world, the measurable elements are clear: quarterly dividends, stock buybacks, and immediate overhead costs. But what truly matters—intellectual growth, adaptability, and long-term relevance—rarely fits neatly into a spreadsheet. Bound to their metrics, it is easy to see how many of these corporate titans could meticulously measure their daily success while remaining entirely blind to the unquantifiable shifts in the world around them.

What do you think the drop-off rate for the Fortune 500 will look like in 20 years?

The trend line is clear. While conservative linear and exponential models based on the last 60 years of data suggest a Fortune 500 drop-off rate between 59% and 62% for 2043, the historical numbers actually reveal a distinct pattern of acceleration. Because of this compounding momentum, I am projecting that within the next 20 years, up to 70% of today's Fortune 500 will drop off the list entirely. I anticipate this accelerating quadratic trend will become our reality given the unprecedented role that AI is taking in reshaping organizations and the sheer speed at which they can move. Let's take a look at the assumptions behind the structural proof of my thesis.

The Mathematics of Mortality: Refactoring the Corporate Equation

To truly understand why established companies are poised to churn from the marketplace at an unprecedented rate, we must look at the structural math. Here's why I believe up to 70% of today's Fortune

500 will drop off the list entirely in the next two decades. Let's look at the limits of my value creation (V) equations for legacy firms and AIDE startups:

- **The Limit of the Legacy Firm:** As an organization tries to scale by adding more people, the coordination complexity ($Latency_{Admin}$) grows faster than the human output. As $Latency_{Admin} \rightarrow \infty$, $V_{Latency}$ plateaus and eventually approaches zero. This is bureaucratic collapse.
- **The Limit of the AIDE:** As $Compute \rightarrow \infty$ and execution costs drop to near zero, the latency shrinks to a fraction of its former self. V_{AIDE} scales exponentially, bottlenecked by only one thing: the magnitude and ambition of human *Intent*.

> If you'd like the complete value creation equations, you can grab them on the book's website: NoOneWorks Here.com/value-creation-equations.

From Vanity Metrics to Real Value

This structural shift is correcting a massive economic distortion. During the dot-com boom (and arguably the SaaS boom of the 2010s), companies were often valued on Vanity Metrics. Page views. Impressions. Clicks. Headcount growth.

Investors poured billions into companies based on "potential" and "eyeballs." Profitability was a problem for "later." That era is over. The AI-Driven Enterprise is held to a higher standard. Because AI allows for the mechanization of cognition, the excuse for inefficiency is gone. You cannot tell an investor, "We are unprofitable because we need to hire 500 sales and support reps to scale." The investor knows you could do it with five agents.

The Headcount Trap

If you were a startup, you measured success by users, revenue, and/or headcount. "We just hired our 500th employee!" was a badge of honor. It signaled scale. It signaled importance. If you were a corporate executive, you measured power by the size of your P&L and the number of direct reports you managed. In a LinkedIn post, Brennan Pothetes perfectly summarized this exact point perfectly in context from David Graeber's *Bullshit Jobs* (Graeber 2018):

> *The premise is simple and brutal: Most dysfunction inside large organizations is incentive driven, not competence driven.*
>
> *Here's a perfect example from one of the Brennan's LinkedIn post:*
>
> *If you're an SVP at a big bank, you get rewarded for one thing: Growing your org chart. It's not about serving customers or increasing leverage or creating value. Just . . . adding people?*
>
> *Which is why these days, you'll meet a "head of product" whose first instinct is to hire five PMs before they've even identified a single real customer problem. This is the default mode in corporate America. But it's the death of early-stage companies.*

I have the privilege of serving as an advisor to the CEO and board of Brennan's company, Infinity Constellation, where we are building a portfolio of AI-first services businesses. The entire model is built in contrast to the incentive of "growing headcount." Still, our limiting factor and risk are people—the best possible architects to build AI-first services businesses—so we are always looking for people to hire.

In the legacy model, hiring was the solution to every problem. In the AIDE model, hiring is a sign that you haven't yet figured out how to automate the outcome.

This shift isn't just theoretical; it's being codified by the world's most successful founders. Tobi Lütke, CEO of Shopify, recently issued a memo to his entire team that signals the end of reflexive hiring. He didn't just suggest using AI; he made it a "baseline expectation." Most importantly, he flipped the burden of proof for growth. Lütke wrote:

> Before asking for more Headcount and resources, teams must demonstrate why they cannot get what they want done using AI. What would this area look like if autonomous AI agents were already part of the team?
>
> **(Lütke 2025)**

Lütke's stance at Shopify represents a radical departure from the "Red Queen" race, a hypothesis in evolutionary biology, proposed by Leigh Van Valen (inspired by Lewis Carroll 2003), of corporate hiring. By requiring teams to prove that an AI agent *cannot* do the job before a human is hired, Shopify is effectively treating human headcount as a last resort rather than a first impulse. This is the "AIDE-first" mentality in action: You don't scale by adding people; you scale by multiplying your current people through reflexive AI usage.

Beyond headcount, we have entered a market correction that is not just cyclical; it is structural. The availability of easy capital when anyone with an idea and pitch deck could raise funding has dried up, but more importantly, the *necessity* of capital has changed. In the AIDE era, headcount is no longer a proxy for success. In fact, it is often a proxy for inefficiency.

When the finance company Block announced it was laying off more than 4,000 employees in February 2026, about half its headcount, its shares skyrocketed as much as 24% in extended trading (Palmer 2026). Investors, boards, and the public markets are no longer rewarding growth at all costs. They are rewarding efficiency. They are looking for organizations that can generate outsized returns with minimal human latency.

The New Arithmetic of Growth

The ratio of revenue to headcount is the single most important metric for the modern founder. The primary metric for the AI era is ARR/FTE: Annual Recurring Revenue per Full-Time Equivalent.

This is a simple ratio: total recurring revenue divided by the number of full-time equivalents, or the number of full-time employee work hours regardless of full-time or part-time employment. This ratio captures how effectively a company converts human capacity into value. It is the ultimate measure of leverage.

The Early 2000s (Human-Powered): To reach $100M in Annual Recurring Revenue (ARR), companies like LinkedIn (LinkedIn Corporation 2011) and Shopify (Shopify Inc. 2015) required 600 to 900 employees. Growth was headcount-intensive. You needed an army.

The 2020s (AI-Powered): Today, we are seeing startups hit $100M ARR with teams of under 50 people. Some examples include:

- **Anysphere (Cursor):** Hit ~$100M ARR with ~20 employees (Kolahdoozan 2025).
- **ElevenLabs:** Hit similar milestones with ~50 employees (Kolahdoozan 2025).

If you're running a legacy organization with 1,000 employees generating $100 million in revenue, your ARR/FTE is $100,000. You are, respectfully, bloatware. You are vulnerable to a competitor with 10 employees generating $20 million, who operates with a fraction of your overhead and 100 times your speed.

The Spectrum of Automation and Decoupling Labor

How do they do it? The legacy enterprise views growth linearly: To process double the output, they usually must hire more people. This creates a crushing "complexity tax." The AIDE plays an entirely different game. When a company like Midjourney (2026) sees its workload double, they don't hire 60 more people; they simply spin up more compute. They treat scale as a function of processing power, not coordinates on a traditional org chart. You are playing a game of addition. They are playing a game of multiplication—checkers versus chess.

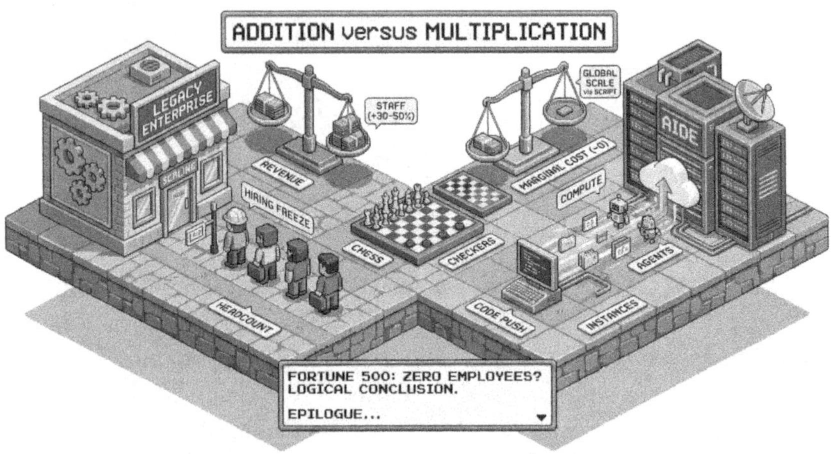

Whether you're moving bits or moving atoms, the goal is the same: to decouple your revenue growth from your headcount growth. If your "scaling" requires an outsized increase in new headcount to new profits, you aren't building a future-proof business; you're just building a bigger bureaucracy.

We must acknowledge that this isn't a binary switch. Every industry sits on a spectrum of "agentic adoption" based on two factors: physicality and regulation. In every industry, the goal remains the same: using technology to strip away the friction, allowing your human talent to operate at maximum efficiency.

Industry Type	Industry Examples	Scaling Mechanism	The Role of the Human	Real-World Example
Pure Digital	Software, media, e-commerce	Infinite compute (Algorithmic execution at zero marginal cost)	Architect and auditor	AI generates thousands of personalized ad campaigns; a human sets the strategy and reviews the top-performing anomalies.
Heavy Asset	Manufacturing, logistics, retail	Predictive optimization (Squeezing maximum yield from physical constraints)	Strategic operator	AI predicts supply chain bottlenecks and suggests rerouting; a human operator makes the final call based on physical ground truths.
Regulated	Financial services, healthcare, legal	Compliant automation (Accelerating prep work without bypassing legal checks)	"Human-in-the-loop" authority	AI reviews decades of case law or medical history to draft a brief or chart; a licensed human legally signs off.

The Efficiency Illusion: Why ARR/FTE Only Tells Half the Story

While ARR/FTE is the headline metric, it is far from the whole story.

I recently led an executive education session at MIT Sloan with CEOs from around the world where we debated the limitations of this ratio. A critical nuance emerged during our discussion, one that is reshaping the economic playbook of Silicon Valley: ARR/FTE measures headcount, but it ignores sky-high outlier salaries *and* "digital labor" expenses.

In the current war for talent, the supply of top-tier AI researchers, the architects of foundation models, is vanishingly scarce. We are seeing compensation packages for individuals approaching $50 million to $100 million per year when factoring in aggressive vesting schedules.

If a company generates $500 million in revenue with only 10 employees, its ARR/FTE is a staggering $50 million. On paper, this is the most efficient organization in history. But if half those employees are "stars" earning $50 million each, their labor efficiency is a mirage.

As we move toward the AI-Driven Enterprise, we are replacing human payroll, or "carbon payroll," with "Silicon payroll," the massive, often volatile costs of AI tokens, model training, data pipelines, and inference. Armand Ruiz (2026b) recently made a startling prediction: "Token budgets will soon surpass human salaries."

Venture capitalist Tomasz Tunguz recently documented this transition. In early 2026, Tunguz shared that his annualized AI inference costs jumped from $7,200 to over $100,000 in just two quarters as he moved to a fleet of browser agents. He highlights a coming reality for the C-suite (Tunguz 2026): "Technology companies are adding a fourth component to engineering compensation: salary, bonus, options, & inference costs."

Today, many companies are operating on "borrowed margins." Token costs and API access are frequently subsidized by venture capital or platform giants to drive adoption. As these subsidies evaporate and companies move from "wrappers" to proprietary fine-tuning, the cost of compute becomes a permanent, structural weight on the P&L.

This creates a new efficiency benchmark for every leader to track: productive work per dollar of inference. You cannot look at ARR/FTE in a vacuum. If your GPU bill is $200 million and your inference costs scale linearly with every new customer, you haven't built a more efficient business. You've simply traded a human HR problem for a technical one.

The "Unicorn" of One

We are rapidly approaching the era of the one-person unicorn, a company with a billion-dollar valuation run by a single human founder and a swarm of AI agents. When that happens (and it will happen soon), the ARR/FTE will be $100 million-plus. This outlier will force every Fortune 500 board to look at their own thousands of employees and ask, "What are we actually doing here?" And while I am extremely excited about the one-person unicorn, I also believe that the most inefficient part of the one-person unicorn will be the one person! This leaves me extremely bullish on the zero-person company, which we will explore later.

Example: General Intelligence Company

This shift from "time" to "intelligence" is being pioneered by builders like Andrew Pignanelli, the founder and CEO of the General Intelligence Company of New York, an AI company I advise. Andrew's thesis is a cold shower for anyone still treating AI as a mere personal assistant or "helper." He isn't building a copilot; he is building a fully autonomous engineering department. His "North Star" is the realization of the first one-person, billion-dollar company.

To reach that milestone, he has replaced traditional success metrics with what he calls the token-to-salary ratio. On peak days, his team actually spends more on AI tokens than on human payroll. As Andrew puts it, "Headcount is a lagging indicator. . . . Capital is shifting from 'Time' (salaries) to 'Intelligence' (APIs). If your token spend isn't climbing, you're not scaling" (Lee 2026).

This is the ultimate validation of the AIDE model: a 400% increase in output velocity achieved not by hiring more desks, but by deploying more compute.

The Binary Choice

This chapter serves as a wake-up call.

If you are leading an established enterprise in "any" industry, you have a choice. You can continue to view AI as a productivity tool, a "copilot" for your existing bureaucracy. If you do this, you will likely gain 10% efficiency in the next couple of years. And you will likely be gone in ten years. Or you can undertake the painful, difficult work of structural reinvention. You can begin to dismantle the hierarchies that create latency and replace them with networks of intelligent agents.

The greatest risk is not that AI will replace your workers. It is that a company built on AI will replace your business. The clock is ticking. And it's running on computer time, not human time.

No One Works Here: The Digital War Room

You've learned the theory; now let's build the machinery. Turn these concepts into immediate ROI for your company by accessing your free resources at NoOneWorksHere.com.

1. Immediate Actions (Do These Today)

- **Calculate Your ARR/FTE Floor:** Divide your total annual recurring revenue by your current full-time equivalents to establish your baseline "human leverage" score. Compare this against the new AI-era benchmark of $1M-plus per employee to identify if you are operating as "bloatware."
- **Audit Your Silicon Payroll:** Review your profit-and-loss statement to identify "Shadow Workforce" costs, including AI tokens, API subscriptions, and compute expenses. Begin tracking "productive work per dollar of inference" to ensure your automation spend is driving exponential output rather than just adding technical overhead.
- **Flip the Burden of Proof:** Implement a "Shopify-style" hiring freeze where any request for new headcount must first be accompanied by a documented failure to achieve the same outcome using autonomous AI agents.

2. The Discussion (Bring This to Your Team)

- The chapter highlights that up to 70% of today's market leaders could vanish due to bureaucratic collapse. Are we currently suffering from the McNamara Fallacy by prioritizing easily measurable, short-term metrics while remaining blind to the exponential speed of AI-driven competitors?

- If we were forced to reach our next revenue milestone with zero additional hiring, which specific "human-heavy" workflows would break first, and how would an AI-first architecture solve them?
- What would happen if, instead of approving new headcount requests, we offered teams in our organization a grant or budget to navigate the messy middle of the J-Curve?

3. The Step-by-Step Implementation

Stop guessing and start building. Use the **Calculus of Scale Workbook** for step-by-step guidance. This digital workbook provides the exact framework you need to implement this chapter's concepts.

Download it at: NoOneWorksHere.com/calculus-of-scale

4. The Unfair Advantage: AI-Powered Tools

Don't just read about AI; use it right now. As a reader of this book, you get exclusive access to interactive AI-software tools designed to do the heavy lifting for you.

Access your tools instantly at: NoOneWorksHere.com

(Or simply scan the QR code with your smartphone camera)

PART

I → II

What happens when you realize the greatest threat to your survival isn't new technology, but your outdated organizational structure?
Moving from the crisis of legacy latency to the context of hybrid intelligence.

THE DANGER IS real, but fear without understanding only leads to noise. The collapse of legacy firms and the crushing pressure for efficiency are symptoms, not causes. To respond intelligently, you first need to see what has changed beneath the surface: the very physics of business.

We have now defined the landscape of the threat:

- **The Bottleneck:** Legacy organizations are biologically incapable of moving at machine speed (Latency).
- **The Trap:** The traditional metric of adding human headcount to scale is now a fatal liability.
- **The Scorecard:** Human leverage and computational efficiency (ARR/FTE) dictate the new arithmetic of growth.

You now understand why you need to change and the structural debt that puts you at risk. But understanding the threat isn't enough. You need to understand the mechanics of the solution.

In Part II, "The Changing Landscape," we are going to open up the black box. We will fundamentally redefine the word "organization" as a hybrid network of human and silicon nodes. We will explore why your leadership style must evolve from manual "captain" to systems "architect," how your business model must shift from seat-based licenses to real-time outcomes, and why the messy friction of our current "dial-up era" of AI is actually your greatest competitive advantage.

The "Threat" is real. But the "Opportunity" is bigger.

Let's turn the page.

PART II
The Changing Landscape

Redefining What It Means to Organize

To lead in the AI era, you must first redefine what you're leading.

The organization didn't disappear. It evolved beyond people.

ONCE YOU SEE the cracks exposed in Part I, the next step is to understand the new foundation. The traditional definition of an organization—a group of people working together toward a shared purpose—no longer fits because intelligence is no longer a human monopoly.

This section builds the new frame. We will open the black box to fundamentally redefine the organization as a dynamic network of human and silicon nodes. From there, we will explore exactly how this reshapes the mechanics of your business:

- **The Leadership Shift:** Why you must move from being a "captain" who manually directs tasks to an "architect" who designs systems and defines intent
- **The Business Model Shift:** How changing buying behavior forces a move away from selling seat-based software licenses to delivering real-time outcomes

- **The Timing:** Why the clunky, messy friction of our current "dial-up era" of AI is not a reason to wait, but actually your greatest window of opportunity

By the end of this section, the confusion that surrounds AI will clear. The vocabulary, logic, and timing of this transformation will come into sharp focus.

3

The Node Architecture

What does it mean to organize when not everyone is human?
Redefining the word "organization" to include intelligent systems.

LANGUAGE IS THE operating system of society. The words we use define the boundaries of what we can imagine.

If you cannot name something, you cannot manage it. If your definition of a core concept is outdated, your strategy will be outdated too. But most of all, alignment on common language is what enables groups of humans to build alignment, clarity, understanding, and ultimately determine direction.

I was fortunate to have a group of 15 senior stakeholders in the entrepreneurship and innovation ecosystem together for a dinner in Belfast, Northern Ireland, in the fall of 2024. As a group, we diagnosed why there was a lack of alignment, and as it turns out, different people had different ideas of what entrepreneurship really means without common language or shared understanding. It's difficult for society to make forward progress without a shared language.

And, right now, the most dangerous bug in the business world isn't in your software code. It's in the dictionary.

In this chapter, you will:

- **Confront Outdated Dictionary Definitions:** Understand why "organization" must evolve beyond just people.
- **Adopt the Node Framework:** Learn to distinguish between carbon nodes and silicon nodes, and rewrite your organizational chart to reflect the AI era.
- **Master Dynamics of Probability:** Understand why LLMs are prediction engines, not truth engines, and how to balance deterministic guardrails with probabilistic innovation.
- **Bridge the Technical Gap:** Distinguish between generative AI, prompt engineering, and context engineering.
- **Architect the Digital Doing:** Define the critical leap from systems that talk to systems that act through AI workflows, agents, and swarms.

The Bug in the Dictionary

I recently wrote an open petition to *Merriam-Webster* because I realized that the way we teach business at business schools, and the way the world actually works, had diverged from the English language.

Open up a dictionary today, and look up "organization." You'll find something like this:

> **organization** /*ˌɔːɡənʌɪˈzeɪʃn* / *noun*
>
> a group of people who work together in an organized way for a shared purpose.

For centuries, that definition was accurate. It made perfect sense. "People" were the only agents capable of cognitive work. But in the last 5 years, the world of work has changed more than it did in the previous 50. We have introduced a new variable into the equation. We have introduced agents—autonomous, intelligent systems—that can "work" without a (physical) heartbeat.

The dictionary is outdated. And because it is outdated, we risk hiring wrong, leading wrong, and building wrong.

The New Definition: The Rise of the Node

We are witnessing the rise of a new kind of entity. It is not exclusively built on biology; it is a hybrid. I propose a new definition—a subtle change in wording, but a massive change in logic.

> **organization** /ˌɔːɡənʌɪˈzeɪʃn/ *noun*
>
> a group of **nodes** working together in an organized way for a shared purpose.

- **Old Unit:** Person
- **New Unit:** Node

A node is any entity capable of receiving an input, processing it, and producing an output that moves the organization closer to its goal. Some nodes are people (carbon-based). Some nodes are AI agents (silicon-based). Together, they form a network. The modern organization is no longer a hierarchy of humans; it is a dynamic web of nodes.

A Warning on Culture

I know what you're thinking: Calling a human being a "carbon node" feels cold. It sounds like engineering-speak that strips away our humanity. I use this language intentionally to protect that humanity. We must be honest about the psychological and existential weight of this shift. As Michelle Sim, senior manager for Trade, Science, and Technology at Scottish Development International—with whom I have the pleasure of working on programs to support scale-up companies in Scotland expand internationally—noted in a critique of this manuscript, we must explore how it will actually *feel* to work in an AIDE. How does this revolution reshape our understanding of "good" work? If we move toward hyper-efficient environments where AI monitors every pulse of productivity, do we disrupt the very models of motivation, like Dan Pink's autonomy, mastery, and purpose (from his book *Drive*; Pink 2011), that drive human fulfillment?

While "node architecture" is the correct engineering framework for designing your business, it is a disastrous framework for communicating with it. Do not walk into your next town hall and call your loyal staff "carbon nodes." They could revolt, and they should. Use this framework to design your systems in the war room, but lead with humanity in the break room. Your people need to know they are the architects of the silicon nodes, not the gears being replaced by them.

The Technical Foundation of the Silicon Node

To operate this way, you need to understand the specifications of your artificial nodes. You need to know when to deploy a human and when to deploy an agent.

The most critical thing for an organizational architect to understand is that modern AI is a prediction engine. In the "Software 1.0" era, we programmed computers with explicit, deterministic rules: If X happens, do Y. Old software returns the exact same result every time.

Generative AI changes this dynamic because it is probabilistic. It does not look up facts in a database; it predicts the most likely next "token" based on patterns in data. Because AI is based on patterns rather than rigid rules, it introduces variance into your operations. Old software returns the exact same result every time, but today AI returns one of the most probable results.

It's important to note that an AIDE does not need to use *generative* AI in every functional area of the business, and in fact there are many scenarios in which that's actually not a good idea, especially in regulated industries. Some functional areas may be better served by deterministic AI that provides additional control.

As you redesign your organization for the AI era, the challenge lies in architectural balance:

- **Deterministic Guardrails:** Certain functions, such as financial approvals, legal compliance, or safety-critical logic must remain programmed with explicit, deterministic rules to ensure absolute consistency and zero "hallucination."
- **Probabilistic Innovation:** Other areas, like creative ideation, strategic drafting, and complex pattern recognition, should leverage the probabilistic nature of AI to find insights a rigid script would miss.

To build an AIDE, you must move beyond "chatting" and master the two pillars of elite orchestration: prompt engineering and context engineering. Prompting is the process of structuring instructions to elicit high-quality responses, while context engineering is the strategic management of the data environment surrounding the AI to ensure outputs are grounded in your specific business reality.

The Architecture of "Doing": Workflows, Agents, and Swarms

To architect an AI-Driven Enterprise, you must look past the "typewriter" (generative AI) and focus on the "factory" (the systems that do the work).

1. AI Workflows: The Digital Assembly Line

An AI workflow is the orchestration layer that strings together data, models, and human approvals to achieve a specific outcome. While traditional workflows are rigid and rule-based, AI workflows use semantic routing to "understand" context and make probabilistic decisions at each step. Crucially, a workflow is the rigid, "hard-coded" track or plumbing that dictates exactly how data and tasks move between different AI nodes and human managers.

2. Agents: The Workers

Agents are autonomous systems designed to act with purpose. While generative AI talks, agents *do*.

The Formula: LLM (Brain) + Tools (Hands) + Permissions (Guardrails) = Agent

To be clear, an agent is an individual "digital worker" that uses "tools," which are simply API connections to your software like Stripe, Slack, or a web browser, to execute a specific task rather than just talking about it.

3. Multi-Agent Systems: The Teams

When multiple specialized agents work together, they form a multi-agent system or "swarm." These systems mirror human departments; you might have a "product manager agent" writing a spec for a "coder agent," who is then checked by a "QA agent." A multi-agent system is essentially a collaborative department of these digital workers that can debate, critique, and fix each other's work to solve complex problems that are too big for a single agent to handle alone.

Case Study: The Hybrid Sales Team

Let's look at how this definition changes a real department: sales.

The "Group of People" Approach: You hire 10 business development reps (BDRs). Their job is to find leads, research them, and write emails.

- *Reality:* They spend six hours a day researching (slowly) and two hours writing (often poorly). They get burned out. They quit after 12 months.
- *Result:* High churn, high cost, inconsistent data.

The "Group of Nodes" Approach: You view the "sales organization" as a network.

- **Node A (Agent):** Scrapes LinkedIn and news sites for buying signals 24/7 (speed)
- **Node B (Agent):** Enriches the data and drafts a personalized email based on the prospect's recent posts (scale)

- **Node C (Human):** Reviews the drafts for the top 10% of high-value targets, adds a personal touch, and hits send (intent and nuance)
- **Node D (Agent):** Handles the scheduling back-and-forth when the prospect replies (latency reduction)
- **Node E (Human):** Takes the Zoom call to close the deal (trust)

In this model, the parts of the "organization" are working together. The AI nodes handle the volume; the human nodes handle the value.

Why This Matters for Leaders

Business schools, including the ones where I teach, have spent a hundred years training leaders to manage "human resources." But we have limited curriculum on "node resources."

If you define your company exclusively as a "group of people," your default reflex for scaling will always be to increase headcount. "Sales are down? Hire more reps." If you define your company as a "group of nodes," you solve problems by analyzing the bottleneck. "Sales are down? Deployment of new prospecting nodes is required."

The best leaders hire those that are experts. To reshape that thinking in the AIDE era, leaders must recruit with this approach: Hire nodes smarter, more efficient, and/or more effective than you!

No One Works Here: The Digital War Room

You've learned the theory; now let's build the machinery. Turn these concepts into immediate ROI for your company by accessing your free resources at NoOneWorksHere.com.

1. Immediate Actions (Do This Today)

- **Conduct a "Node Audit":** Review your current team's weekly task list and categorize every activity as either a "carbon" task (requiring empathy, judgment, or high-level intent) or a "silicon" task (repetitive data processing or 24/7 monitoring).

- **Identify the "Chatter" Versus the "Doer":** List three repetitive tasks in your department and categorize them: Are you currently using AI just to "talk" (generative AI) about them, or can you deploy an agent to "do" them via API access?
- **Define Your Guardrails:** Identify one high-stakes process where you currently use AI and implement a "human-in-the-loop" break to ensure probabilistic outputs are verified by deterministic human judgment.

2. The Discussion (Bring This to Your Team)

- If we redefined our department as a network of "nodes" rather than just a group of people, which of our current manual processes would immediately appear obsolete or inefficient?
- Looking at our current customer journey, where could an "AI Swarm" (specialized agents for sentiment, policy, and drafting) replace a slow human committee to reduce our response latency from hours to seconds?
- Are we currently suffering from the illusion of AI integration by only using generative AI to "chat" and draft documents, instead of deploying autonomous agents that actually execute tasks via our APIs?

3. The Step-by-Step Implementation

Stop guessing and start building. Use the **Node Architecture Workbook** for step-by-step guidance. This digital workbook provides the exact framework you need to implement this chapter's concepts.

Download it at: NoOneWorksHere.com/nodes

4. The Unfair Advantage: AI-Powered Tools

Don't just read about AI; use it right now. As a reader of this book, you get exclusive access to interactive AI-software tools designed to do the heavy lifting for you.

(*continued*)

(*continued*)

Access your tools instantly at: NoOneWorksHere.com
(Or simply scan the QR code with your smartphone camera)

4

The Architect and the Moat

What happens when leaders can't lead through intelligence?
The constraints are human leadership and decision-making, not technology.

In this chapter, you will:

- **Define the Human Moat:** Identify the specific cognitive skills, social skills, and roles that AI cannot replicate.
- **Understand the Prediction Limit:** Learn why AI is excellent at providing answers but subpar at asking questions.
- **Audit Your Decision Latency:** Identify where your personal involvement is slowing down the organization.
- **Shift Your Leadership Style:** Move from being a "captain" who directs tasks to an "architect" who designs systems.
- **Navigate the Accountability Gap:** Understand the critical concept of the "moral crumple zone" and why legal liability cannot be delegated.
- **Audit for False Empathy:** Identify where you are using humans to do robotic work, and robots to do human work.

I have stood on stages from Cambridge to Silicon Valley and all around the world, speaking to rooms full of founders, executives, and investors. Over the last 18 months, I have started asking a simple, uncomfortable question.

I ask them to imagine a scenario five years from now. You have two options for the CEO of the company managing your retirement portfolio, or the logistics firm handling your supply chain.

- **Option A:** A human CEO: experienced, credentialed, but prone to fatigue, bias, and ego
- **Option B:** An AI CEO: data-driven, tireless, capable of processing millions of variables per second with zero latency

I ask for a show of hands: "Who would you bet on?" Two years ago, the room would have laughed. They would have voted for the human out of solidarity. Today, the hands go up for the AI CEO, a reality I have now invested significant research and development efforts to bring "to life." More on that in the epilogue.

While of course most would prefer an option C, in which a human CEO leads empowered with AI by their side, this is a remarkable shift in market sentiment. We are reaching a tipping point where society is beginning to trust the consistency of code more than the variability of human judgment.

However, the "vote" isn't monolithic. When I poll a room of fintech founders, the buy-in for Option B is near-total. But when I speak to leaders in aviation, biotech, or heavy manufacturing, the room tightens. And if I'm speaking to a room of public servants, the hands stay down, usually because in a world of "gotcha" politics, a human scapegoat is still much easier to haul before a subcommittee than an algorithm.

These leaders recognize what the "move fast and break things" crowd often forgets: In industries governed by physical constraints, safety-critical systems, and geopolitical nuance, the cost of an "AI hallucination" isn't a lost trade. It's a lost life or a national security crisis.

We are witnessing a fragmented revolution. While a SaaS company or quantitative hedge fund might move toward a fully autonomous AI leadership model within the decade, a global titan like Nestlé or Boeing operates in a different reality. These organizations require a "human-in-the-loop" architecture where AI handles the massive computational load of R&D and supply chain optimization, but a human captain navigates the turbulent waters of government affairs, public relations, and customer empathy.

This presents a thought-provoking paradox for the modern leader. The question is no longer whether AI can out-decide a human, but where we will permit it to do so. We are moving toward a world of "bimodal leadership," which builds off Gartner's concept of bimodal IT, a practice of managing two separate styles of work with one focused on predictability, the other on agility:

- **High-Determinism Sectors:** Finance, logistics, and digital marketing, for example, where AI decision-making will become the primary driver
- **High-Criticality Sectors:** Aviation, healthcare, and energy, for example, where AI acts as the ultimate copilot, but the moral and legal "stop" remains human

The New Constraint: From Captain to Architect

You may have spent your career climbing a hierarchy or building your business based on the assumption that you were the smartest person in the room. You were the "super-processor" of information. But in the age of intelligent systems, you are no longer the processor. You are the bottleneck.

We are witnessing a shift in the physics of business, and thus, leadership:

- **Old Model:** The leader provides the intelligence (answers the questions).
- **New Model:** The leader provides the intent (designs the questions).

The constraint is no longer compute power. The constraint is your ability to let go of the controls without introducing unnecessary risk to the business. I tell my students that they need to stop thinking of themselves as the "captain of the ship." That is a romantic, 19th-century idea. It assumes a slow feedback loop.

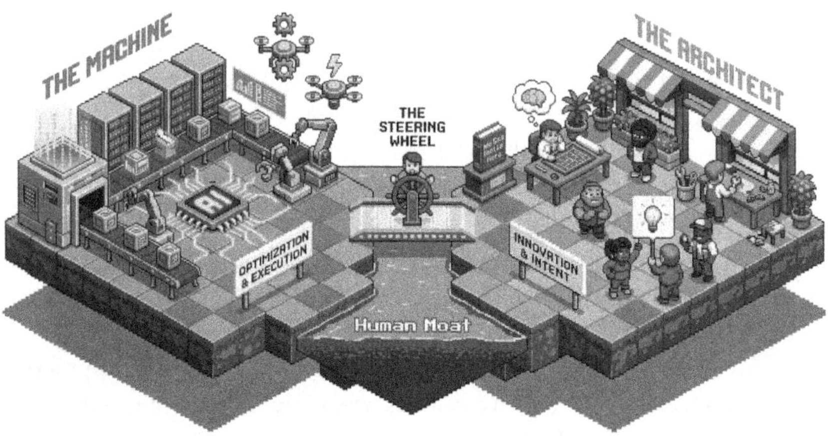

Instead, they need to think more like a modern evolution of the systems architect, one who orchestrates the high-level structure of complex agentic systems. In a world where intelligence is a commodity, the value of *doing* the work drops to near zero. The value of *designing* the work skyrockets.

The Three Shifts of AI Leadership

1. **From Directing to Programming:** You are no longer telling people what to do. You are programming systems to understand what "good" looks like. You are setting the parameters, the guardrails, the objective functions, and providing examples of excellence.
2. **From Intuition to Data-First Hypotheses:** The "gut feeling" of a founder is often just pattern recognition based on limited data.

AI has better pattern recognition. Your job is to frame the hypothesis: "If we lower CAC by 20%, does LTV hold?" Then let the agents run the experiment. It's important to note that this assumes the AI hasn't already proactively created such a hypothesis.

3. **From Managing People to Orchestrating Nodes:** Remember the definition from our proposal: An organization is a dynamic network of human and nonhuman nodes. You are orchestrating a hybrid workforce. You need to know which tasks require a human touch (empathy, high-stakes negotiation) and which require an API call.

Probabilistic Management: Leading the Black Box

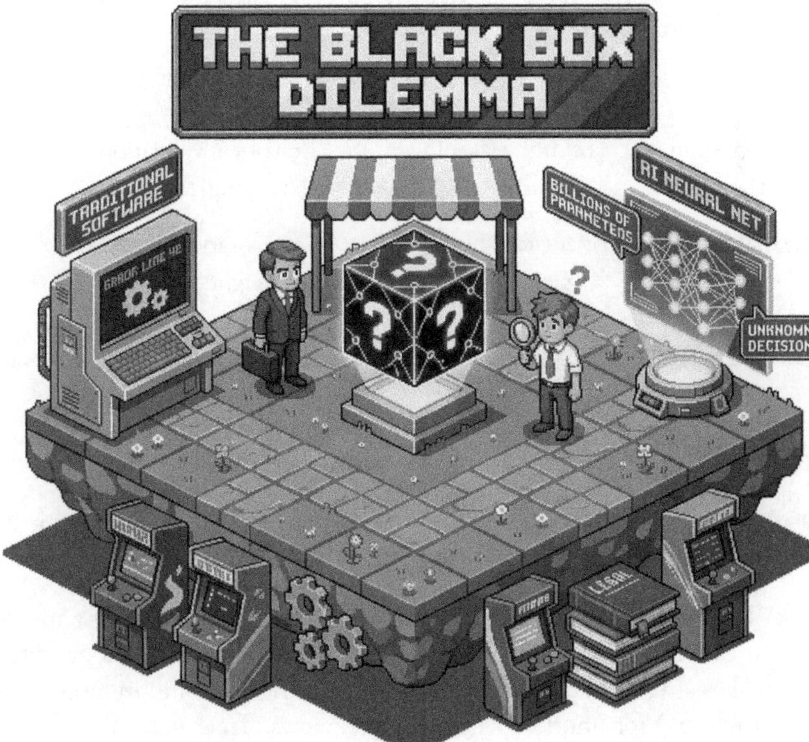

Engineering students love certainty (2 + 2 = 4), but AI is "fuzzy." Leading an AIDE requires shifting from instruction to intent:

- **Instruction:** "Click this button, then type this word."
- **Intent:** "Optimize this email for a 20% click-through rate, keeping the tone professional."

You are no longer debugging code; you are guiding outcomes and checking results. You must accept the black box, the fact that we often cannot explain in a linear way exactly *why* a neural network made a specific decision.

The Transparency Double Standard

Interestingly, leaders have been managing "black boxes" their entire careers: human employees.

Feature	Human Employee	AI Node
Primary Audit Method	Post hoc reasoning (interviews)	Statistical validation (testing)
Internal Logic	Biological "black box" (neurons)	Computational "black box" (weights)
Consistency	Variable (mood/fatigue)	High (controlled)

Case Study: The Marketing Bottleneck

Let's look at a real-world friction point. A B2B SaaS company needs to pivot its messaging:

- **The Legacy Approach (Human Latency):** The CEO calls a meeting. The team debates. The VP briefs a copywriter. The copywriter takes a week to draft. The VP of marketing edits and iterates with the CEO for another week. Legal reviews. *Time elapsed: 4 weeks. Result: One campaign launched.*
- **The AI-Driven Approach (Orchestration):** The founder acts as the architect. They do not write the copy; they define the intent:

"Test 50 variations of value propositions for the healthcare sector. Optimize for click-through rates above 2.5%. Maintain a tone of 'authoritative but scrappy.'" They input this intent into a multi-agent stack composed of a healthcare research expert agent, a conversion copywriter agent, a brand critic agent, and a media buyer agent. *Time elapsed: 4 hours. Result: 50 experiments run, winning message identified, data collected.*

The legacy approach traps an executive's most valuable asset—their time—in manual review cycles. The AI-driven leader is highly effective because the technology frees them to act as the ultimate orchestrator.

The Human Moat: The "How" Versus the "Why"

If you stopped reading there, you might assume my worldview is bleak. You might think I believe humans are destined to become "pet humans" for super-intelligent algorithms, or that the future of work is a barren landscape where no one is needed. That is not the case.

The title of this book is *No One Works Here*. It is not *No One Matters Here* or *No One Creates Value Here*.

Strip away the marketing hype. LLMs function by predicting the next "token" in a sequence. This creates a fundamental paradox: AI is forward-facing in its output, but backward-looking by design. It is trained on data that already exists. It is the ultimate lagging indicator. AI can mimic the "new," but it cannot inhabit the "novel."

This creates a clear boundary line:

- **AI solves the "how."** If you know you need to optimize a supply chain for cost, AI can run the math.
- **Humans own the "why."** Why are we optimizing for cost instead of resilience? Is that ethical? Is it the best use of our brand capital?

I tell my students: In the age of AI, the answer is cheap. The question is expensive. As Thomas Watson, founder of IBM, said, "The ability to ask the right question is more than half the battle of finding the answer."

The Delimitation of Value

As you restructure your organization, you need a filter to decide what to automate and what to keep human. Use this framework.

The Domain of AI (The Machine)	The Domain of Humans (The Architect)	Why?
Optimization: Making an existing process faster/cheaper.	Innovation: Creating a process that didn't exist.	AI excels at refining known variables. Humans still hold the "spark" for entirely new paradigms.
Execution: Performing the task defined by the prompt.	Intent: Defining the prompt and the definition of success.	LLMs and agents are already becoming the "hands." The human remains the "commander."
Consistency: Doing the same thing 1,000 times without error.	Novelty: Doing something new or counterintuitive.	Silicon doesn't get tired. Humans provide the "erratic" genius that breaks ruts.
Answers: Retrieving known information.	Questions: Framing the problem.	Search is dead; synthesis is here. However, knowing what to ask requires deep contextual empathy.
Simulation: Predicting likely outcomes based on data.	Accountability: Taking responsibility for the outcome.	AI can model a crash, but it can't "own" the consequences. Ethics and liability stay with the architect.

The machine is the engine; you control the steering wheel. If you let go of the wheel, the engine will keep running, but it will drive you off a cliff. To move from this theoretical "delimitation of value" to practical organizational design, we must plot our tasks against the primary

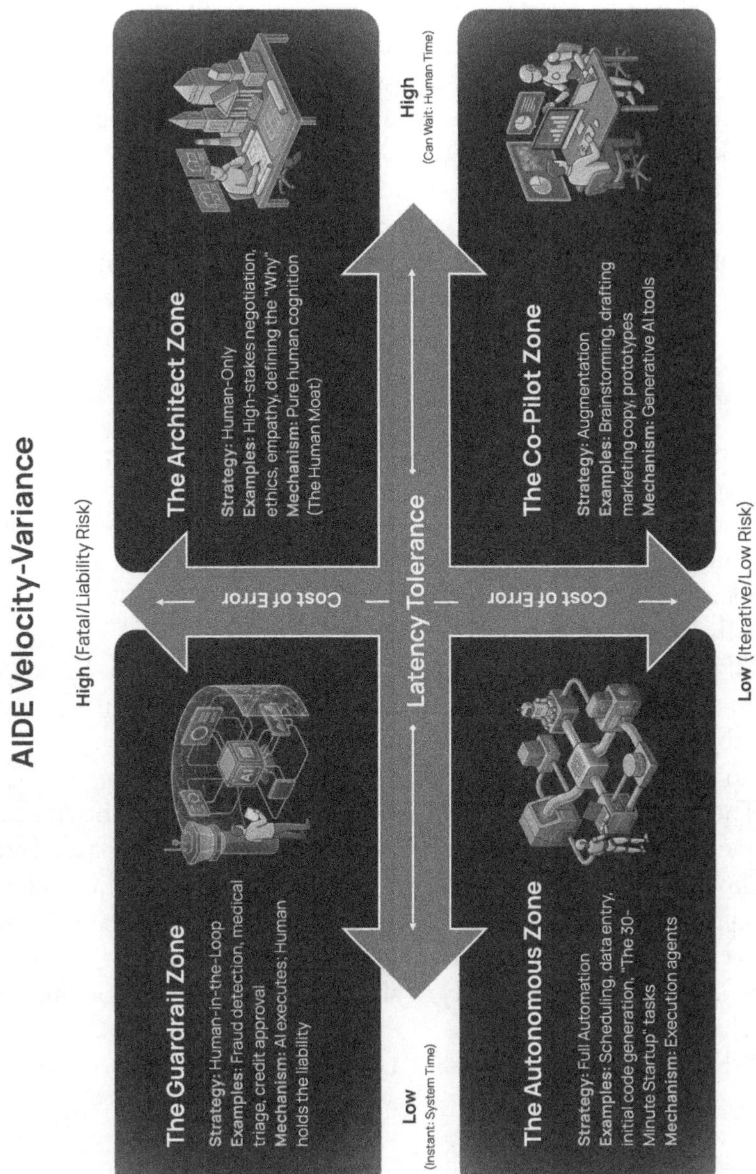
AIDE Velocity-Variance
High (Fatal/Liability Risk)
Cost of Error
Latency Tolerance
Cost of Error
Low (Iterative/Low Risk)
Low (Instant: System Time)
High (Can Wait: Human Time)
The Guardrail Zone
Strategy: Human-in-the-Loop
Examples: Fraud detection, medical triage, credit approval
Mechanism: AI executes; Human holds the liability
The Architect Zone
Strategy: Human-Only
Examples: High-stakes negotiation, ethics, empathy, defining the "Why"
Mechanism: Pure human cognition (The Human Moat)
The Autonomous Zone
Strategy: Full Automation
Examples: Scheduling, data entry, initial code generation, "The 30-Minute Startup" tasks
Mechanism: Execution agents
The Co-Pilot Zone
Strategy: Augmentation
Examples: Brainstorming, drafting marketing copy, prototypes
Mechanism: Generative AI tools

constraints of the AIDE era: latency tolerance and the cost of error. While the machine handles the high-velocity engine of execution, the human "architect" must determine where high-stakes liability requires a permanent human firewall. The AIDE velocity-variance framework provides the operational map for these decisions, identifying where the "human moat" remains a strategic necessity and where autonomous agents can be safely deployed at machine speed.

By categorizing workflows into these four zones—the guardrail, the architect, the autonomous, and the copilot—leaders can systematically reduce human labor while ensuring that the value of human intent and accountability rises to meet the risk of the outcome.

Accountability and Liability in an AIDE

There is one specific reason why humans will never be fully removed from the loop: Liability cannot be delegated.

In risk management, there is a fundamental law: You can delegate a task, but you cannot delegate the liability. If an autonomous agent routes a shipment of perishable goods to the wrong port, the lawsuit doesn't name the algorithm. It names you.

I'll never forget a keynote I gave in Bratislava, Slovakia. During the Q&A, the Slido board lit up with a singular, anxious theme: Who is the "one throat to choke"? If an AI agent effectively runs a company, who goes to jail?

The "accountability gap" is the growing chasm between the AI's computational agency and the human's legal liability. This creates a dangerous paradox. As AI tools search, digest, and interpret 99% of the evidence, the human decision-maker risks becoming a "moral crumple zone." Just as a car's crumple zone is designed to absorb the impact of a crash, the human in the loop may soon exist only to absorb the legal and ethical impact of a machine's failure.

When an AI hallucinates, it's a glitch. When a human acts on that hallucination, it's negligence.

Example: The Medical Diagnosis

AI is already better at reading radiology scans than human doctors. It identifies patterns the human eye misses.

- **What Changes:** The radiologist no longer spends hours squinting at screens. The "work" of detection is gone.
- **What Stays the Same:** The conversation with the patient. The interpretation of risk. The decision to operate. An AI can say, "There is a 95% probability of a tumor." Only a human can look another human in the eye and say, "Here is how we are going to fight this."

False Empathy

One of the biggest mistakes I see founders make is trying to use AI to fake humanity. We have all interacted with customer support chatbots that try to be "empathic." They say, "I am so sorry to hear you are having trouble," but we know it's a script. It lands in the "uncanny valley."

Don't use AI to fake empathy. Instead, it's important to use AI to deliver competence. If I'm calling my bank because my card was stolen, I don't want a robot to tell me it "feels my pain." I want a robot to cancel the card and issue a new one in three seconds. That is competence.

The Pack and the Wolf

My mentor, Bill Aulet, often cites Rudyard Kipling's law of the jungle:

> *For the strength of the pack is the wolf, and the strength of the wolf is the pack.*

In the context of this chapter, the wolf is the individual, whether that is you, the architect, or the human employee providing the "human moat" of empathy and novelty. The pack is the hybrid system you have designed.

One cannot function without the other:

- **The Strength of the Wolf Is the Pack:** Even your most talented human employees, your "wolves," are crippled if they are forced to do "robotic work." Their strength is only realized when the organization provides an AI-driven "pack" to handle the high-latency, deterministic tasks, freeing them to focus on high-value intent.

- **The Strength of the Pack Is the Wolf:** Conversely, an autonomous system without human "wolves" is just a black box. It lacks the "why," the accountability, and the "human moat" that protects the organization from the risk of a machine-speed hallucination.

The architect's job is to ensure that the machine provides the power, while the humans provide the purpose. You aren't just building a faster company; you are building a stronger pack.

No One Works Here: The Digital War Room

You've learned the theory; now let's build the machinery. Turn these concepts into immediate ROI for your company by accessing your free resources at NoOneWorksHere.com.

1. Immediate Actions (Do This Today)

- **Define Your "Intent Stack":** Stop telling your team or your software exactly how to do their jobs. Rewrite your current quarterly objectives as clear, measurable parameters and guardrails that an autonomous agent could understand and optimize against.
- **Conduct a "Why/How" Audit:** Review your top three most time-consuming projects and categorize every task as either "the how" (data synthesis, routine coding, optimization) or "the why" (ethical oversight, intent, novelty). Immediately slate one "how" task for AI automation to free up human capacity for "why" strategy.
- **Identify Your "Moral Crumple Zones":** Pinpoint where in your workflow a human is simply "pressing the button" on AI-generated data. Assign a "licensed auditor" role to that person.
- **Kill "False Empathy" Scripts:** Audit your automated customer touchpoints and remove any language where the AI attempts to "feel" for the customer. Replace these scripts with "competence triggers."

2. The Discussion (Bring This to Your Team)

- Be brutally honest: Are our leaders currently operating as 19th-century "captains" manually steering the ship, or as modern "architects" orchestrating complex systems?
- In our current structure, who is the "one throat to choke" for our automated processes? If our AI-driven systems caused a significant legal or ethical failure, do we have a clear firewall of accountability, or are we operating in a dangerous "accountability gap"?
- If our execution costs (the "how") dropped to zero tomorrow, what novel "why" questions would we be asking that we are currently too busy to consider?

3. The Step-by-Step Implementation

Stop guessing and start building. Use the **Architect's Leadership Workbook** for step-by-step guidance. This digital workbook provides the exact framework you need to implement this chapter's concepts.

Download it at: NoOneWorksHere.com/leadership

4. The Unfair Advantage: AI-Powered Tools

Don't just read about AI; use it right now. As a reader of this book, you get exclusive access to interactive AI-software tools designed to do the heavy lifting for you.

Access your tools instantly at: NoOneWorksHere.com

(Or simply scan the QR code with your smartphone camera)

5

Business Models and Changing Buying Behavior

Can your organization move at the speed of a digital pulse?
The shift from retrospective data to real-time reflexes defines the new market leaders.

FOR DECADES, THE "corporate scorecard" was a lagging indicator. We looked at quarterly reports to see what happened 90 days ago. We looked at market research to see what consumers liked last year. In the AI era, latency is the enemy.

The winners are no longer those with the most "seats" or the most features. The winners are those who can close the gap between a consumer's latent desire and the enterprise's delivery. Just as macroeconomists and meteorologists rely on real-time data to understand current conditions, organizations must do the same. We are moving from a world of quarterly forecasts to a world of real-time now-casts. To survive, your organization must transition from a slow-moving hierarchy to a responsive nervous system.

In this chapter, you will:

- **Master Real-Time Reflexivity:** Learn to pivot from "rearview mirror" data to a responsive nervous system that fulfills latent demand the moment it peaks.
- **Win the Attention War:** Understand why "feature fatigue" is the hidden killer of modern margins and why shipping more code can actually decrease your market value.
- **Innovate Your GTM Strategy:** Shift your go-to-market approach from selling the complexity of the "build" to selling the measurable "delta" of the outcome.
- **Uncouple Revenue from Seats:** Break the linear growth trap by uncoupling your income from your customer's headcount, transforming your business model into a high-velocity utility.
- **Adopt the Orchestrator Mindset:** Transition from "destination apps" built for human eyeballs to Invisible UIs designed for agent experience (AX) and proactive execution.

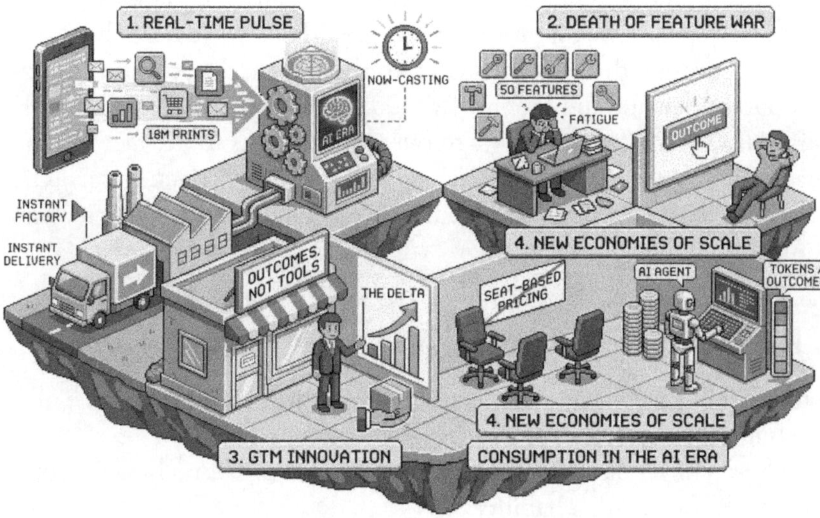

1. The Pulse of the Machine: Consumption in the AI Era, from Retrospective Trends to Real-Time Reflexes

The traditional rhythm of consumption, once a slow dance of quarterly reports and annual projections, has been replaced by a frantic, real-time pulse. We are entering an era where the gap between a consumer's desire and an enterprise's delivery is shrinking toward zero.

What? A shift from "rearview mirror" data (learning what people liked last quarter) to "now-casting" (identifying demand as it happens).

Why? In the "old world," companies relied on the "big three": Mintel, Kantar, and Nielsen. These provided invaluable data, but the product development cycle was perpetually chasing a ghost. AI-Driven Enterprises use real-time digital footprints to respond to demand before it peaks.

Imagine you are a food and beverage titan. On a random Tuesday night, a contestant on a reality show like *Big Brother* whips up an improvised, unconventional spicy pumpkin soup. It wasn't a planned marketing stunt, but the internet explodes. Within an hour, an AI insights platform registers 18 million digital prints, searches, tags, and mentions of people craving that specific flavor profile. In the pre-AI era, you'd hear about this at a board meeting three months later. In the AI era, the goal is instantaneous latent demand fulfillment. By 8:00 the next morning, your supply chain software has automatically rerouted ingredients to the factory, and your marketing agents have already pre-sold the first production run. The enterprise becomes a nervous system that reacts to the consumer's whim as quickly as a muscle flinches.

2. The Death of the Feature War

As the cost of production (the "build") drops toward zero, we hit the ultimate human wall: attention.

What? The realization that shipping more features is no longer a competitive advantage, it's a liability.

Why? Users are drowning in "feature fatigue." If you ship 50 new AI-powered tools, but the user only has the mental bandwidth to learn three, the other 47 represent wasted capital. In the AI era, the goal is to do more things *for* the user so they don't have to pay attention at all.

3. GTM Innovation: Selling Outcomes, Not Tools

What? A radical shift in "go-to-market" strategy that focuses on the *delta* (the result) rather than the complexity of the code. This is not new, exactly, and reflects Clayton Christensen's "jobs to be done" theory (Christensen 2016), as well as Theodore Levitt's famous marketing axiom ("People don't want to buy a quarter-inch drill. They want a quarter-inch hole").

Why? If a buyer knows an AI helped you build a tool in a weekend, they won't pay for your "effort."

This forces two shifts:

1. **From "How It Works" to "What It Does":** Buyers care about the measurable difference between their problem and your solution. This is what we refer to as the Quantified Value Proposition (QVP) in *Disciplined Entrepreneurship*.
2. **Invisible Enablement:** The product or service becomes proactive. Instead of a user searching for a "trend" button, the AI pushes the insight to them.

4. The Death of the "Seat": Uncoupling Revenue from Headcount

For decades, the SaaS (Software as a Service) model thrived on seat-based pricing. It was a simple proxy for value: More users meant more utility. But in the AI era, this model creates a fundamental "revenue/people paradox." If an AI agent performs the work of 10 people, a provider charging for a single "seat" is effectively punishing themselves for their own efficiency. To maintain a high revenue-to-people cost ratio, the business model must shift from charging for access to charging for outcomes.

The assumption in the manual era was that revenue was relatively fixed per employee. To grow, you added seats. In the AI era, we move from charging per human "license" to charging per unit of work (tokens, computes, or business outcomes). When revenue is tied to seats, it is inherently linear. When revenue is tied to consumption or outcomes, it becomes exponential. You are no longer limited by the customer's hiring plan; you are limited only by the volume of work your AI can handle.

When companies like Lovable, led by executives like CRO Ryan Meadows, move to a consumption-based model, they remove the psychological barrier of the "license." When a user doesn't have to ask procurement for permission to add a new seat, they let the AI run. As Meadows (2026) notes, "Seat-based pricing is a relic of the manual labor era. If AI is doing the work of 10 people, charging for one 'seat' is a race to the bottom."

By shifting to usage or outcome-based models, the revenue-to-people cost ratio improves drastically because:

- **Revenue Is No Longer "Fixed":** It scales with the AI's performance, not the customer's office size.
- **Zero Marginal Cost of Distribution:** Doubling your revenue through increased AI usage doesn't require doubling your support or sales staff.

5. The Invisible UI: Solving the Attention Bottleneck by Moving from "Active Search" to "Proactive Presence"

In the "manual era," success was measured by "time on website" or in-app. In the AI era, the most valuable software is the kind you never have to look at.

This shift isn't just about efficiency; it's about a fundamental change in our relationship with technology. As Armand Ruiz, vice president of AI platform at IBM, recently noted, "The moment I stopped thinking of myself as a 'user' and started thinking of myself as an orchestrator, everything changed. I set goals. I define constraints. I verify outcomes. That's it. The entire middle, the actual work, I don't touch it anymore" (Ruiz 2026a).

Ruiz argues that we are currently building "obsolete" software because we are still designing for humans to operate. In the AIDE era, the software we build won't have traditional dashboards or onboarding flows; it will be built of APIs and feedback loops designed for agents. The real question for any modern leader, as Ruiz puts it, isn't how to use AI to help humans use a feature, but rather, "If no human ever had to touch this, what would we build from scratch?" (Ruiz 2026a).

This "orchestrator mindset" is the psychological bridge to the zero-touch enterprise. It requires us to stop building UIs for human eyeballs and start building "agent experience" (AX) for machine intelligence. The final evolution of this shift is the zero-touch enterprise. It doesn't wait for a human to sit in a seat to create value.

No One Works Here: The Digital War Room

You've learned the theory; now let's build the machinery. Turn these concepts into immediate ROI for your company by accessing your free resources at NoOneWorksHere.com.

1. Immediate Actions (Do This Today)

- **Audit Your Latency:** Identify the time gap between a market shift and your operational response to determine where "rearview mirror" data is slowing your growth. Set up one real-time social listening AI agent today to monitor your brand, moving you from "rearview mirror" quarterly data to "now-casting."
- **Kill One Button:** Select a single manual feature in your product, workflow, or customer experience and transition it into an automated background process that requires zero human intervention.
- **Review Your Pricing Logic:** Calculate how much revenue you are leaving on the table by charging per "seat" instead of per unit of work or successful outcome.
- **Hunt for Vertical Vendors:** Identify one horizontal software platform your company heavily relies on. Spend 30 minutes today researching emerging, AI-native vertical tools in your industry that sell the final cognitive result rather than just the software itself.

2. The Discussion (Bring This to Your Team)

- If our customers didn't have to pay for individual "seats," or our current pricing unit how much more work would they allow our product to perform, and how would that data accelerate our AI's intelligence?

(*continued*)

(*continued*)

- Are we currently suffering from "feature fatigue" by shipping code that adds complexity rather than solving for the "delta" of a measurable customer outcome?
- If no human ever had to touch our interface again, what would we build from scratch to serve an "agent experience" (AX) rather than a human "user experience" (UX)?

3. The Step-by-Step Implementation

Stop guessing and start building. Use the **AIDE Business Model Workbook** for step-by-step guidance. This digital workbook provides the exact framework you need to implement this chapter's concepts.

Download it at: NoOneWorksHere.com/business-models

4. The Unfair Advantage: AI-Powered Tools

Don't just read about AI; use it right now. As a reader of this book, you get exclusive access to interactive AI-software tools designed to do the heavy lifting for you.

Access your tools instantly at: NoOneWorksHere.com

(Or simply scan the QR code with your smartphone camera)

6

The Dial-Up Era of AI

What is the true cost of waiting for "perfect" technology during the messy, fragmented "dial-up era" of AI?
The runway ahead is long . . . and you are an early adopter.

IF YOU OPEN X (Twitter) right now, it feels like the world is accelerating away from you. You see 22-year-olds building unicorns. You see new AI models released every Tuesday. You feel the anxiety of the "late adopter." You worry that the train has left the station.

I have good news for you: The train hasn't left. We are still laying the tracks. We are currently living in the dial-up era of AI.

In this chapter, you will:

- **Contextualize the Current Friction:** Understand why AI feels magical yet clunky
- **Use the "LimeWire Test":** A mental model for recognizing early-stage technology
- **Identify the Infrastructure Gap:** Why the lack of standards is your biggest opportunity
- **Prepare for the "Broadband" Moment:** What happens when the friction disappears

The Illusion of Maturity

Because AI can pass the bar exam and write poetry, we assume the technology is mature. It isn't.

While the *intelligence* is high, the *integration* is low.

Think back to the early days of the internet. The promise was "information at your fingertips." The reality was a screeching modem noise, a blocked phone line, and a web page that loaded pixel by pixel. We are in the exact same phase with artificial intelligence. We have the "capability" (the internet connection), but we lack the "bandwidth" (the smooth integration).

The LimeWire Moment

Let me take you back to a specific moment in time to illustrate this.

Remember the mid-2000s? Before you could instantly stream "Boom Boom Pow" by the Black Eyed Peas on Spotify or Apple Music, you had to struggle.

You went to LimeWire or Napster. You searched for the file. You clicked "Download." Then you went to have dinner. You came back two hours later, hovered your mouse over the progress bar, and saw: 17% downloaded.

It was miraculous—you were getting music for free from the ether, but it was painfully slow and unreliable.

This is exactly where we are with AI today.

Consider one of the many vibe coding tools available on the market today, miraculous tools that allow you to build software just by describing it. Or an AI spreadsheet tool that enables you to build a five-year pro forma financial model with a basic prompt. If you prompt a vibecoding tool to build a complex application or ask for a financial model, you don't get it instantly. You wait. It might take 5 or 10 minutes to generate v1. You might have to "debug" the prompt. You might have to wait for the "server busy" error to clear.

We tolerate this friction because the result is magic. But make no mistake: Waiting 10 minutes for an app is the modern equivalent of waiting two hours for a Black Eyed Peas song.

The Five Signs of the Dial-Up Era

How do we know we are still in the early, "dial-up" phase of the AI transition? We look for the friction. In the history of technology, friction isn't a reason to stop; it's a sign that the infrastructure is still catching up to the vision. Look for these five signals to understand why the "broadband era" of AI-Driven Enterprises has yet to reach its full velocity.

1. High Latency

As discussed in Chapter 1, latency is the enemy. Right now, talking to an LLM takes time. Chaining agents together takes even more time. We are measuring responses in seconds, sometimes minutes. In the "broadband era" of AI, this will be measured in milliseconds.

2. Fragmentation (No DNS)

In the early internet, finding things was hard until we invented Domain Name System (DNS) and search engines. Today, AI is fragmented. Your "sales agent" doesn't know how to talk to your "calendar agent" without custom setup. There is no universal protocol, no HTTP, for agents to communicate. While model context protocol (MCP) aims to fill this void, the reality is that there are far more MCP servers than clients, meaning that people aren't using it to its fullest potential. (Although I am excited about the work that many are doing to establish these norms!)

3. The "Waiting Room" Fallacy

Leaders ask, "Why should I invest millions in integrating this LLM today when a faster, cheaper, and more capable model will be released in six months?" This is the Waiting Room Fallacy. It assumes that the value of AI is in the software itself. It isn't. The value is in the organizational muscle memory you build by learning how to integrate AI into your workflows.

Jeff Seibert, CEO of Digits, describes a world where he no longer "codes" in the traditional sense, but instead dictates intent in plain English to AI agents. "I can now ship more software every day than I ever have in my life, but the thing I spent my entire life being good at? That's now gone" (Seibert 2026). If you wait for the technology to "settle," you will be attempting to build a high-speed organization on a foundation of zero experience. By the time you start, your competitors will have already iterated through a hundred experiments.

4. The Sovereignty Imperative

There is a second danger in the dial-up era: building on rented land. If your entire AIDE relies on a closed-source model (like GPT-X), you are vulnerable to pricing spikes, censorship, or model degradation. While you may start by renting intelligence for speed, your long-term roadmap must include a path to "owning the weights," fine-tuning open-source models (like Llama or Mistral) on your own infrastructure to ensure your company's brain cannot be turned off by a third party.

5. Mainstream Skepticism

Just as critics famously dismissed the internet as a "fad" for hobbyists, many legacy leaders today dismiss AI as a "gimmick." This skepticism is a leading indicator of early adoption. When the skeptics finally capitulate and admit that AI is the new standard, the "alpha," your competitive advantage, is gone.

The Infrastructure Gap

The lag of generative AI is a feature of early adoption. And for the entrepreneurs and intrapreneurs reading this, it is the opportunity. If AI were perfect, if it were instant, integrated, and standardized, the market would be saturated. The winners would already be established. Because infrastructure, policy, literacy, and integration are all in their infancy, the field is wide open. We are not just building companies; we are building the protocols, standards, and behaviors that will enable a new era of intelligent organizations.

No One Works Here: The Digital War Room

You've learned the theory; now let's build the machinery. Turn these concepts into immediate ROI for your company by accessing your free resources at NoOneWorksHere.com.

1. Immediate Actions (Do This Today)

- **Audit Your Friction Points:** Identify two internal software tools that currently do not talk to each other. Use a tool like Zapier with AI or an integration agent to bridge that specific gap today without having to deal with the complexities of data structures.
- **Kill the Waiting Room Fallacy:** Select one low-risk internal workflow and implement a "good enough" AI solution today to begin building the organizational muscle memory required for the broadband era.
- **Assess Your Sovereignty:** Review your current AI tech stack to determine whether you are "building on rented land" and identify one open-source model (like Llama or Mistral) you could test for long-term data independence.

(*continued*)

(continued)

2. The Discussion (Bring This to Your Team)

- If our primary AI tools were suddenly a hundred times faster and perfectly integrated (the "broadband moment"), which parts of our current business model would become obsolete overnight?
- Are we acting as "waiters" or "operators"? Specifically, what is the hidden cost of delaying our AI integration while our competitors are already iterating through their first hundred experiments?
- As AI shifts the "Unit of Work" from generating output to setting strategy, which roles in our department are at the highest risk of being "LimeWired" out of relevance?

3. The Step-by-Step Implementation

Stop guessing and start building. Use the **Dial-Up to Broadband Transition Workbook** for step-by-step guidance. This digital workbook provides the exact framework you need to implement this chapter's concepts.

Download it at: NoOneWorksHere.com/dial-up-era

4. The Unfair Advantage: AI-Powered Tools

Don't just read about AI; use it right now. As a reader of this book, you get exclusive access to interactive AI-software tools designed to do the heavy lifting for you.

Access your tools instantly at: NoOneWorksHere.com

(Or simply scan the QR code with your smartphone camera)

PART

II → III

How do you take the mechanical advantage of a machine-speed organization and translate it into a billion-dollar moat?
Turning the physics of the new enterprise into actionable, exponential strategy.

THIS CONCLUDES PART II, "The Changing Landscape." We have fundamentally redefined the organization as a hybrid network of human and silicon nodes. We have shifted the leadership mandate from a manual "captain" to a systems "architect." We have explored the radical evolution of business models from seat-based licenses to real-time outcomes. And we have pinpointed our exact location in time: the dial-up era of AI.

You now have the context. You understand the physics, the history, and the timing. You know that you are not late; you are arguably the earliest you could possibly be while the technology is actually useful.

With the mechanics exposed, the picture sharpens. You now understand how AI redefines work, scale, and structure. What began as a threat now looks like leverage. The same technologies that dismantle outdated systems also create new ones that move faster and cost less.

So what do you do with this advantage?

The transition from LimeWire (dial-up) to Spotify (broadband) didn't just make music faster. It changed the business model of music.

- **Dial-Up Era:** You owned files. You managed storage. Value was in *access*.
- **Broadband Era:** You stream everything. You own nothing. Value is in *curation*.

We will see the same shift in AI.

- **Current Era:** You prompt a model. You check the work. Value is in the *output*.
- **Future Era:** You set a goal. The stream of intelligence handles it. Value is in the *strategy*.

How do you take this "LimeWire" technology and build a billion-dollar "Spotify" business? How do you capitalize on the efficiency of the AIDE model to grow exponentially?

In Part III: "The Opportunity," we shift from theory to practice. We will show how founders, deep tech innovators, established SMEs, private equity investors, and entire national economies are using this new logic to build organizations that learn and operate on their own. We will go deep on the AI-Driven Enterprise model of growth, the new superpower of creation speed, and how to execute while the rest of the world is still buffering.

PART III

The Opportunities

Building the Next Generation of Intelligent Organizations
AI didn't just change business. It changed what a business is. Intelligence is the new infrastructure.

ONCE YOU UNDERSTAND the mechanics exposed in Part II, the opportunities become undeniable. Every industry, every function, and every profession is being rewritten by AI's ability to think, decide, and act at scale. We are moving from theory to operational reality.

This section is your guide to seizing the opportunities. We will look at how the AI-Driven Enterprise (AIDE) model is rewriting the rules of scale across the entire economic spectrum:

- **The New Mechanics of Growth:** How to flatten your org chart, decouple revenue from headcount, and operate with a fraction of the traditional friction
- **The Shift in Scarcity:** Why the unprecedented speed of creation—the ability to build a company in 30 minutes—has moved the ultimate competitive bottleneck from *Development* to *Distribution*

- **The Universal Application:** How this logic applies everywhere, empowering local SMEs to break out of linear growth and allowing Deep Tech and Big Pharma to compress decades of scientific R&D into computational simulations
- **The Capital and Global Race:** How private equity, venture capital, and national governments are fundamentally rewriting their scorecards to prioritize "Swarm" resilience and computational efficiency over massive capital deployment

You are about to see the emergence of a new kind of company: one that is autonomous, data-driven, and relentlessly experimental. The opportunities are no longer hypothetical. It is ready to be built.

7

AI-Driven Enterprises

The New Model of Growth

What does a company look like when AI is embedded in every functional area at every seniority level?
Explore the structure and economics of AIDEs.

IF WE ARE currently in the "dial-up era" of friction and clunky tools, how are some companies already moving at lightspeed? The answer lies in their architecture. They aren't waiting for the tools to become perfect; they are designing their organizations to absorb the friction and exploit the speed.

How does an entrepreneur achieve the exponential "hockey stick" growth curve sought after by high-impact startups without the need to raise significant funding or blitz-hire?

For decades, the answer to that question was "You don't." If you wanted massive growth, you needed massive capital and a sizable team. You needed to hire an army of engineers, a legion of salespeople, and a fleet of support staff. You had to burn cash to fuel the rocket ship.

But as we established in Parts I and II, we are no longer limited by the speed of human hiring or the depth of our bank accounts. Human training, onboarding, and ramping usually take months, but training an AI agent to understand a code base can be done in seconds.

Consider your next hire. You face a fundamental choice: Do you spend three months ramping up a person to perform a function, or do you spend three months designing a system that can perform that function, ramp instantly, and be replicated 10 times over at marginal cost?

The entrepreneur's new superpower is the ability to determine the optimal hybrid combination. You must decide which outputs require the unique creative judgment of a human and which require the tireless, high-velocity execution of an AI node.

In this chapter, you will:

- **Define the AIDE Category:** The third category of entrepreneurship that bridges the gap between local businesses and global startups
- **Analyze the New Arithmetic:** How companies are reaching $100M ARR with fewer than 50 people
- **Understand Product Development Debt:** How AI shrinks the "Valley of Death"
- **Examine the Lovable Case:** How a team of 15 people built a $17M ARR business in months

The Two Old Models: SME Versus IDE

To understand where we're going, we have to look at the framework we have used at MIT for years, which I touched on in the introduction. My mentor and colleague, Bill Aulet, and Professor Fiona Murray famously distinguished between two types of entrepreneurship. Treating them as a single category is an "important mistake" (Aulet and Murray 2013).

On one side are Small and Medium Enterprises (SMEs), the local restaurants or service firms that grow linearly, require limited upfront capital, and serve a local market. On the other are Innovation-Driven Enterprises (IDEs), the high-growth tech companies like Google or Uber that target global markets, fueled by significant capital and massive R&D.

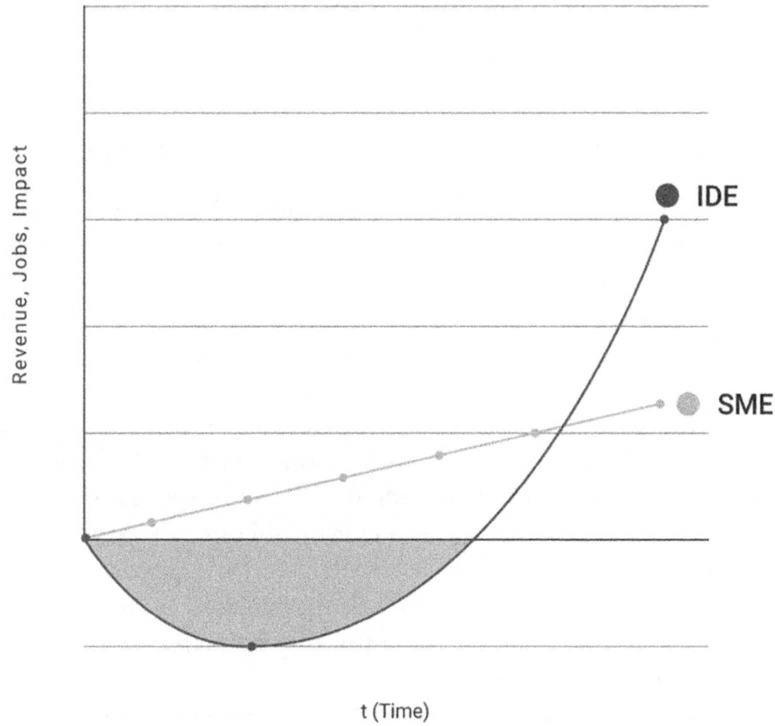

1. **Small and Medium Enterprises (SMEs)** Think of a local restaurant, a dry cleaner, or a consulting shop.
   - **Market:** Local or regional
   - **Innovation:** Low or incremental
   - **Growth:** Linear
   - **Capital:** Self-funded or bank loans
   - **Team:** Small (four employees, on average)
2. **Innovation-Driven Enterprises (IDEs)** Think of Google, Tesla, or Moderna.
   - **Market:** Global
   - **Innovation:** High (technological or business model)
   - **Growth:** Exponential (the hockey stick)
   - **Capital:** High risk (VC, angel, grants)
   - **Team:** Starts small, scales to thousands.

For a long time, you had to choose. You could be small and profitable (SME), or you could be huge and burn cash (IDE).

The Third Model: The AI-Driven Enterprise (AIDE)

For decades, the path seemed binary: stay small and profitable, or go big and scale globally. However, this framework misses a dangerous middle ground that I see all too often, particularly in emerging tech hubs. Many founders find themselves trapped in a "growth purgatory" of startups that possess the DNA of an IDE but the execution of an SME.

These companies often stall due to hesitant decision-making, or what Noam Wasserman (2013) calls the Founder's Dilemma: the choice between being "king" (maintaining total control) or being "rich" (scaling the company). By postponing the difficult structural decisions required for scale, like professionalizing management or diluting equity for capital, these founders create "zombie" startups. They burn through resources without achieving escape velocity. While the economy needs both SMEs and IDEs, it has little room for those stuck in between—too large to be agile, yet too hesitant to truly lead.

That binary is gone, however. We are witnessing the rise of a third category: the AI-Driven Enterprise, which combines the global ambition and innovative edge of an IDE with the lean operational footprint of an SME. It's truly the best of both worlds.

By leveraging AI tools and intelligent agents to handle functions ranging from code generation to customer support, these companies decouple revenue growth from headcount growth. They do not need an army of employees to scale; they need AI-literate humans paired with a fleet of agents.

To be clear, these AIDEs are not exclusively AI companies—any company (including yours!) can be an AIDE by leveraging AI in every functional area across the business.

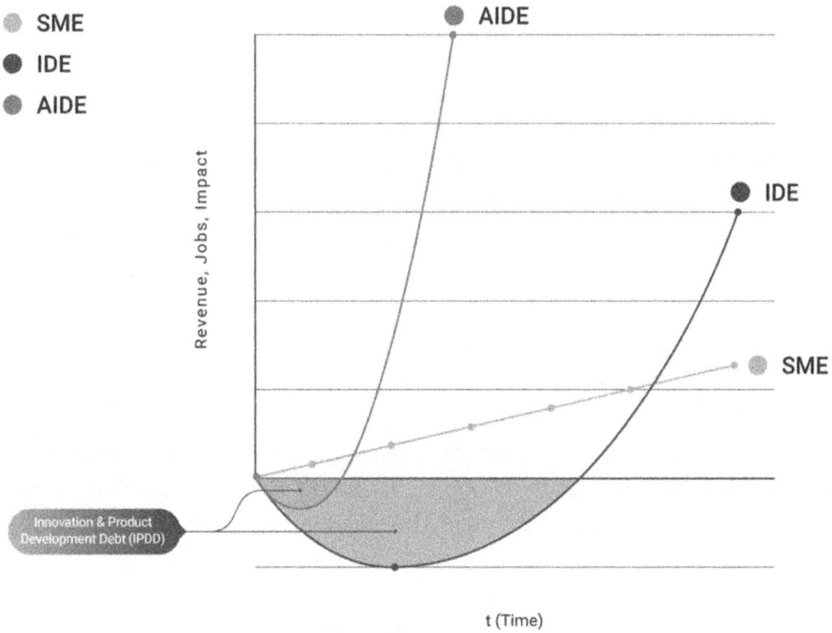

Download this graph and other resources on the AI-Driven Enterprise model: NoOneWorksHere.com/downloads/graphs.

Factor	SME (The Shop)	IDE (The Unicorn)	AIDE (The New Standard)
Ambition	Local/Regional	Global	Global
Innovation	Low/Incremental	High/Disruptive	High/Automated
Capital Need	Low	Very High	Low to Moderate
Time to Market	Short	Long (Years)	Fast (Weeks)
Headcount	Small	Large (Scaling)	Lean (Fixed)
Profitability	Immediate	Long-Term	Accelerated

AIDEs leverage artificial intelligence to drive all aspects of their business, market research, product development, go-to-market, finance, and HR. Because they substitute some *labor* with *compute*, they decrease execution risk and increase the odds of success.

The hallmark of an AI-Driven Enterprise isn't the integration of machines and hardware, but the integration of intellect. While industries have relied on machines to extend our physical reach for over a hundred years, we are now entering an era where machines extend our mental capacity. The AI-Driven Enterprise model rewrites the arithmetic of business. Where a traditional tech company might need 500 employees to generate $100 million in revenue, an AIDE can achieve the same outcome with fewer than 50, often in one-tenth the time. This shift, from labor-intensive scaling to compute-intensive scaling, is the central thesis of this book. We are not automating tasks; we are redesigning the architecture of the firm to move at the speed of software rather than the speed of hiring.

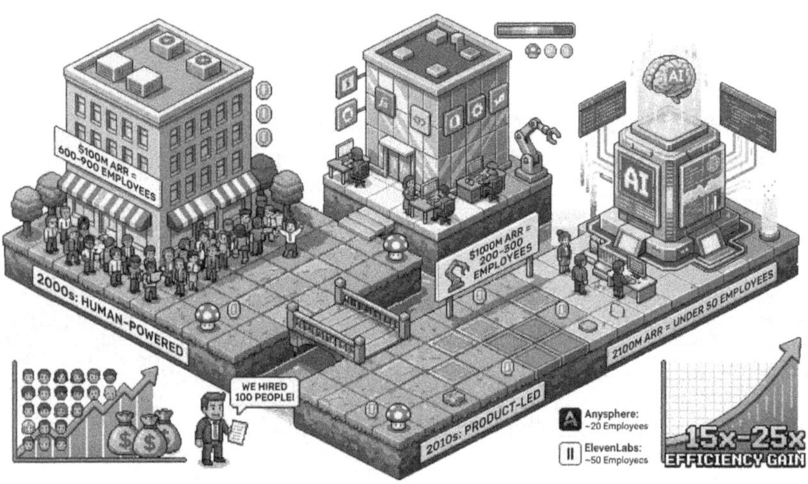

A central pillar of this model is the recognition that technical proficiency, specifically coding, has historically acted as a high-friction gatekeeper, restricting creation to a select guild of experience and educated engineers and forcing the general public into a state of dependency. The AI-Driven Enterprise model decouples risk capital accessibility from entrepreneurial opportunity and economic growth.

For decades, the gap between having an idea and executing it could only be bridged by those fluent in complex programming languages. However, the defining characteristic of the impending "AI era" is the radical democratization of this capability. By decoupling logic from syntax, AI acts as a universal translator, allowing nontechnical visionaries to bypass the traditional engineering bottleneck. This shift implies that the future of technology will be defined not just by new algorithms, but by the unprecedented unleashing of creativity from those who previously lacked the tools to build.

This isn't a prediction. This is reality. To understand the magnitude of this shift, look no further than the trajectories of companies like Cursor (Anysphere) and Lovable. In the traditional software era, reaching $100 million in Annual Recurring Revenue (ARR) was a marathon that typically took 5–10 years and required a headcount of hundreds.

Cursor, an AI-powered code editor led by MIT undergraduate founder and CEO Michael Truell, shattered this ceiling in early 2025, hitting $100 million ARR in just 12 months (Cursor Team 2025) with a team of only 12 people. Lovable accelerated this pace even further, reaching the same milestone in a mere 8 months (AI Giants) with a team of 45 employees (Loizos 2025). For context, compare Lovable's $2.2M revenue per employee to the $203,760 venture-backed Software as a Service (SaaS) industry median ARR/employee in the same year, 2025, for SaaS companies with ARR greater than $20M of revenue (Perry 2025).

Despite raising massive amounts of capital, with Cursor securing over $2.3 billion (Cursor Team) and Lovable raising more than $330 million (Lovable) to fuel their compute-heavy operations, neither felt the need to balloon their workforce. They proved that modern companies can scale revenue exponentially while keeping their human footprint astonishingly small.

Importantly, I must highlight that the AIDE model also helps to achieve one of the primary goals that I have for the entrepreneurs I advise: I want entrepreneurs to own as much of their businesses as possible. In the AIDE model, entrepreneurs generally have the opportunity to retain more equity because they may not need to raise significant risk capital until they have proven traction when they can justify higher valuations.

The Calculus of Compounding: Why AIDE Growth Is "More" Exponential

To understand why the AIDE model is disruptive, we have to move beyond the colloquial use of "exponential" as a synonym for "a lot" and look at the actual math of the curve. In a traditional IDE, growth often feels parabolic, governed by quadratic functions where we add resources to gain output. While some parts of a parabolic curve are steeper than some exponentials, they eventually hit the friction of human scaling. A true exponential function, defined technically as $y = c \times a^x$, is characterized by increasing at an increasing rate.

For the business leader, the distinction is vital: While an IDE's growth graph often struggles to stay "above the line" during the hiring-heavy early years, an AIDE behaves more like a pure mathematical exponential, starting nearly asymptotic to the x-axis before exploding upward. Because the "constant" in our equation is driven by compute rather than headcount, we avoid the trap of thinking exponential is just "one slope." Instead, we leverage a model where the rate of change itself is accelerating. In an AIDE, we aren't just moving fast; we are widening the gap between the parabolic limits of human-centric organizations and the frictionless trajectory of AI-driven scale.

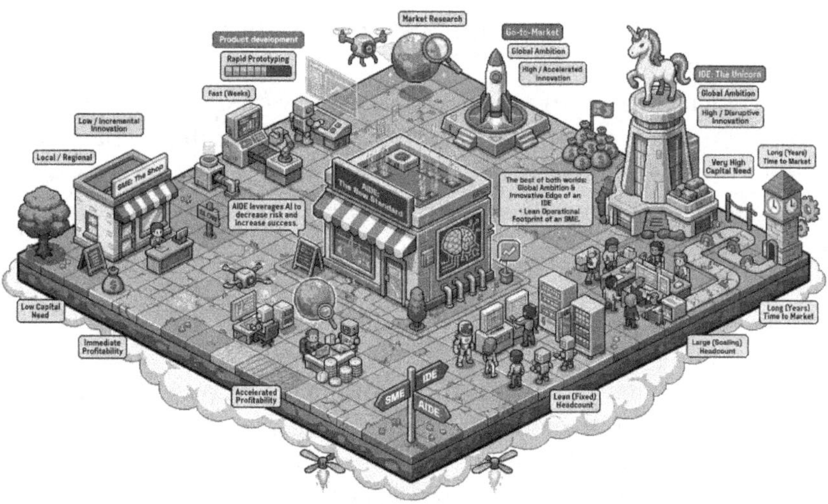

The Collapse of the Valley of Death

Why are AIDEs able to move so fast?

In a traditional IDE, you face a massive gap between having an idea and having a sellable product. Bill Aulet coined Innovation and Product Development Debt (IPDD), a way to measure the Valley of Death (the gap requiring significant investment between developing an early prototype and successfully commercializing it as a scalable, profitable product). You have to hire engineers, build prototypes, fail, iterate, and burn cash for 18 months before you make a dollar. AI collapses this debt.

Clockspeed, a concept defined by MIT's Charlie Fine in his book *Clockspeed: Winning Industry Control in the Age of Temporary Advantage*, refers to the rate at which an industry or company moves, iterates, and evolves (Fine 1998):

- **IDEs** had a faster clockspeed than SMEs.
- **AIDEs** have a clockspeed that is near-instant.

When you use generative AI to code your MVP. (minimum viable product, a concept coined by Frank Robinson and popularized by Eric Ries 2011), market and sell to customers, generate your marketing assets, and set up your legal structure, you are not paying down debt over months. You are paying it down in hours.

The Democratization of Impact

This model changes the geography of innovation. Historically, to build a "unicorn," you needed to be in Silicon Valley, New York, or London. You needed access to the deep pockets of Sand Hill Road because you needed $20 million just to get through the Valley of Death.

The AIDE model democratizes this. I see entrepreneurs building AIDEs in Lagos, in Santiago, Beijing, Sydney, and in rural America. If a small team with laptops and cloud credits can create a globally competitive service, then the limiting factor is no longer capital. The limiting factor is talent.

The Implications

For You, the Founder: You need to become the "top 1% of AI users." Your skill is no longer just "management." It is orchestration. You are an entrepreneur commanding an army of agents.

For Investors: The math has changed. Investors are looking for ARR/FTE ratios that were previously thought impossible at the early stages of new company formation.

For Policy Makers: We need to stop measuring success by "jobs created" in the short term. An AIDE might employ only 20 people, but it generates the wealth and economic impact of a company that used to employ 500. We need to prepare the workforce to be the *founders* of these companies, not just the employees (more on that in Chapter 17).

Part III Continues

The AIDE model is the vehicle. Once you understand the new arithmetic of growth, the next step is to redefine the very map you use to navigate it, leading us directly to the architectural blueprint of the future: the New Age Organization Chart.

Further Reading

If the concepts we've explored have you wondering how the **AI-Driven Enterprise Model** translates from the page to your specific boardroom, you're asking the right questions. Moving beyond the "automation" buzzwords requires a structural shift in how an organization breathes, decides, and scales. To dive deeper into what this evolution looks like for your unique business landscape, and to bridge the gap between theory and operational reality, I invite you to explore our dedicated resources. It's the best way to turn these insights into a tangible, intelligence-led strategy for your team. Learn more here: PaulCheek.com/articles/ai-driven-enterprises

No One Works Here: The Digital War Room

You've learned the theory; now let's build the machinery. Turn these concepts into immediate ROI for your company by accessing your free resources at NoOneWorksHere.com.

1. Immediate Actions (Do This Today)

- **Audit the Engineering Bottleneck:** Identify one product feature or internal tool currently stalled in "development debt" and use an AI code editor to build a functional MVP prototype in hours rather than weeks.
- **Calculate Your IPDD (Innovation and Product Development Debt):** Identify one new product or market expansion currently stalled by resource constraints. Calculate the traditional capital and time required to build an MVP, then task an internal team to use AI to build a functional V1 by the end of the week for under $500.

2. The Discussion (Bring This to Your Team)

- Are there new product lines or market expansions we have abandoned because the traditional Valley of Death (the time and capital required) was too wide? How could an AI-first approach shrink that innovation debt and make those initiatives viable today?
- Are we currently operating in "growth purgatory," possessing the high-reaching goals of an Innovation-Driven Enterprise but the slow, linear execution of a small business?
- How can we shift our internal culture from "management" (overseeing people) to "orchestration" (commanding an army of AI agents), and what specific technical skills does the team need to acquire to lead this transition?

(*continued*)

(*continued*)

3. The Step-by-Step Implementation

Stop guessing and start building. Use the **AIDE Growth Architecture Workbook** for step-by-step guidance. This digital workbook provides the exact framework you need to implement this chapter's concepts.

Download it at: NoOneWorksHere.com/aide-model

4. The Unfair Advantage: AI-Powered Tools

Don't just read about AI; use it right now. As a reader of this book, you get exclusive access to interactive AI-software tools designed to do the heavy lifting for you.

Access your tools instantly at: NoOneWorksHere.com

(Or simply scan the QR code with your smartphone camera)

8

Everywhere in Every Organization

How does a traditional business survive when every competitor inevitably becomes an AI company?

Deploying the AIDE model as a horizontal nervous system across all legacy industries.

THE MOST COMMON pushbacks I hear from executives are "But I'm not an AI company. I make airplane parts," or "I process poultry," or "I manage a logistics fleet."

And they are half-right. You cannot "vibe code" a jet engine or prompt a poultry processing plant into existence. The physical world has friction that code does not. But while your product may be atoms, your process is bits. The AIDE model in heavy industry doesn't replace the factory; it wraps the factory in a nervous system that moves at the speed of thought.

This is a fundamental misunderstanding of the era we have entered. In the 1990s, leaders said, "I'm not an internet company." By 2010, they said, "I'm not a software company." Today, those distinctions are dead. Every company is an AI company, or they are an endangered species.

To be an AIDE does not mean your *product* is an LLM; it means your operating model is built on the backbone of intelligent automation. AI isn't a vertical industry; it is a horizontal layer that can be "dropped in" to virtually any legacy workflow.

In this chapter, you will:

- **Understand the Horizontal Layer:** Learn why AI isn't a vertical industry, but a system that wraps around legacy workflows.
- **Explore the "Drop-In":** See how AI is deployed across sector-agnostic physical industries and functional back-office zones.
- **Identify the Threshold of Trust:** Learn when "agentification" must pause to allow for high-stakes, human-to-human accountability.

The Sector-Agnostic Drop-In

Whether you are moving physical atoms or digital bits, the friction points in your business are likely the same: data silos, manual inspection, and "human-in-the-loop" bottlenecks. Here is how AI is being deployed across "non-AI" industries today:

- **Aerospace and Heavy Manufacturing:**
  - **Generative Design:** Instead of an engineer spending weeks drafting a single turbine bracket, AI generates 1,000 permutations optimized for weight and stress in minutes.
  - **Predictive Maintenance:** Acoustic AI sensors "listen" to factory floor bearings, predicting a failure 48 hours before it happens, preventing millions in downtime.
- **Food and Agriculture:**
  - **Computer Vision Quality Control:** In poultry or produce processing, high-speed cameras use AI to identify contaminants or grading defects at a speed and consistency no human eye can match.
  - **Supply Chain Optimization:** AI models ingest weather patterns, fuel prices, and harvest yields to reroute logistics in real time, shaving 15% off carbon footprints and waste.
- **Professional Services and Legal:**
  - **Automated Due Diligence:** A junior associate no longer spends 40 hours reviewing contracts for "change of control" clauses. An AI agent does it in four seconds with a higher accuracy rate.
- **Construction and Real Estate:**
  - **Site Safety and Progress:** Drones equipped with LiDAR and AI compare daily site progress against BIM (Building Information Modeling) blueprints to catch structural errors before the concrete sets.

AI Opportunities Matrix — Paul Cheek

	Product/Service	Operations	Marketing/Sales	Supply Chain
Manufacturing	Predictive Maintenance	Quality Inspection	Demand Forecasting	Inventory Optimization
Financial Services	Fraud Detection	Risk Assessment	Customer Analytics	Algorithmic Trading
Healthcare	Medical Imaging	Clinical Workflow	Patient Engagement	Drug Optimization
Energy	Production Optimization	Grid Management	Customer Insights	Predictive Logistics
Retail	Personalized Recommendations	Inventory Management	Customer Sentiment Analysis	Supply Chain Forecasting
Education	Adaptive Learning Systems	Student Performance Monitoring	Enrollment Prediction	Course Material Distribution
Transportation	Route Optimization	Fleet Management	Passenger Experience Analytics	Freight Optimization
Telecommunications	Network Optimization	Service Assurance	Churn Prediction	Logistics Routing
Real Estate	Smart Property Valuation	Building Management Automation	Targeted Campaigns	Smart Leasing Systems
Agriculture	Crop Monitoring	Yield Prediction	Market Demand Prediction	Agri Supply Forecasting
Media & Entertainment	Content Personalization	Content Scheduling	Audience Targeting	Content Delivery Optimization
Hospitality	Dynamic Pricing	Operational Efficiency	Loyalty Program Optimization	Procurement Planning
Construction	Design Automation	Site Monitoring	Bid Management	Materials Supply Tracking
Automotive	Autonomous Driving	Predictive Maintenance	Vehicle Demand Forecasting	Parts Forecasting
Legal Services	Contract Review Automation	Legal Research AI	Client Acquisition	Case Flow Forecasting
Government	Citizen Services Chatbots	Resource Allocation	Public Opinion Analysis	Crisis Logistics Management

The Functional Drop-In

Regardless of your industry, every organization has a "back office" and a "growth engine." These are the universal zones where AI becomes the ultimate labor multiplier:

Functional Area	The Old Model (SME/IDE)	The AIDE Model (Drop-In AI)
Customer Support	Tier 1 agents reading scripts.	Multimodal agents resolving 80% of queries with voice/text instantly.
Finance and Audit	Monthly manual reconciliation of invoices.	Real-time, autonomous "continuous audit" that flags fraud instantly.
HR and Recruiting	Screening 500 resumes for one role.	AI agents conducting initial technical screenings and culture-fit assessments.
Sales and Marketing	One-size-fits-all email blasts.	Hyper-personalized video and text outreach generated per prospect.

The question is no longer "Are we an AI company?" The question is "Which of our human-led bottlenecks are we willing to let our competitors automate first?"

The Threshold of Trust: Where Human Agency Remains Essential

While the AIDE model aggressively pursues "compute over labor," the level of achievable autonomy is not uniform across all functional areas or business models. We must distinguish between transactional efficiency and relationship-based trust.

For enterprises with high Lifetime Value (LTV) that sell complex solutions into government (B2G) or large corporations (B2B), the sales cycle is rarely just a data transfer; it is a high-stakes exchange of accountability. In these sectors, "agentification" may handle the top-of-funnel research and personalized outreach, but the final mile, the closing of a multi-million-dollar contract, will likely remain a human-to-human endeavor in the short and medium term.

In these instances, the "high-cost customer acquisition" isn't a bug to be automated away; it is a verification of commitment. The AIDE doesn't seek to remove the human from these high-trust interactions, but rather to use AI to ensure that when a human does sit down with another human, they are armed with such a high degree of intelligence and preparation that the outcome is nearly certain.

No One Works Here: The Digital War Room

You've learned the theory; now let's build the machinery. Turn these concepts into immediate ROI for your company by accessing your free resources at NoOneWorksHere.com.

1. Immediate Actions (Do This Today)

- **Evaluate Where Efficiencies Live:** Map your organization by functional area and seniority. Determine where AI literacy, and thus efficiency, lives. For each intersection of functional area and seniority, rate the level of AI literacy to identify where gaps exist.
- **Deploy a Horizontal Drop-In:** Identify your most expensive, legacy SaaS tool (e.g., an outdated CRM or HR platform). Spend 30 minutes researching AI-native "wrapper" agents that can be integrated directly over the top of this software to automate data entry without requiring a system migration.
- **Map the Trust Threshold:** Categorize your upcoming client meetings or deals for the week into "transactional" (delegate research/prep to AI) and "relational" (high-stakes; protect human bandwidth).

2. The Discussion (Bring This to Your Team)

- Where are the most entrenched "data silos" in our legacy back-office systems, and how could deploying a horizontal "wrapper agent" extract that value instantly without requiring a multi-million-dollar software migration?

(*continued*)

(*continued*)

- In our specific industry, are we treating AI as a "shiny new tool" for a vertical department, or are we integrating it as a horizontal nervous system that wraps around our entire legacy operation?
- Looking at the "Lovable" case study (see Chapter 7), where is our "self-healing loop"? Do we have processes that can currently "unstick" themselves without human intervention, or are we building an endangered IDE (Internally Driven Enterprise)?

3. The Step-by-Step Implementation

Stop guessing and start building. Use the **AIDE Universal Integration Workbook** for step-by-step guidance. This digital workbook provides the exact framework you need to implement this chapter's concepts.

Download it at: NoOneWorksHere.com/everywhere-aide

4. The Unfair Advantage: AI-Powered Tools

Don't just read about AI; use it right now. As a reader of this book, you get exclusive access to interactive AI-software tools designed to do the heavy lifting for you.

Access your tools instantly at: NoOneWorksHere.com

(Or simply scan the QR code with your smartphone camera)

9

The New Age Organization Chart

What does the map of your company look like when your most productive "employees" don't have heartbeats?
The shift from a traditional hierarchy to an organized system of nodes is not a technology update; it is an architectural reorientation of leadership.

IN CHAPTER 3, WE fundamentally redefined the word *organization*. We established that the modern firm is no longer just a group of people; it is a dynamic network of human and nonhuman nodes. But if we have redefined the core unit of business, we must also redefine how we interpret and implement that structure operationally. We need a new map.

The organization chart was originally introduced as a tool for operational clarity and a testament to aesthetic and functional design. In 1855, Brigadier General Daniel McCallum, then general superintendent of the New York and Erie Railroad, created the world's first organizational chart. McCallum, a multidisciplinary mind with a background in architecture and civil engineering, faced a massive "latency problem" of his era: managing over 500 miles of track and a geographically scattered workforce of thousands. The Erie Railroad was plagued by disorganization because the informal, improvised management styles that worked for short roads were inadequate for such an extensive network. McCallum noted, "Any system which might be applicable to the business and extent of a short road would be found entirely inadequate to the wants of a long one" (Geraghty 2023).

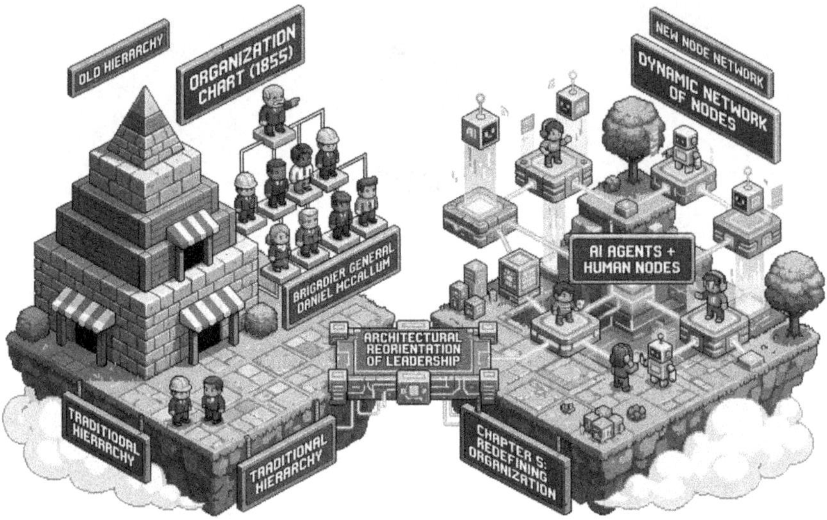

To manage this complex enterprise and the influx of data from the newly invented telegraph, McCallum designed a system to map human hierarchy, reporting lines, and task delegation. For over a century, the org chart remained a manual for human communication, designed to solve the problem that one person cannot manage 1,000 people.

Today, the paradigm has shifted once again. The "nodes" on your chart are no longer exclusively human; they now include AI agents that think, act, and execute at machine speed. Mapping out this new structure is not merely an administrative exercise. The map dictates the direction of your organization and fundamentally changes its orientation and capabilities.

In this chapter, you will:

- **Analyze the Historical Shift:** Track the evolution from human-only hierarchies to hybrid node networks
- **Compare the Startup Advantage:** Evaluate how new entrants scale faster than established firms undergoing transformation
- **Master Five Org Chart Stages:** Move your company systematically toward a "self-driving" organizational state
- **Understand Flipping Progression Dynamics:** See how the ratio of agents to humans inevitably inverts
- **Examine the Swan AI Case:** Observe the New Age Org Chart operating in breakneck action

The Evolving Org Chart: New Versus Established Companies

If your internal map still looks like a 19th-century pyramid, you are effectively trying to navigate a digital-first economy with a paper map of a city that has been demolished. Or perhaps it's like trying to follow a MapQuest printout while traveling cross-country when the exit numbers have since changed and the "Old Exit 33" signs are long gone.

The AIDE startup advantage is real and dangerous for incumbents. New companies can spin up rapidly with a redefined, AI-native org chart from day one, bypassing the "legacy bloat" and "innovation debt" that anchors established firms. For established organizations, the path is more complex. I see two primary routes:

1. **The Retrofit Approach:** Organizations reinvent themselves within specific departments, functional areas, or business units, allowing certain divisions to skip ahead to higher levels of AI integration. This is much like leveraging intrapreneurship to build a new, nimble speedboat to move alongside your sailing ship.
2. **The Phased Transformation:** Organizations set up formal transformation projects to slowly redesign the org chart step-by-step.

This evolution is driving the Great Flattening. We are seeing a massive shift from tall hierarchies of humans to significantly flattened structures to reduce communication latency. Even traditional tech giants are forcing this shift. Giants like Amazon famously solved for this by flattening their organizational structures, allowing them to experiment (Jassy 2024), fail fast, and operate at "weeks speed." Amazon's mandate under Andy Jassy was to cut middle management and increase the individual contributor-to-manager ratio by 15%, proving that even established titans must force flatter structures to improve speed and reduce latency.

Regardless of whether you're predicting triangle, diamond, circle, tree, or other shaped org charts in the future, I believe that to survive you must move from being a "captain" directing tasks to an "architect" designing systems.

The Five Stages of Org Chart Transformation

Most organizations will not reach the theoretical limit of efficiency overnight. Based on my collaborations with many of the large consulting firms that are working through this transformation with clients, I have identified a potential sequential path for this transformation stylistically illustrated below:

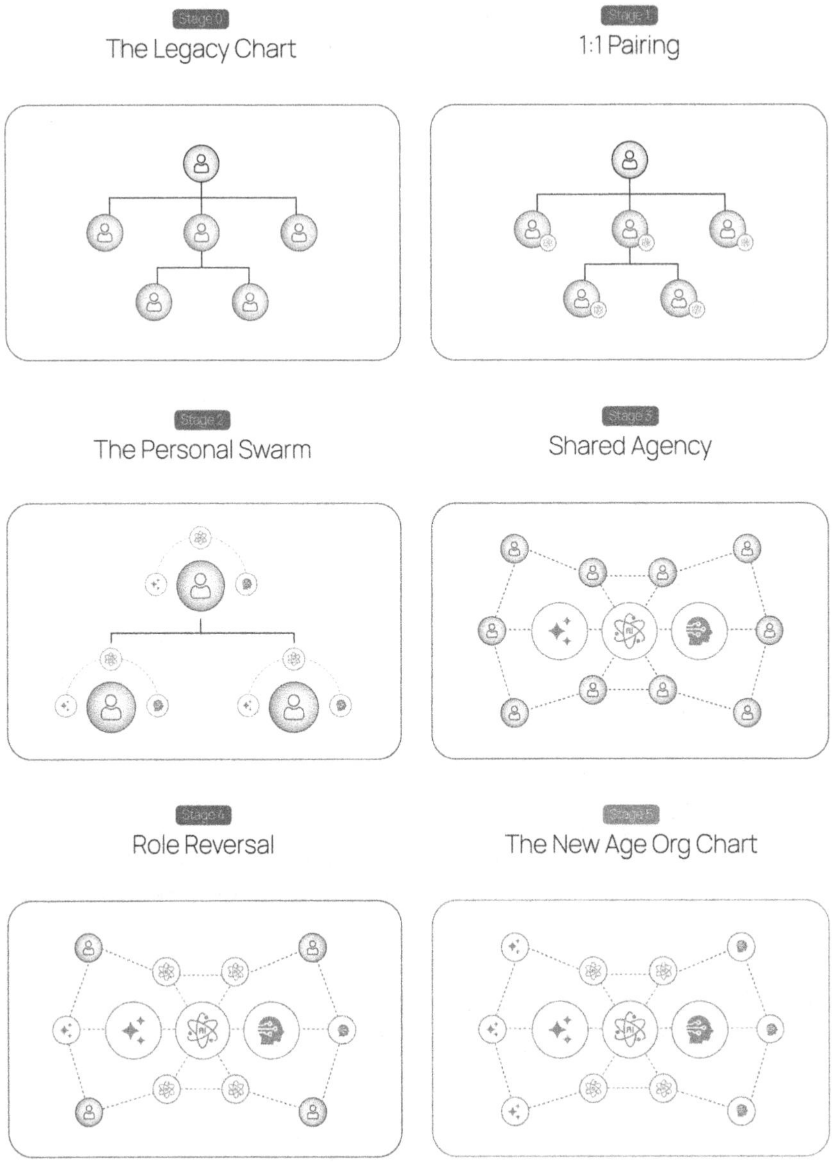

Stage	Description	Agent-to-Human Ratio	Difficulty of Transformation	Level of Culture Change	Key Executive Challenge
Stage 0: The Legacy Chart	The exclusively human org chart where every node is a person. This is the easy, status quo approach where AI is viewed merely as a tool.	Zero (or Near-Zero)	Low (Maintaining status quo)	None to Minimal	Complacency: Recognizing the risk of obsolescence and falling behind early adopters.
Stage 1: 1:1 Pairing	The pairing of individuals with a single, dedicated AI agent. This "Copilot" era acts as a general assistant to increase personal efficiency.	Low	Low	Low (Adopting a new daily tool)	Adoption and Security: Driving daily utilization, ensuring equitable access, and establishing basic data boundaries.
Stage 2: The Personal Swarm	Each individual is paired with their own personalized swarm of specialized AI agents to support them in their specific job functions.	Medium	Moderate	Moderate (Shift from "doing tasks" to "managing outputs")	Tech Sprawl: Managing licensing costs, identifying high-ROI use cases, and helping employees redesign their own workflows.
Stage 3: Shared Agency	Humans work alongside shared AI agents that support multiple different humans across the organization chart, acting as connective tissue.	High	High	High (Trusting AI as a reliable, cross-functional team member)	Enterprise Governance: Breaking down departmental data silos, standardizing AI operations, and managing workforce anxieties about redundancy.
Stage 4: Role Reversal	The inverted report. Some humans begin following the direction or outputs of AI agents, while maintaining shared agents throughout the organization.	Very High	Very High	Severe (Overcoming traditional human management hierarchies and ego)	Accountability: Establishing clear legal/ethical frameworks for AI-led decisions and redefining the core value proposition of human employees.
Stage 5: The New Age Org Chart	A fully self-driving organization. Shared agents run execution, humans work directly for AI systems managing the business, and AI serves as a mentoring coach.	Exponential	Extreme	Transformational (A complete reimagining of the firm and human labor)	Visionary Leadership: Shifting the executive role entirely away from operational management to focus strictly on human empathy, ethics, and extreme strategic pivots.

This collapse of middle management allows AI to step in as a mentoring coach to junior employees or those with fewer years of experience, providing the high-level guidance once reserved for human managers.

Progression Dynamics in the AI-Driven Enterprise

As you ascend from Stage 0 to Stage 5, your unit of scale changes. You are no longer playing a game of addition; you are playing a game of multiplication.

The Flipping Ratio: In a legacy firm, growth requires a linear increase in headcount. In an AIDE, the ratio flips. As you progress, the number of agents to humans increases significantly, allowing you to decouple revenue growth from headcount growth.

The Ascension Curve: While Stages 0 and 1 are accessible, Stages 3, 4, and 5 require immense structural and cultural shifts, making them increasingly difficult to achieve. It requires moving from a world where "status" equals the size of your team to a world where status equals the speed of your ship.

The Rise of the Tech-Savvy Junior: We are seeing a unique transition dynamic where employees with fewer years of experience, but who are highly technologically savvy, are increasingly finding themselves in managerial roles with AI agents reporting directly to them. This self-driving organization eliminates administrative latency, positioning humans to do only their best, highest-leverage work.

Visualizing Stage 5: The Self-Driving Org Chart

To fulfill the promise of a company without heartbeats, we must completely discard the traditional top-down pyramid. You cannot fit autonomous AI agents into rigid reporting boxes designed for middle managers.

The Stage 5 organizational chart does not look like a pyramid; it looks like a solar system or a neural network.

- **The Core (the Execution Engine):** The center of the chart may be entirely nonhuman. This is an interconnected mesh of specialized AI agents handling operations, customer service, data processing, and initial code generation. There are no "departments" here, only workflows. These agents do not need one-on-ones, they do not have interpersonal conflicts, and they communicate with each other instantly via APIs.

- **The Perimeter (the Human Architects):** The human employees no longer sit at the top of a pyramid, dropping tasks down. Instead, they sit on the perimeter of the AI core. They are the architects, editors, and exceptions handlers. They plug into the core to set strategic parameters, train the models, handle highly empathetic customer escalations, and pivot the company's direction.
- **The Connective Tissue:** Middle management is entirely replaced by the system's own analytics and reporting dashboards. In Stage 5, AI steps in as a mentoring coach to junior employees, providing the high-level operational guidance once reserved for human managers.

In a legacy firm, growth requires a linear increase in headcount. In a self-driving organization, the ratio flips. You decouple revenue growth from headcount growth entirely. We'll explore this in more detail in the epilogue, but for now we should look at a concrete example of this in the real world.

Concrete Evidence: The Autonomous Business Model

For new companies, this structural shift is happening at breakneck speed. The prime example of the *New Age Org Chart* in practice is Swan AI, led by CEO Amos Bar-Joseph.

Swan AI's metrics rewrite the arithmetic of business:

- **Speed:** They scaled to $1 million in Annual Recurring Revenue (ARR) in just nine weeks.
- **Scale:** They acquired over 200 customers during that window.
- **The Chart:** They achieved this with only the three co-founders and a swarm of AI agents, employing zero traditional employees.
- **Efficiency:** They are targeting an unprecedented $10 million in revenue per employee.

As Amos puts it: "We don't think the next competitive edge is hiring faster. It's relocating engineering burden into systems. Swan is built to scale with intelligence, not headcount" (Bar-Joseph 2026). He argues that building amazing products is now table stakes; the real war is fought over attention and the ability to build a company that simply needs less to do more.

Once you have architected the new map of your organization, the next challenge is understanding how rapidly you can populate it, leading us directly into the entrepreneur's new superpower: the unprecedented speed of creation.

No One Works Here: The Digital War Room

You've learned the theory; now let's build the machinery. Turn these concepts into immediate ROI for your company by accessing your free resources at NoOneWorksHere.com.

1. Immediate Actions (Do This Today)

- **Target the Middle Management Latency:** Identify one internal reporting process where information is manually summarized and passed up a chain of command. Replace that human reporting chain today with an automated AI dashboard that pulls directly from the source data.
- **The 1:1 Pairing Mandate:** Assign every team member a dedicated AI "Copilot" today to move from Stage 0 (Legacy) to Stage 1 (Pairing), focusing on increasing individual personal efficiency.
- **Identify Your "Architects":** Review your leadership's daily tasks and identify three operational responsibilities that can be shifted to a system, moving the leader's role from a "captain" of tasks to an "architect" of systems.

2. The Discussion (Bring This to Your Team)

- If we were to aggressively flatten our organizational chart today, which layers of middle management currently exist solely to route information, and how could a "shared agency" AI model safely eliminate that communication latency?

- Looking at the Five Stages of Org Chart Transformation, honestly assess which stage our team resides in today. What is the single biggest cultural or technical "innovation debt" anchoring us to the traditional pyramid?
- As AI begins to handle mentoring and high-level guidance for junior employees, what does the "unique value proposition" of our human middle management become, and how must their skills evolve to stay relevant?

3. The Step-by-Step Implementation

Stop guessing and start building. Use the **AIDE Org Chart Transformation Workbook** for step-by-step guidance. This digital workbook provides the exact framework you need to implement this chapter's concepts.

Download it at: NoOneWorksHere.com/org-charts

4. The Unfair Advantage: AI-Powered Tools

Don't just read about AI; use it right now. As a reader of this book, you get exclusive access to interactive AI-software tools designed to do the heavy lifting for you.

Access your tools instantly at: NoOneWorksHere.com

(Or simply scan the QR code with your smartphone camera)

10

Speed of Creation

The Entrepreneur's New Superpower

How fast can value now be created?
See how AI compresses the entrepreneurial timeline to days, not months.

I HAVE FOR years told entrepreneurs I advise: Never do a live demo.

There are too many variables. The code might break. The API might time out. And yet there I was in Europe, standing on a stage with 30 minutes on the clock and a challenge I hadn't fully thought through. I was going to build an entirely new AI-Driven Enterprise (AIDE) live. This wasn't a rehearsed parlor trick; it was the culmination of an intensive personal pivot. When I left the Martin Trust Center for MIT Entrepreneurship, I realized I was at a crossroads. I spent the subsequent six months learning everything possible about how to start and scale a company in the AI era. Before that transition, I didn't fully understand the mechanics of this shift, and, frankly, I didn't have the time to dig in. I had to treat myself like a student again, refactoring my own knowledge of business building from the ground up. In Chapter 6, I warned you that we're in the dial-up era, where tools can be clunky and fragmented. That is true. But as I discovered during my six-month immersion, even with that friction, the architecture of business has changed so fundamentally that the speed of creation has collapsed from months to minutes.

My first hesitation wasn't about creativity or process; it was about the Wi-Fi. The only thing worse than a bad startup idea is a live demo that fails because of a slow internet connection. But within a few minutes, that hesitation faded. I realized that if this worked, if I could start a credible company using only AI tools in real-time, it would prove something extraordinary. It would prove that the age of the AI-Driven Enterprise isn't coming. It is here.

In this chapter, you will:

- **Witness the 30-Minute Startup:** A step-by-step breakdown of how to build the first draft of a company in half an hour
- **Learn Chain of Thought:** How to pass context from one AI application to another
- **Master AI Meta-Prompting:** Using AI to write the instructions for other AI
- **Understand Speed as Moat:** Why velocity is the only defense against unlimited competition

The New Approach to Building

The AIDE model we discussed in Chapter 7 is the natural evolution of modern entrepreneurship. It merges the timeless first principles of company creation with the applied capabilities of artificial intelligence.

At MIT, we teach frameworks like *Disciplined Entrepreneurship* and *Startup Tactics*. We force founders to answer hard questions:

- Who is your customer?
- What problem are you solving?
- How will you scale sustainably?

In the past, answering these questions took months of market research, weeks of prototyping, and days of financial modeling.

AI doesn't replace these steps. I argue they are more important now than ever. Rather, it accelerates them. The experiment I ran on that stage was designed to test the limits of this acceleration. I mapped out a stack of AI tools to mirror the MIT process, identifying a customer, zeroing in on their biggest problem, validating it, designing a solution, and building the infrastructure. Here is the playbook I used. You can, and should, replicate this today. Do so by grabbing the detailed step-by-step process and exclusive discount codes reserved for readers of this book for relevant AI tools on the book's website at NoOneWorksHere.com.

The Orchestrated Workflow

To execute this live, I didn't rely on a single piece of software. I built a "chain of thought" workflow where the output of one AI agent became the context and instruction for the next. By acting as the system architect, I orchestrated a seamless sequence of value creation:

- **Problem Discovery:** Instead of guessing, we mined real-time public forums to identify organic, urgent pain points being discussed by our target demographic.
- **The Central Brain:** We fed those raw insights into a foundational language model, creating a dynamic, centralized knowledge base that governed every subsequent decision.
- **Strategic Planning and Validation:** The "brain" generated a formal business model, which we immediately stress-tested against

synthetic, AI-generated customer personas to expose hidden objections and kill bad ideas fast.

- **Meta-Prompted Execution:** Using meta-prompting, asking our central AI to write expert-level instructions for other specialized AIs, we instantly generated a brand identity, a professional pitch deck, and most importantly, a fully coded, functional prototype.
- **Go-to-Market and Economics:** Finally, specialized agents spun up a targeted outbound sales campaign and a five-year financial projection to prove unit economics.

The Result: Velocity as a Moat

In exactly 30 minutes, we went from a blank slate to possessing a validated problem, a strategic plan, simulated customer feedback, a live product, and an outbound sales campaign.

Was it a billion-dollar unicorn right out of the gate? No. A product built in half an hour has exactly zero value until a real human validates it in the market.

But that is exactly the point. You haven't built a final business; you have built a highly testable hypothesis at near-zero cost. The superpower isn't just that you built it fast; it's that you can now afford to iterate based on real customer feedback, or ruthlessly discard the idea if the market rejects it, without losing months of your life or thousands of dollars.

Build This Today: The 30-Minute Playbook

Because the AI landscape is evolving at breakneck speed, the specific platforms I use for this workflow change constantly. Rather than printing an outdated list of tools in this book, I have published the exact, step-by-step technical playbook online. To access the current AI tool stack, copy my meta-prompt templates, and grab exclusive software discounts to build your own AIDE today, visit: NoOneWorksHere.com/30-minute-startup.

Lessons from the 30-Minute Startup

1. Speed Is the New Moat

In a world where everyone has access to the same AI models, the winner is the one who iterates fastest. The cycle time from idea to execution has collapsed to zero. If you spend a week debating your logo, you're very far behind your competition.

2. The Power Is in Orchestration

Notice that no single AI tool did it all. The magic wasn't in Lovable or NotebookLM individually; it was in the chain.

- The output of Step 1 became the input of Step 2.
- The output of Step 2 became the prompt for Step 5. Your job as a founder is to be the system architect who connects these nodes.

3. Human Judgment Is the Multiplier

AI simulated the customers, but it didn't *feel* their pain. I had to choose which problem on Reddit mattered. I had to look at the product prototype and say, "Change the vibe." The AI provided the *acceleration*; the human provided the *direction*. And of course I need to validate the output from this system with real customers in the real world to build conviction.

4. Democratization

The most profound realization there on that stage wasn't technical; it was social. The AIDE model democratizes company building. You don't need a computer science degree from MIT. You don't need $100,000 in savings or a vast network of venture capitalists. You need curiosity, creativity, and the courage to press "Generate."

What Will You Build?

As the final seconds ticked down, the Wi-Fi held. A new company existed. The crowd's reaction wasn't to the novelty of the tech, but to the sheer *possibility* it represented. The tools are here. The methods are clear. The friction is gone. The only question left is this: What will you build in your 30 minutes?

No One Works Here: The Digital War Room

You've learned the theory; now let's build the machinery. Turn these concepts into immediate ROI for your company by accessing your free resources at NoOneWorksHere.com.

1. Immediate Actions (Do This Today)

- **Audit Your "Problem-Market Fit":** Use an AI empathy engine or social listening tool to extract the top three recurring frustrations from your target audience's online communities.
- **Build Your Central Brain:** Upload your current business plan, customer feedback, and market research into a context-aware knowledge base to ground all future AI prompting in your specific business logic.
- **Execute a 30-Minute Sprint:** Select one stalled project and attempt to move it from concept to a functional prototype or pitch deck using a chained AI workflow, focusing on orchestration over manual pixel-pushing.

2. The Discussion (Bring This to Your Team)

- If our competitors can now launch a credible, functioning prototype and sales campaign in under an hour, what is our actual "moat"? How much of our current competitive advantage is based on slow processes that no longer provide protection?
- Looking at our current product development cycle, where are we "moving pixels" manually when we should be acting as system architects? Which specific stages of our workflow can be replaced by meta-prompting and AI orchestration?
- How can we integrate synthetic customer personas into our weekly brainstorming? If we could pressure-test every new idea against 10 diverse, simulated AI buyers in minutes, how would that change our tolerance for experimentation?

(*continued*)

(continued)

3. The Step-by-Step Implementation

Stop guessing and start building. Use the **30-Minute Startup Workbook** for step-by-step guidance. This digital workbook provides the exact framework you need to implement this chapter's concepts.

Download it at: NoOneWorksHere.com/30-minute-startup

4. The Unfair Advantage: AI-Powered Tools

Don't just read about AI; use it right now. As a reader of this book, you get exclusive access to interactive AI-software tools designed to do the heavy lifting for you.

Access your tools instantly at: NoOneWorksHere.com
(Or simply scan the QR code with your smartphone camera)

11

Development Versus Distribution

The New Bottleneck

If everyone can build, who can sell?
How to compete in an attention-scarce economy.

In Chapter 10, we proved that you can build a company in 30 minutes. You can vibe-code a product, spin up a brand, and generate a financial model before your coffee gets cold. This sounds like a utopia for entrepreneurs. But it creates a massive, terrifying problem.

If *you* can build a product and launch a go-to-market campaign in 30 minutes, so can your neighbor. So can a student in Mumbai. So can a 12-year-old in Chicago. For the last 30 years, the defining struggle of the technology startup was development.

- "Can we build this?"
- "Do we have the engineers?"
- "Can we afford the server costs?"

Today, the answer to all of those questions is "Yes, easily, and for free." Of course some businesses require R&D beyond what we've described here, such as drug development, and we'll explore the implications for them in Chapter 13. We have now entered a new era where the scarcity has shifted. When the cost of creation drops to zero, the volume of noise rises to infinity. More so than ever before, the adage "If you build it, they will come" (from the *Field of Dreams*, an American baseball movie from 1989) rings true. Just because you can build a new product does not mean that, as soon as it's ready, customers are going to emerge from the woodwork with cash in hand, ready to pay.

There is an old Silicon Valley adage popularized by Ben Horowitz that the battle between a startup and an incumbent comes down to whether the startup gets distribution before the incumbent gets innovation. In the AI era, that dynamic is absolute: The new bottleneck is no longer development; it is distribution.

In this chapter, you will:

- **Analyze the CAC Crisis:** Why acquiring customers is getting more expensive while building products gets cheaper
- **Identify the Retention Trap:** Why "Land and Expand" is challenging in the AI era
- **Navigate the Technical Founder's Dilemma:** The trap of falling in love with the code
- **Identify the New Moats:** Community, brand, and the human touch
- **Examine the Gladly Case:** How centering the human relationship wins in an AIDE world

The Supply Shock

We are currently witnessing a "supply shock" in software.

In 2010, if you had a problem—say, "I need a better way to manage my dog walking business"—there might have been two or three software solutions. If you built a fourth one that was slightly better, you could win.

In 2026, because of the many vibe-coding tools available at low cost in the marketplace, there can be 500 solutions for that problem. Next week, there could be 1,000.

Put directly by Amos Bar-Joseph, the CEO of Swan AI, "In 2026, GTM innovation is more important than product innovation. Building amazing products becomes table stakes, earning attention becomes the most competitive war to fight—and the most important one." (Bar-Joseph 2026) By the way, if you're looking for one of the individuals best leveraging founder brand and founder content on LinkedIn, Amos is worth a follow.

When supply becomes infinite, price trends toward zero. We are seeing a race to the bottom in software utility. This creates a new economic reality: Efficiency is no longer a moat; it is table stakes.

If any competitor can spin up a clone of your product in 30 minutes, what are you actually selling? You are selling trust. In a world of infinite AI-generated noise, "slop," and deepfakes, the premium asset is no longer the code, it is the verification that the code does what you say it does. The "human touch" discussed later isn't just about being nice; it's the only way to prove you aren't just another hallucinating wrapper. Distribution isn't just about getting eyeballs; it's about retaining belief.

I hear this the refrain of the AIDE era constantly from the entrepreneurs I advise at MIT: "We've built the product. It works perfectly. But we can't get anyone to use it."

In the past, this was the curse of the technical founder, the brilliant engineer who built a complex tool but couldn't talk to humans. The barrier to entry for software creation has collapsed. Today, with the right AI tools, any founder with clear intent and domain expertise can orchestrate software creation and build functional prototypes. Therefore, everyone faces the technical founder's dilemma: You've built a solution, but you haven't built a path to the customer.

The CAC Crisis

While development costs have plummeted, customer acquisition cost (CAC) has skyrocketed. Why? Because It's been on an upward trajectory for years, and now the same AI tools that help you build product also help other companies generate noise.

- Inboxes are flooded with AI-written cold emails.
- Social media feeds are flooded with AI-generated content.
- Search results are flooded with AI-generated SEO (search engine optimization) spam.

The "signal-to-noise" ratio of the internet has crashed. To cut through that noise, you have to pay more, either in ad dollars, creative effort, or human generated content.

The New Equation:

- **Old World:** Spend $100k building, $10k marketing.
- **New World:** Spend $100 building, $100k marketing. Or prove you have the scrappiest growth hacks.

If, for example, your software business plan allocates 80% of your budget to R&D and 20% to sales and marketing, you're designing for 2015. Flip the ratio.

The Retention Trap

However, getting a user to click "Sign Up" is only half the battle. The true crisis in the AIDE era isn't just getting them in the door; it's keeping them there.

For a very long time, venture capitalists such as Nico Bonatsos have evaluated companies and their customer cohorts with metrics like:

- Daily active users (DAU)
- Weekly active users (WAU)
- Monthly active users (MAU)

But as he flags in this new era, the metrics are changing, and those become irrelevant given that AI agents can actually serve as users and customers of a business's products and services: "DAU, WAU, MAU ratios and retention across cohorts just became irrelevant in the Moltbook era. As AI agents are chronically online and can be omnipresent, these traditional metrics are going to be 100% at all times" (Bonatsos 2026).

Further, in my work advising startups at MIT, I see a recurring pattern: a founder uses AI to launch a slick tool, runs a viral LinkedIn campaign, and signs 50 pilots in a month. But 60 days later, those customers are gone. They've moved on to the *next* AI tool that promised a 5% better interface.

In the old world of SaaS, we focused on customer acquisition. In the AIDE world, you must obsess over net revenue retention (NRR), a metric that measures the percentage of recurring revenue retained from existing customers over a set period, including expansion revenue (upsells) and accounting for churn.

Factor	Legacy SaaS Model	AI-Driven Enterprise (AIDE)
Primary Cost	R&D/Engineering	Marketing/Distribution
Competitive Moat	Proprietary Code	Trust and Community
Key Metric	Monthly Active Users (MAU)	Net Revenue Retention (NRR)
Sales Strategy	Product-Led Growth[1]	Relationship-Led Growth

If your NRR is below 100% in the AIDE era, your growth model is highly fragile; you are pouring capital into a leaky bucket. Because it's so easy to "pilot" a new AI tool, lifetime value (LTV) is collapsing for companies that don't provide deep, integrated value.

Distribution Is Not an Afterthought

Most first-time founders treat distribution like a sprinkle on top of the cupcake. They bake the cupcake (build the product) and then ask, "How do we sell this?" In the AIDE era, distribution isn't just the cupcake; distribution is the nearly the only moat left.

[1] Product-led growth (PLG) is a go-to-market methodology and industry framework coined by OpenView Venture Partners.

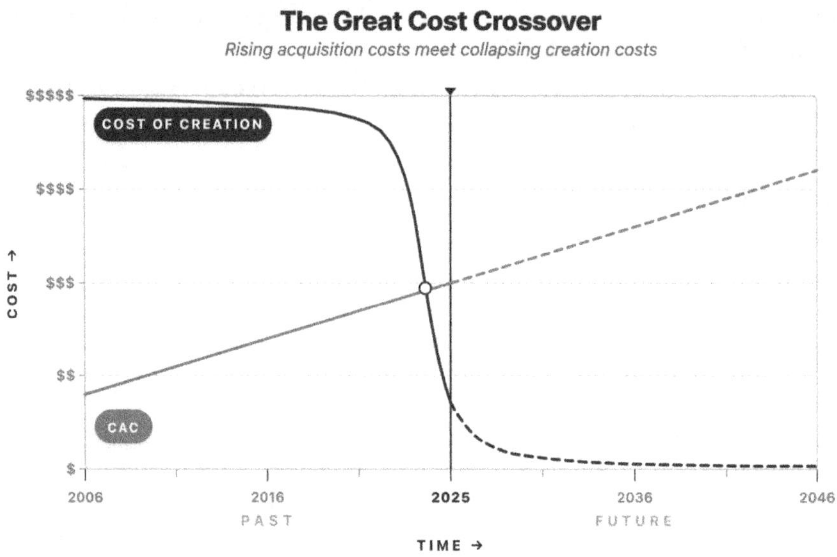

When the cost of code hits zero, product becomes a commodity. Your competitors can clone your features in an afternoon. They cannot clone your community, your brand trust, or your integrations. If you are building a "better mousetrap" but don't have a unique channel to sell it, you will be eaten by a wrapper that does.

- Can you build an audience?
- Can you build a community?
- Can you partner with an existing aggregator?

If you cannot answer, "How will people find this?" you should not write a single line of code (or generate a single prompt).

With distribution as one of the only remaining moats, this is where the incumbent strikes back.

If you're an established organization with 20 years of history, the "30-minute startup" is terrified of *you*. They have speed, but you have trust. They can generate a landing page in seconds, but they cannot generate a 10-year track record of fulfilling contracts. Your defense against the AI swarm is to weaponize your reputation and your existing infrastructure. For incumbents, decades of CRM data, established vendor portals, and massive customer email lists are the ultimate distribution moats.

You don't need to hack a viral launch on social media, because you already own the channels. While the startups compete on "new features," you must compete on "verified reliability" and direct access. In an era of infinite AI noise, being the boring, reliable partner with a direct line to the buyer becomes a premium asset.

The New Moats: What AI Can't Copy

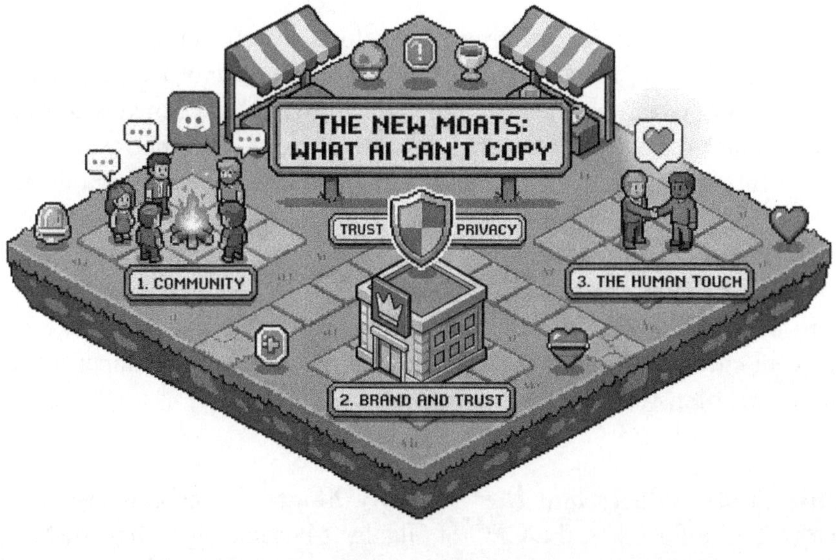

If your competitor can copy your features in 30 minutes using the same AI agents you used, what is your defense? What is your "moat"? It is no longer your code. It is your relationship. Here are the only durable advantages left when software is a commodity:

1. Community

Software can be copied; a tribe cannot. If you have a Discord server of 5,000 passionate users who help each other, that is a moat. People stay for the people, not the features.

2. Brand and Trust

In a world of deepfakes and AI spam, trust and privacy are the most valuable currencies. A personal brand, your reputation as a founder, your history of delivering value, cannot be prompted into existence. It takes time.

3. The Human Touch

Founder-led sales and doing things that don't scale is an approach that originates from a 2013 essay by Paul Graham, co-founder of Y Combinator. In an era of AI-generated spam, the "human touch" moat means getting on a plane to shake a client's hand, hosting intimate dinner events for prospects, or personally onboarding your first hundred users. It's about unscalable trust as a distribution channel, not customer service ticketing.

This brings us to a paradox. The more the world becomes AI-driven, the more humans crave human connection. In an era where your competitors can clone your features over the weekend, the only friction keeping your customers from switching to a slightly cheaper AI wrapper is the human relationship they have with your team.

Case Study: Gladly and the Empathy Moat In my conversations with Charlie Besecker, the CEO of Gladly, it became clear that the true "human touch" isn't just about branding; it is a vital growth and retention strategy.

Gladly is a customer service platform that moves away from traditional, ticket-based legacy systems. Instead of treating every customer interaction as a numbered case to be "closed" as cheaply as possible, Gladly centers the entire platform around the person. It creates a single, lifelong conversation thread so the agent always knows exactly who they are talking to.

What makes Charlie's approach a masterclass for the AIDE era is how he navigates the "efficiency versus empathy" trade-off to drive NRR. Most of the industry is racing to use AI to deflect customers away from humans to save a buck, effectively building walls between the company and the buyer. But when you deflect your customers, you commoditize your relationship with them. If they have no relationship with you, they may churn the second a cheaper alternative appears.

Gladly uses AI to empower the human, not replace them. They ensure that a customer gets to a human as quickly as possible, leveraging AI in the background to summarize previous issues so the human agent can focus entirely on relationship-building.

In the AI era, empathetic customer support is no longer a cost center; it is a GTM strategy. When you keep the human at the center, your customers don't just stay; they become your evangelists. In a world where your competitors are using AI to build walls between themselves and their customers, your greatest competitive advantage is using AI to tear those walls down.

Social Media Reach as Infrastructure

In the AIDE model, your social media following is not "vanity." It is Infrastructure. If you have 50,000 LinkedIn followers, you have a zero-marginal-cost distribution channel. You can launch a product for $0. If you have zero followers, you have to pay Google or Meta $50 per click to get a user.

For example, when Anton Osika launched Lovable, he didn't buy Super Bowl ads. He leveraged the community he built with GPT-Engineer. He had distribution *before* he had the finished product.

The Pivot: From Builder to Broadcaster

This requires a difficult psychological shift for many of you.

You picked up this book because you want to build the most efficient companies. You want to engineer the systems. You want to play with the agents.

But as the CEO of an AIDE, your primary job is no longer engineering. The agents do the engineering. Your job is evangelism. You must be the chief storyteller. You must be the face that cuts through the AI sludge. You must build the partnerships that allow your efficient little engine to reach the tracks.

Part III Summary

We have explored the opportunity:

- Chapter 7: The AIDE Model (Efficiency)
- Chapter 10: The Speed of Creation (Velocity)
- Chapter 11: The Distribution Bottleneck (The Challenge)

We know *what* to build, *how fast* to build it, and *why* selling it is hard.

Now, we need to look at the timeline. Different industries will adopt this at different speeds. You need to know if you are in a "fast-moving" zone or a "slow-moving" zone.

In the next chapter, we'll discuss "The Rate of Entrepreneurial Experiments" and why the sheer volume of "shots on goal" is about to change the global economy.

No One Works Here: The Digital War Room

You've learned the theory; now let's build the machinery. Turn these concepts into immediate ROI for your company by accessing your free resources at NoOneWorksHere.com.

1. Immediate Actions (Do This Today)

- **Flip Your Budget Ratio:** Move away from the 2015 model of heavy R&D spending and reallocate 80% of your resources toward distribution and storytelling. If your code can be cloned in 30 minutes, your only surviving asset is your ability to reach the customer first.
- **Audit Your "Moat" Integrity:** List your product's top three features and ask if an AI agent could replicate them by next week. If the answer is yes, immediately initiate a "human touch" project, such as a founder-led webinar or a community Discord, to build a defense based on trust rather than software.
- **Review Your Retention Metrics:** Stop prioritizing "monthly active users," which can be inflated by AI agents, and calculate your current NRR. Identify the bottom 20% of

your customer base and reach out personally to ensure your tool is integrated into their human workflow, not just their tech stack.

2. The Discussion (Bring This to Your Team)

- If a competitor used vibe-coding to clone our entire platform over the weekend and offered it for free, why would our customers stay? We need to identify if we are selling a commodity utility or a trusted relationship that is immune to software price-crashing.
- Are our current AI implementations building "walls" or "bridges" with our customers? We must discuss whether our automation is merely deflecting human interaction to save costs or empowering our team to provide the high-empathy support that drives long-term loyalty.
- Is our social media presence being treated as a "vanity metric" or as critical business infrastructure? We need to evaluate if we have the zero-marginal-cost distribution channels necessary to launch new products without being held hostage by skyrocketing ad costs.

3. The Step-by-Step Implementation

Stop guessing and start building. Use the **Distribution & Retention Strategy Workbook** for step-by-step guidance. This digital workbook provides the exact framework you need to implement this chapter's concepts.

Download it at: NoOneWorksHere.com/moats

4. The Unfair Advantage: AI-Powered Tools

Don't just read about AI; use it right now. As a reader of this book, you get exclusive access to interactive AI-software tools designed to do the heavy lifting for you.

(*continued*)

(*continued*)

Access your tools instantly at: NoOneWorksHere.com
(Or simply scan the QR code with your smartphone camera)

12

The Rate of Entrepreneurial Experiments

What happens when failure is cheap and learning is fast?
Experimentation as the new norm of innovation.

For the last 20 years, the narrative of entrepreneurship has been the narrative of the "big bet." You have an idea. You quit your job. You raise friends-and-family money. You spend six months building an MVP. You launch. And then, if the market doesn't want it, you crash and burn.

In that model, the cost of failure is catastrophic. It costs you your savings, your reputation, and a year of your life. Because the cost is so high, people are naturally risk-averse. They only take the shot if they are 100% sure. But what happens when the cost of failure drops to near-zero?

What happens when you can build the MVP, write the business plan, and test the market in an afternoon, for the cost of a $20 AI subscription? We are entering a new era where entrepreneurship is no longer about taking one big bet. It's about taking more shots on goal.

In this chapter, you will:

- **Adopt the Scientist Mindset:** Why your business is a hypothesis, not a baby

- **Understand Mathematics of Experimentation:** Why a higher failure rate is actually a good sign (provided the cost is low)
- **Differentiate Startups and Experiments:** Learn the difference between a startup and an experiment
- **Identify Digital Platform Risk:** How to avoid being wiped out by a single API update
- **Embrace Parallel Entrepreneurship Models:** How to run multiple tests simultaneously using agents

The Cost of Curiosity

In economics, when the price of a resource drops, the consumption of that resource rises.

AI has caused the price of *experimentation* to collapse. In the past, testing a business idea required a minimum viable product (MVP). But even a "minimum" product often required $50,000 and three engineers. Today, as we saw in the speed of creation from Chapter 10, the MVP can be generated by AI. The landing page can be vibe-coded. The ads can be agent-generated.

The barrier to entry has not simply been lowered; it has been removed. This means that far more individuals will pursue entrepreneurial experiments. The "cost of curiosity" is effectively zero. This is great news for everyone, especially those in regions with limited risk capital access but demands the highest quality entrepreneurship education.

The "More Shots on Goal" Philosophy

In sports, you cannot score if you do not shoot. If you are playing a game where you are only allowed one shot per year, you will be paralyzed by pressure. You will wait for the *perfect* opening. You will hesitate.

But if you are allowed to take a thousand shots per year, your strategy changes. You shoot from everywhere. You test angles. You look for deflections. You don't need to be perfect, but you do need quality and volume.

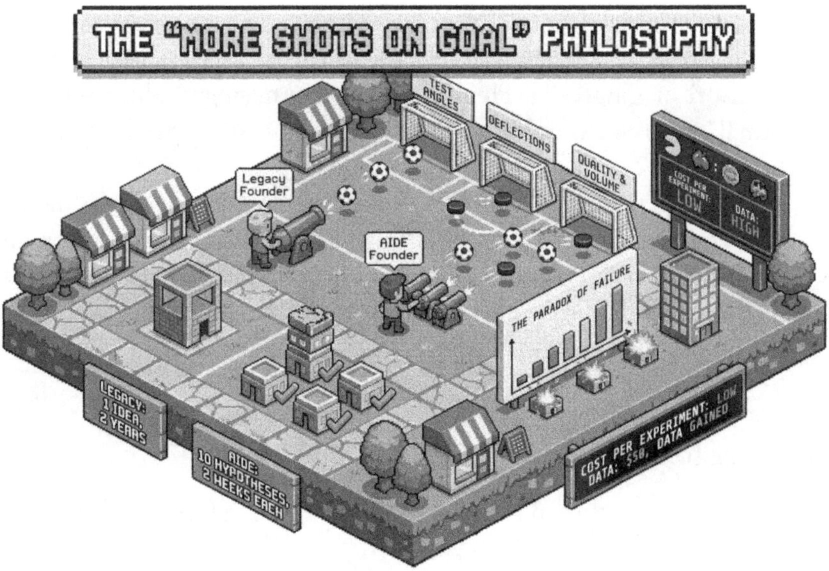

The AIDE Advantage: Because AI agents can execute the heavy lifting of company building, you can now afford to test 10 ideas in the time it used to take to test one.

- **Legacy Founder:** "I have one idea. I will spend two years building it." (high risk)
- **AIDE Founder:** "I have 10 hypotheses. I will spend two weeks testing each one. I will double down on the one that gets traction." (de-risked)

This is a fundamental shift from prediction (trying to guess what will work) to empiricism (seeing what actually works).

The Fragility of the "Wrapper"

However, a lower cost of experimentation does not mean a lower risk of obsolescence. Many entrepreneurs are currently falling into the "wrapper trap," building simple interfaces on top of existing models without adding unique value.

When the underlying platform updates, these companies often vanish overnight. We saw this clearly when OpenAI introduced specialized features like "GPTs" or industry-specific tools. As noted in recent coverage of OpenAI's move into healthcare, specifically their introduction of ChatGPT Health, the platform began absorbing the functionality that hundreds of third-party startups had spent months building.

If your "experiment" is simply a thin layer on someone else's engine, you aren't building a moat or an AIDE; you're renting a storefront on an active volcano. To survive the "more shots on goal" era, your experiments must focus on proprietary data, unique distribution, or complex workflow integration that a general AI update cannot easily replace.

The Paradox of Failure

Here is a prediction that might scare you, but shouldn't: In the AIDE era, the failure rate of startups will skyrocket.

We will see millions of "companies" launched that go nowhere. They will get zero users. They will generate zero revenue. They will be shut down in a week. Headlines may scream, "The AI Startup Bubble Burst! 90% of AI Companies Fail!" when of course these "companies" are merely experiments.

Ignore those headlines. They are applying old metrics to new realities. If a "failure" costs you $1 million, that is a tragedy. If a "failure" costs you $50 and four hours of tinkering, that is data.

We need to stop stigmatizing failure, which I've found to be a massive challenge, especially in regions of the world where failure is culturally unacceptable, given that this limits their economic growth potential, and start calculating the cost per experiment.

Metric	Traditional Era	AIDE Era
Unit of Work	The Startup	The Experiment
Time to Validate	6, 18 Months	6, 48 Hours
Cost to Validate	$50k, $500k	$0, $100
Failure Consequence	Bankruptcy/Burnout	"Okay, next idea."
Optimal Strategy	Focus/Conviction	Volume/Iteration

Redefining the "Startup"

I teach my students to be precise with their language. We need to stop calling everything a "startup."

- A **startup** is a temporary organization designed to search for a repeatable and scalable business model (Steve Blank's definition).
- An **experiment** is a discrete test of a specific value proposition.

In the AIDE era, you should stay in the "experiment" phase much longer. Do not print business cards. Do not rent an office. Use AI to run the experiment.

These experiments are extremely simple. (I document them in detail in Chapters 5 and 6 of the market testing stage of my book *Startup Tactics*.) Only now, with the power of AI, can these experiments be created and run in less time with less money. In short, a mousetrap experiment looks like this:

- Spin up a landing page.
- Run ads.
- Collect emails.

Only when the experiment yields statistically significant signal (revenue or high relative engagement) do you graduate it to a "startup." This "more shots on goal" approach de-risks the venture much earlier in the process. You are not betting on hope; you are betting on evidence.

Parallel Entrepreneurship

This dynamic enables a new behavior called parallel entrepreneurship.

Historically, investors hated "part-time" founders. They wanted you "all in." They believed you couldn't focus on two things at once. But in an AIDE, the *agents* do the work. You can theoretically run three different experiments in three different industries simultaneously.

- **Experiment A:** An AI tool for dentists
- **Experiment B:** A direct-to-consumer brand for pet owners
- **Experiment C:** A newsletter for finance professionals

You set the intent. The agents execute the research and marketing. You watch the dashboards. If Experiment B takes off, you kill A and C, and *then* you go all in.

An Environment of Flourishing Innovation

Critics argue that this will lead to a world filled with "spam" startups. I argue it will lead to a world of unprecedented innovation.

When the cost of trying is high, only the privileged get to try. Only those with rich parents or VC connections can afford to fail. When the cost of trying is low, *everyone* gets to try.

We will see weird ideas. Niche ideas. Ideas that no VC would ever fund, but that find a passionate audience of 10,000 people. This messy, chaotic, high-volume environment is exactly where breakthroughs come from. I also believe that it will result in more businesses solving more problems for more people in far more personalized ways. Instead of one CRM company, such as Salesforce, you could have thousands of CRM companies that all cater to extremely niche market segments and these can all be sustainable businesses. There will still be many big businesses, but there can also now be more businesses that cater specifically to niche audiences.

And these businesses are moving faster than ever. Payment processing company Stripe offers Stripe Atlas, which helps founders incorporate their business and begin charging customers. They highlighted in their 2025 report that founders are generating revenue faster than ever before, that "In 2025, more Atlas startups hit $100,000 of revenue in their first 6 months, 56% more than in 2024, and they got there nearly 11% faster (108 days versus 121)" (Carey 2025).

Evolution works through random mutation and selection. AI allows us to speed up the mutation rate of the economy.

A Note on Patience

However, there is a trap. Just because you *can* build fast doesn't mean *everything* should be built fast.

The "more shots on goal" methodology works perfectly for software, consumer apps, and digital services. It works for the "bits" world.

But what about the "atoms" world? What about curing cancer? What about fusion energy? You cannot run a 30-minute experiment to build a nuclear reactor.

In the next chapter, we will discuss the exception to the rule. We will look at Deep Tech, Medtech, and Pharma, and why these industries operate on a fundamentally different timeline, even in the age of AI.

No One Works Here: The Digital War Room

You've learned the theory; now let's build the machinery. Turn these concepts into immediate ROI for your company by accessing your free resources at NoOneWorksHere.com.

1. Immediate Actions (Do This Today)

- **Calculate Your Cost Per Experiment:** Audit your last three "new ideas" and determine the total time and capital spent before you received a market "yes" or "no." Identify how AI agents could have slashed those costs to under $100.
- **Launch a "Mousetrap" Test:** Select one stagnant hypothesis sitting in your backlog and use AI to generate a landing page and ad copy by end-of-day. Run a low-budget traffic test to collect emails and measure "statistical signal" rather than relying on gut feel.
- **Audit for "Wrapper Risk":** Review your current digital projects and ask if a single API update from OpenAI or Google would render them obsolete. If you are just a "thin layer," document one proprietary dataset or complex workflow you can integrate to build a moat.

2. The Discussion (Bring This to Your Team)

- Are we treating our current business projects like "babies" to be protected or "hypotheses" to be tested? How would our roadmap change if we prioritized a high failure rate in exchange for a 10-time increase in experiment volume?

(*continued*)

(*continued*)

- If the cost of curiosity is effectively zero, why are we still requiring six-month lead times for MVPs? What cultural or technical bottlenecks are preventing us from moving at the speed of "parallel entrepreneurship"?
- Look at our current competitive advantage: Is it based on a "storefront on a volcano"? How can we pivot our digital experiments to focus on unique distribution or "atoms-based" complexity that general AI models cannot easily replicate?

3. The Step-by-Step Implementation

Stop guessing and start building. Use the **Rapid Experimentation Workbook** for step-by-step guidance. This digital workbook provides the exact framework you need to implement this chapter's concepts.

Download it at: NoOneWorksHere.com/entrepreneurial-experiments

4. The Unfair Advantage: AI-Powered Tools

Don't just read about AI; use it right now. As a reader of this book, you get exclusive access to interactive AI-software tools designed to do the heavy lifting for you.

Access your tools instantly at: NoOneWorksHere.com
(Or simply scan the QR code with your smartphone camera)

13

Deep Tech, Medtech, and Pharma

A Different Timeline

> How do you shrink a ten-year, billion-dollar scientific R&D cycle into a computational simulation?
> *AI's role in reducing R&D friction and risk.*

In the previous chapter, I told you that you should be running rapid, cheap experiments. I told you that you could build a company in 30 minutes. I told you to fail fast and move on.

If you're building a SaaS app, a newsletter, or a marketplace, that is absolutely true. But what if you're trying to cure sickle cell anemia?

What if you're engineering a new carbon-capturing concrete? Or navigating the complex world of Green Tech? Currently, many Green Tech firms are considered "tech" only because of the technology pathway they use, not because they're leveraging AI or data to their fullest potential. To drive the uptake of renewables and stay competitive for scarce capital, these firms must use AI for more than just research; they must use it for outcome-driven optimization, determining how to use feedstock most optimally between competing sectors to drive down prices. In the atom world, the AIDE model is the difference between a high-cost experiment and a price-competitive market leader.

What if you're building a quantum computer? You cannot "vibe-code" a new drug (yet, anyway!).

For decades, Deep Tech, Medtech, and Pharma ventures have faced a different reality. They face a decade-long gauntlet of massive capital demands and crushing scientific risk. They do not operate on "internet time." They operate on "science time."

But that is changing.

In this chapter, you will:

- **Confront the Valley of Death:** Why hard science has historically been a challenging venture bet
- **Apply AIDE to Atoms:** How AI is compressing the "lab-to-fab" journey
- **Learn How AI De-Risks Science:** Moving from brute-force discovery to predictive simulation
- **Explore Democratization of Science:** Why the next great biotech company might come from Canada, for example, not Cambridge

The Impossible Mission

I work with brilliant scientists every day. I have the opportunity to collaborate with those around the world who are catalyzing the next generation hard-tech innovations. They are not trying to optimize ad clicks. They are trying to save lives and save the planet.

Beyond the innovators I work with and teach daily at MIT, I've worked closely with the national leadership team at Labs4, a Canada-wide network of 38 colleges and universities working in partnership to empower researcher-entrepreneurs to turn academic breakthroughs into real-world ventures, products, and solutions, to determine how best to ensure that the scientists, engineers, and researchers developing these new innovations can leverage the AI-Driven Enterprise model to commercialize them and create an impact in society. Our goal has been to help these researcher-entrepreneurs not just increase their technology readiness level (TRL), a spectrum of technology readiness developed by NASA from 1 to 9, used to indicate how mature a technology is, but also to make sure that they're best equipped to bring it to market.

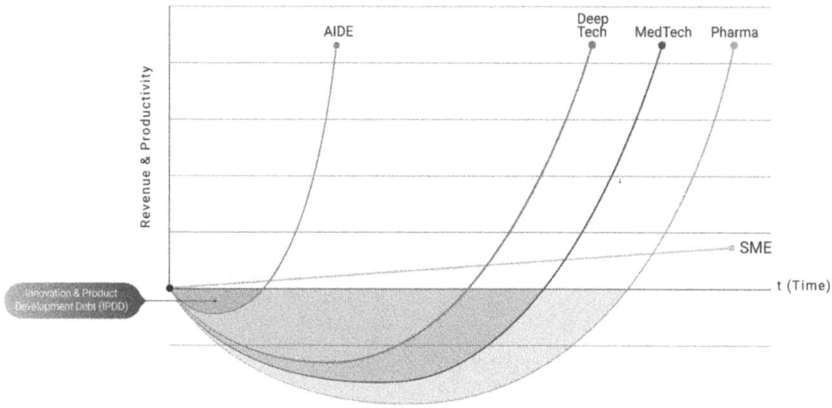

The ventures they're creating fall into the category my colleagues Bill Aulet and Fiona Murray call Innovation-Driven Enterprises (IDEs). But unlike a digital IDE (like Shopify), a Deep Tech IDE has a massive anchor dragging behind it in the form of significant Innovation and Product Development Debt (IPDD). In software, IPDD is time. In Deep Tech, IPDD is 10 years and $100 million. The transition for these entrepreneurs is a societal benefit I've explored in detail with Jeff Larsen, my friend and collaborator at Dalhousie University who launched one of the world's first AIDE education programs.

Unlike the software startups in Chapter 10 where distribution is the new bottleneck, in Deep Tech, discovery and scale remain the primary walls.

The Traditional Gauntlet:

1. **Discovery:** Spend years in a lab
2. **Validation:** Spend millions proving it works in a petri dish
3. **Scale-Up:** Spend tens of millions proving you can manufacture it
4. **Regulation:** Spend hundreds of millions proving it is safe (clinical trials)
5. **Market:** Finally, after 12 years, try to sell it

This timeline creates a "Valley of Death" as ventures climb in technology readiness level (TRL) so wide that most investors refuse to cross it. It is why we have a thousand food delivery apps and very few new antibiotics.

The Acceleration Engine

However, a new force is dismantling these barriers. Artificial Intelligence is mechanizing the scientific method.

AI is no longer just a side tool for data analysis. It is a core driver of value that compresses timelines and de-risks science. When you apply the AI-Driven Enterprise (AIDE) model to the physical world or across MedTech, Deep Tech, and Pharma, you don't just get efficiency; you get *possibility*.

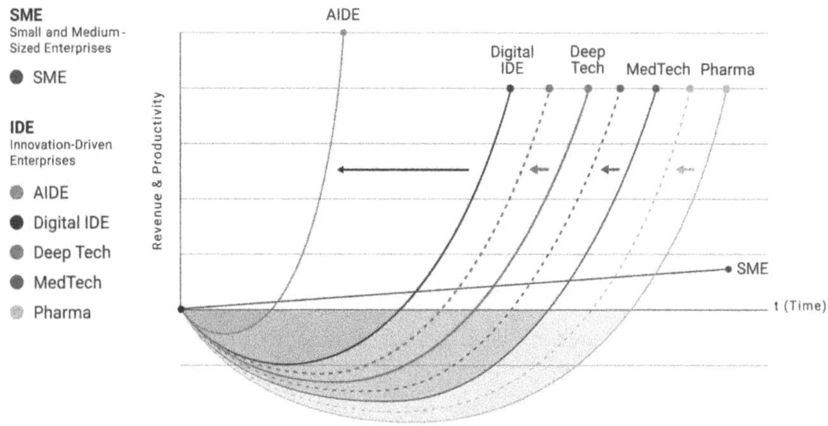

> Download this graph and other resources on the AI-Driven Enterprise model: NoOneWorksHere.com/downloads/graphs.

The AIDE model can be applied to all companies. Just as with software companies where an AIDE incorporates AI into every functional area, a Deep Tech company can similarly incorporate AI into market research, technoeconomic analysis, operations, finance, HR, and so much more. But for these companies there are also additional benefits introduced by the AIDE model, which is rewriting the rules across three critical sectors. Following are a few stylized examples.

1. Deep Tech and Advanced Materials: From Lab to Fab

Historically, developing a new material (like a better battery electrolyte) was a linear process of physical trial and error. You mix chemicals, test them, fail, and repeat.

The AI Shift: Digital Twins

Now, we use AI to create "digital twins."

- **Simulation:** Instead of physically building 1,000 battery prototypes, we simulate 1,000,000 variations in a virtual environment. The AI predicts the material properties.
- **Automated R&D:** We only physically build the top 1% that the AI identifies as promising.

This turns a physical manufacturing problem into a computational problem.

2. Medtech: From Passive to Predictive

Medical devices used to be passive hardware. An MRI machine took a picture; the doctor did the work.

The AI Shift: Actionable Insight

Now, the device is the diagnostic tool.

- **Predictive Analytics:** AI doesn't just show the x-ray; it highlights the fracture. It detects the anomaly in the heart rhythm before the cardiac event happens.
- **Value Prop:** For a hospital, paying for a machine that *prevents* errors is a much easier sell than paying for a machine that just takes pictures.

3. Pharma: From Luck to Logic

Drug discovery has traditionally been an extremely risky and capital intensive endeavor. You screen millions of molecules hoping one sticks to a disease target. It is brute-force luck.

The AI Shift: Generative Design

Companies like Insilico Medicine and Recursion Pharmaceuticals are using generative AI to design drugs.

- **Target ID:** AI analyzes genomic data to find the disease target.
- **Molecule Design:** Generative models build a custom molecule to fit that target, atom by atom.
- **Clinical Trials:** AI identifies the right patients for trials, reducing the failure rate of the most expensive phase of development.

The Multiplier Effect

Why does this matter to an investor or a founder? Because of the AIDE compound effect.

If AI can reduce the cost of a Stage 1 trial by 30%, and the time of a Stage 2 trial by 30%, and the manufacturing failure rate by 30%, the cumulative effect is not linear. It is exponential.

The "At-Bats" Theory

Venture capital is a game of probability. A fund has a finite amount of money.

- **Old Model:** $100M fund can back 5 drug companies (high risk).
- **AIDE Model:** $100M fund can back 10 drug companies because each one is cheaper and faster to validate.

By de-risking the science, AI increases the number of "shots on goal" humanity gets at curing cancer.

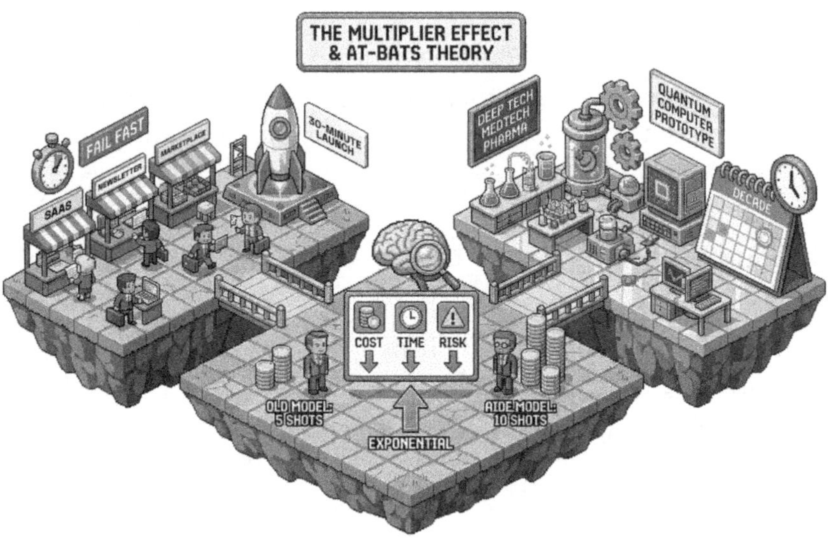

Democratizing Deep Tech: The Canada Case Study

This shift also breaks the geographic monopoly of innovation. Historically, if you wanted to build a biotech company, you had to be in Kendall Square (Cambridge, Massachusetts) or South San Francisco. You needed to be near the big labs and the big money. But if the primary work is moving from the "wet lab" to the "server farm," geography matters less.

Look at Canada, which has always been a powerhouse in fundamental research. It's in the top quartile of the Organisation for Economic Co-operation and Development's (OECD) data on countries for high-technology innovation. But it has historically lagged at commercializing that research (OECD 2024).

Today, Canada is pivoting. It is home to world-renowned AI institutes like Mila and Vector. It has 1,500 PhD-level AI researchers.

- **BenchSci** (Pharma)
- **Deep Genomics** (Genetic Medicine)
- **Xanadu** (Quantum)

These companies are proving that you don't need to be in Silicon Valley to change the world. You just need the compute and the talent. The AIDE model allows regions with strong *science* but limited *capital* to compete globally.

The New Directive

If you're a founder in these spaces, the message is clear. For founders: Stop treating AI as a "feature" you add later. You must architect your venture to be an AIDE from day one.

- Don't just hire biologists; hire data scientists who speak biology.
- Don't just build a lab; build a data loop.

For investors: Your risk models may need to change. The timelines you accepted as "standard" are now "slow." You need to seek out founders who are bilingual, fluent in both deep science and deep learning.

Part III Summary

We have looked at the AIDE model across the spectrum of the startup and Deep Tech companies. Now we'll look at those companies operating as SMEs, and explore how they can adopt the AIDE model to expand their impact.

No One Works Here: The Digital War Room

You've learned the theory; now let's build the machinery. Turn these concepts into immediate ROI for your company by accessing your free resources at NoOneWorksHere.com.

1. Immediate Actions (Do This Today)

- **Audit Your IPDD:** Identify the specific stages in your R&D pipeline where Innovation and Product Development Debt, time and capital, is highest. Determine which of these physical bottlenecks can be converted into computational simulations to compress your lab-to-fab timeline.
- **Recruit "Bilingual" Talent:** Shift your hiring strategy to prioritize "bilingual" experts who are fluent in both your deep-science domain (biology, chemistry, physics) and deep learning. Rewrite one open technical job description today to explicitly require "bilingual" fluency in both your hard-science domain and generative AI prompting.
- **Deploy Digital Twins:** Transition from physical trial and error to predictive modeling by creating virtual environments for your hardware or materials. Before your next physical prototype, ensure you have simulated at least 1,000 variations to identify the top 1% most likely to succeed.

2. The Discussion (Bring This to Your Team)

- If we were to shift 50% of our current physical R&D budget into predictive simulation and generative design, how would that change our "shots on goal" over the next three years? Are we currently limited by the speed of our science or the weight of our traditional processes?

- In what ways is our organization treating AI as a "feature" rather than the architectural foundation of the enterprise? If we had to rebuild our workflow as an AIDE from scratch today, which "standard" industry timelines would we refuse to accept?
- How can we leverage the democratization of compute to compete with larger, better-funded incumbents in traditional innovation hubs? What specific proprietary data assets do we possess that, when fed into an AIDE model, give us an "unfair advantage" regardless of our geographic location?

3. The Step-by-Step Implementation

Stop guessing and start building. Use the **Deep Tech & Pharma Acceleration Workbook** for step-by-step guidance. This digital workbook provides the exact framework you need to implement this chapter's concepts.

Download it at: NoOneWorksHere.com/deep-tech

4. The Unfair Advantage: AI-Powered Tools

Don't just read about AI; use it right now. As a reader of this book, you get exclusive access to interactive AI-software tools designed to do the heavy lifting for you.

Access your tools instantly at: NoOneWorksHere.com

(Or simply scan the QR code with your smartphone camera)

14

The AI-Augmented SME

How does a lean, local business break the gravity of linear growth to achieve global, exponential scale?
The AI-Driven Enterprise model is the key to transforming linear growth into a scalable, high-velocity engine for the global economy.

In the previous chapters, we have focused on the extremes. We looked at the pure digital startup and the Deep Tech (hard science and massive risk) companies.

But what about the middle, the SMEs?

In this chapter, you will:

- **Discover the AI-Augmented SME:** How to turn a linear business into an exponential one
- **Learn Vectors of AI Adoption:** Enhancing operations (efficiency) versus enhancing products (value)
- **See Real-World AI Examples:** From smart brake pads to predictive fishing nets
- **Explore the Industrial Application:** Hear from Mike Wandler, the CEO of an industrial firm, about how they're scaling their impact by embracing AI

What about the company that makes brake pads in Sandusky, Ohio? What about the dairy farm equipment manufacturer in rural Iowa? What about the family-owned business that services wind turbines? The restaurant with just one location but the ambition to open additional locations? Or perhaps the classic German "Mittelstand" company, a firm with fewer than 500 staff and under $1 billion in revenue that remains one of the top three in its global niche. These typically manufacturing-heavy firms are the prime candidates for an AIDE transformation. When a C-suite in a specialized niche—whether it's maritime, rolling stock, or precision components—extracts full value from AI, they don't just grow their company; they advance their economy.

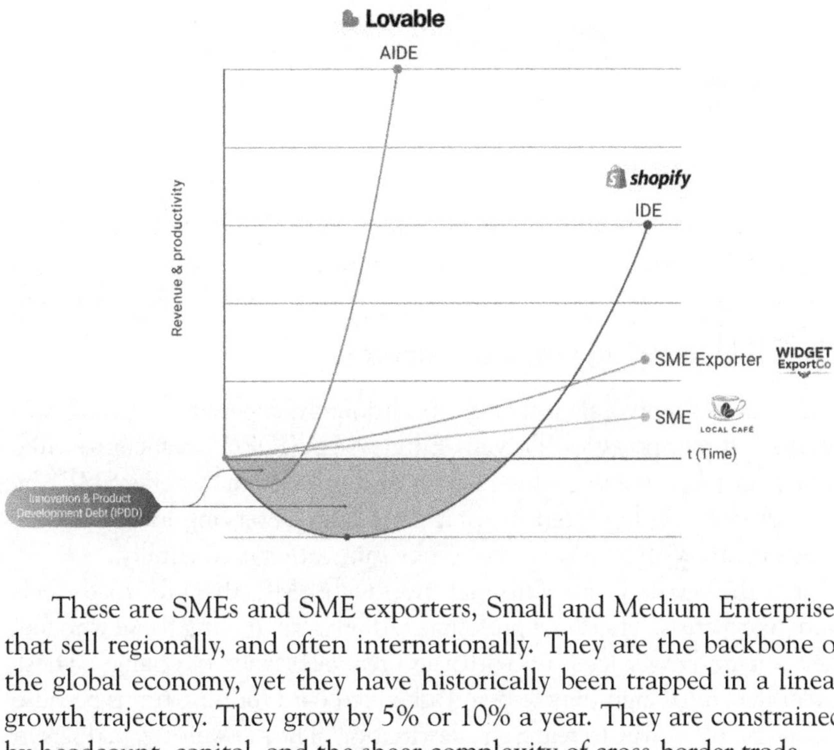

These are SMEs and SME exporters, Small and Medium Enterprises that sell regionally, and often internationally. They are the backbone of the global economy, yet they have historically been trapped in a linear growth trajectory. They grow by 5% or 10% a year. They are constrained by headcount, capital, and the sheer complexity of cross-border trade.

The AIDE model is not just for startups in Silicon Valley. It is the key to unlocking exponential growth for the businesses that make the world run.

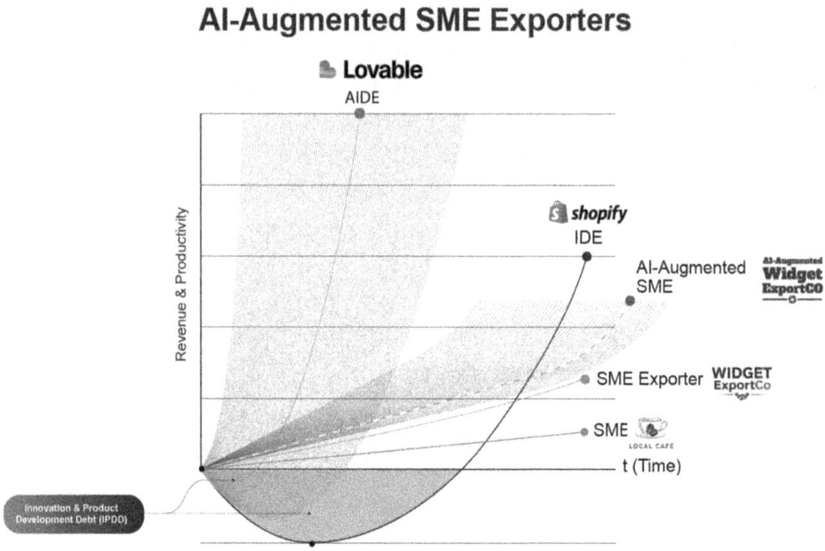

Download this graph and other resources on the AI-Driven Enterprise model: NoOneWorksHere.com/downloads/graphs.

The Hidden Engine of the Economy

SMEs stand at a pivotal crossroads. Traditionally, exponential growth was reserved for Innovation-Driven Enterprises (IDEs), companies like Shopify or Uber that were designed for disruption from day one. SMEs, by contrast, are deeply rooted in their communities serving local markets. They operate with lean resources. They innovate incrementally.

For the owner of a traditional, non-tech SME, this crossroads feels more like a crisis. There is a profound "AI anxiety" among those who feel they can no longer keep up with the breakneck pace of change. These leaders feel as though they're being asked to board running trains because there is no other way to reach the destination. They're waiting, perhaps in vain, for the trains to halt for just a second so they can make a calculated, safe decision on which one to board. My message to these SME owners is that the train will not stop, but the AIDE model provides the "boarding ramp" needed to integrate these tools without losing your local identity or your mind.

But SMEs have a secret weapon: They already have customers. They have specialized knowledge, niche products, and established supply chains. And we need to support them. As Aneesh Raman shares in the LinkedIn "How Small Business Can Win in 2026" report, "We should all be rooting for small businesses right now. They create the majority of new jobs globally, especially in emerging markets, and AI gives them a real shot to compete in ways that weren't possible before. The entrepreneurial skills you develop building something from nothing—resourcefulness, speed, creativity—are exactly what this economy will reward most" (LinkedIn 2025).

The challenge is that they are bottlenecked.

- **Limited Capital:** They can't burn cash to grow.
- **Complex Logistics:** Selling across borders is a nightmare of compliance and shipping.
- **Talent Gaps:** They may struggle to hire data scientists in their local areas.

AI bends the vector. It allows these lean teams to punch far above their weight.

Bending the Vector: Operations Versus Product

How does a 50-person manufacturing firm become an AIDE? It happens on two fronts.

Front 1: Operational Efficiency (Doing Things Better)

This is the low-hanging fruit. AI can streamline the friction of international trade.

- **Market Research:** Instead of hiring a consultant to study the German market, an AI agent can predict demand and analyze local regulations in seconds.
- **Logistics:** AI automates the nightmare of customs paperwork and optimizes shipping routes to shave days off delivery.
- **Support:** Multilingual AI agents allow a small team in Nova Scotia to support customers in Tokyo in fluent Japanese, 24/7.
- Among other operational efficiencies . . .

Front 2: Product Innovation (Making Better Things)

This is the transformative shift. AI allows SMEs to add a layer of *intelligence* to their physical products.

The "Widget ExportCo" Example: Imagine a 200-person firm in the industrial heartland that makes brake pads.

- **Old Model:** They sell a slab of metal and ceramic. It wears out. The customer buys a new one (commodity).
- **AI-Augmented Model:** They embed sensors in the brake pad. An AI model analyzes the wear patterns in real time. It predicts failure before it happens. It automatically notifies the fleet manager and reorders the part.
- **Result:** They are no longer selling a part; they are selling *safety-as-a-service*. They have transformed from a manufacturer to a tech company.

The Dairy Farm Example: Consider a manufacturer of milking equipment.

- **Old Model:** Sell the machine.
- **AI-Augmented Model:** Add cameras and wearables for the cows. The AI detects disease, determines reproduction readiness, and optimizes feed dispersion. The SME now owns the data layer of the farm.

Example: L&H

To understand how the AIDE model hits the industrial sector with the force of a hammer on steel, we must look at L&H, a heavy industrial manufacturing and repair firm. This is a company operating in what President and CEO Mike Wandler refers to as "real steel and real dirt," generating about $115M in revenue through custom parts, welding, and engineering. (Data provided via author interview with Mike Wandler.)

For most industrial SMEs, growth is traditionally linear and constrained by human coordination. At L&H, a dozen job coordinators historically spent two weeks every month quoting $1B worth of work. The knowledge required to quote these complex projects was buried in 20 years of ERP data—data so deep it took new employees five years to truly master.

By building a custom AI infrastructure in AWS to make that ERP data readable and writable, L&H is compressing that quoting cycle from two weeks to two days. The math of this clockspeed shift is transformative: If AI allows them to quote $5B instead of $1B at the same 11% win rate, potential revenue jumps from $115M to $575M without a proportional increase in headcount.

However, Mike, the CEO of L&H, warns that this isn't just about efficiency; it's about survival. He argues that my thesis hits industrials hardest because many leaders dismiss AI as irrelevant to "real manufacturing." This dismissal leads to a predictable, fatal pattern: first margin compression, then a loss of competitiveness, and finally capital starvation.

In the industrial world, the latency problem we discussed in Chapter 1 isn't a minor annoyance; it is an existential cliff. Mike is clear: Laggards in this sector won't experience a slow decline; they will fall off a cliff. He believes his own firm is already so far ahead that competitors can no longer even understand the language of his advantage.

This transformation also redefines the role of the worker. L&H is not cutting people to win; they are elevating them. Mike envisions a 2030 horizon where a master machinist works four half-days, earns more, and manages a fleet of 24/7 CNC machines and four humanoid assistants. In this AIDE model, "work" is no longer about grinding hours; it is about managing intelligent systems.

Internally, L&H is blunt about the stakes: Everyone is invited to the future, but those who choose not to adapt will eventually become too slow, too expensive, or too inconsistent to remain. As Mike puts it, this isn't a punishment; it's the reality.

The Barriers to Entry (and How to Break Them)

If this is so obvious, why isn't every SME doing it?

1. **High Perceived Cost:** AI sounds expensive. (Solution: Use off-the-shelf services, not custom models.)
2. **Talent Gap:** A brake pad factory doesn't know how to hire an ML engineer. (Solution: Use "vibe-coding" tools, specialized vendors, and partnerships.)
3. **Data Silos:** Their data is locked in old ERP systems. (Solution: AI agents that can read and structure legacy data.) You don't need to rip and replace the ERP (a $2M project). You use "wrapper agents," AI tools specifically designed to act as a translation layer. They "screen scrape" or query the clunky legacy interface just like a human would, extracting the data into a modern dashboard without touching the fragile underlying code. It's messy, it's a Band-Aid, but it works immediately.

The opportunity for entrepreneurial, ambitious SMEs is to use the AIDE mindset to knock down these barriers. You don't need a PhD in AI; you need "entrepreneurial AI literacy," knowing just enough to be dangerous.

The Path Forward

If you run an SME, or if you advise one, the call to action is urgent. You are being hunted. Somewhere, a startup is using AI to build a cheaper, smarter version of your product. Or a competitor is using AI to slash their logistics costs by 30%. You cannot afford to stay linear in an exponential world.

For Entrepreneurs: Look at "boring" industries. The biggest AIDE opportunity might not be a new social app; it might be buying a plumbing supply exporter, working collaboratively with the previous owner and their team, and adding an AI logistics layer.

For Policy makers: Stop subsidizing the past. Policy makers and investors shouldn't just chase the next Google; they should help a thousand local manufacturers become AI-augmented SMEs. Fund AI literacy. Build the "digital roads" that allow your local companies to access the global AI grid and export opportunities.

Part III Summary

We have now covered the full spectrum of the AIDE opportunity:

- **Startups:** The 30-minute unicorn
- **Deep Tech:** The science accelerator
- **SMEs:** The linear-to-exponential pivot

We have seen *how* to build and *who* can build. Now we need to talk about money.

Who is going to fund this revolution? How are VCs evaluating opportunities? And how does the role of private equity change when companies become efficient cash-generating machines?

In the next two chapters, we will explore private equity and venture capital.

No One Works Here: The Digital War Room

You've learned the theory; now let's build the machinery. Turn these concepts into immediate ROI for your company by accessing your free resources at NoOneWorksHere.com.

1. Immediate Actions (Do This Today)

- **Identify Your "Brake Pad" Opportunity:** Audit your physical products or services to identify where adding a layer of "intelligence" (sensors, predictive alerts, or automated reordering) transforms a one-time commodity sale into a high-margin "service-as-a-subscription" model.

(continued)

(*continued*)

- **Deploy a "Wrapper Agent" on Legacy Data:** Instead of a multi-million-dollar ERP overhaul, task your technical lead with identifying one "clunky" database and using an AI agent to "screen scrape" or query it, instantly creating a modern, real-time leadership dashboard.
- **Audit Your Quoting Efficiency:** Map your current sales quoting process; if it takes weeks of human coordination to price complex jobs, implement an AI infrastructure to compress that cycle by 80%, allowing your team to bid on five times more volume without increasing headcount.

2. The Discussion (Bring This to Your Team)

- If a lean, AI-native startup launched a "smarter" version of our core product tomorrow, one that used predictive data to solve the customer's problem before it happened, how long would it take for our current margins to compress to zero?
- Are we currently viewing AI as a tool to cut our existing workforce, or are we building a 2030 vision where our master craftspeople/experts are "agent orchestrators" managing a fleet of automated systems and humanoid assistants?
- Which part of our international or regional expansion is currently "bottlenecked" by human language skills or regulatory complexity, and how could multilingual AI agents move us from a local player to a global exporter overnight?

3. The Step-by-Step Implementation

Stop guessing and start building. Use the **AI for SMEs Workbook** for step-by-step guidance. This digital workbook provides the exact framework you need to implement this chapter's concepts.

Download it at: NoOneWorksHere.com/sme

4. The Unfair Advantage: AI-Powered Tools

Don't just read about AI; use it right now. As a reader of this book, you get exclusive access to interactive AI-software tools designed to do the heavy lifting for you.

Access your tools instantly at: NoOneWorksHere.com

(Or simply scan the QR code with your smartphone camera)

15

AI and Private Equity

The Next Frontier

How does AI change the investment playbook?
How capital allocators evolve from analysis to orchestration.

PRIVATE EQUITY (PE) has always been about one thing: efficiency.

For the last 40 years, the playbook was simple. Buy a bloated company. Cut costs. Optimize the supply chain. Add leverage. Sell for a profit. It was financial engineering, and it worked.

But the "low-hanging fruit" of capital arbitrage has been picked. The three primary value levers—growth, delevering, and multiple expansion—now require more than just a cheap loan. In a world of contracting multiples, the traditional tactics of mindless cost-cutting are yielding diminishing returns.

The next frontier for private equity is less financial; it is operational. And the engine of that operation is the AI-Driven Enterprise (AIDE) model.

In this chapter, you will:

- **See the Shift:** Why PE is moving from "financial engineering" to "intelligent orchestration"

- **Learn the Playbook:** How to use AI to diligence, acquire, and transform portfolio companies
- **Meet the AI Operating Partner:** The new role emerging to support portfolio companies demanding expertise
- **Explore the "Roll-Up" 2.0:** Using agents to integrate fragmented industries
- **Understand the New Exit:** Why the most valuable companies of the future will be the ones with the highest **ARR/FTE**

The End of the LBO Era?

The leveraged buyout (LBO) was the hammer of the 1980s. Today, the LBO is no longer a strategic advantage; it is a necessity to "win" a deal because most firms share the same lenders and cost of capital. The real advantage has shifted from capital arbitrage to cognitive arbitrage—the ability to extract second-level insights that others miss.

The Thesis: There are thousands of "zombie" companies in the middle market—logistics firms, insurance brokerages, medical billing services—that are profitable but inefficient. They are run on spreadsheets and manual labor. They have massive amounts of unstructured data they don't use. These companies are prime targets for an AIDE transformation. PE firms (and search funds) are capitalizing.

Phase 1: AI-Powered Diligence

The revolution starts before the check is written.

Traditional diligence is slow. You hire a consulting firm (Bain, McKinsey, BCG) to spend weeks analyzing the target's data room. They interview customers. They build Excel models.

The AIDE Approach:

- **Data Ingestion:** Use AI to scan the entire data room in hours.
- **Sentiment Analysis:** Scrape Glassdoor, LinkedIn, and customer reviews to build a real-time sentiment map of the culture and brand.
- **Code Audit:** Use AI agents to read the target's codebase. Is it spaghetti code? Is it scalable? The AI can tell you the "technical debt" score instantly.

This allows PE firms to evaluate more targets, faster, and with deeper insight than human analysts ever could.

Phase 2: The Transformation (The "AI Turnaround")

Once the company is acquired, the real work begins. The goal is no longer to mindlessly reduce headcount, but to multiply the operating profit per employee by a hundredfold. You aren't sending in a "hatchet man" to fire people; you are sending in a "systems architect" to augment the workforce. You replace friction with compute, allowing the company to do much more with much less.

The Playbook:

1. **The "Back Office" Wipeout:** Accounts payable, payroll, HR compliance—these are rules-based tasks. Deploy agents to automate them.
2. **The Sales Upgrade:** Instead of hiring more business development reps, equip the existing team with AI tools that automate prospecting. Turn your sales team into "sales architects."
3. **Customer Support:** Deploy a customized LLM trained on the company's historical support tickets. Move from "call center" to "resolution engine."
4. More of the same tactics can also be applied across other functional areas.

The Rise of the AI Operating Partner

This transformation isn't just happening top-down; it is being pulled by the portfolio companies themselves.

CEOs of mid-market companies are often overwhelmed by the noise of AI. They know they need to adapt, but they don't know where to start. They are looking to their board and the PE firm for a roadmap.

To meet this demand, PE firms are evolving their structure. Traditionally, firms employed "operating partners" focused on finance (to audit books) or talent (to hire executives).

Now, firms are hiring dedicated AI execution partners—technical experts who connect the dots between business needs and available solutions. Their job is to manage the "build versus buy" framework: deciding whether to develop proprietary internal tools or hire a specialized startup to provide the service. They parachute into a portfolio company (Portco), audit the tech stack, set up the initial agent workflows, and hire the necessary AI talent. They serve as the "chief AI officer" for the entire portfolio, bringing Silicon Valley expertise to Ohio manufacturing firms.

Roll-Ups 2.0: The Integration Engine

One of the most common PE strategies is the roll-up: buying 50 small dental practices or HVAC companies and combining them into one platform.

The problem with roll-ups is integration. Merging 50 different IT systems, 50 different databases, and 50 different cultures is a nightmare. It usually fails or takes years. AI solves the integration problem.

- **Data Harmonization:** AI agents can map data fields from 50 different legacy systems into a single schema automatically.
- **Process Standardization:** Instead of retraining 500 employees on a new handbook, you give them an AI "copilot" that guides them through the new standard operating procedure in real time.

AI allows PE firms to roll up fragmented industries at a speed that was previously impossible.

The Exit: Selling the "Self-Driving" Company

When it comes time to sell, what are you selling?

In the past, you were selling a stream of cash flows. In the future, you are selling a self-driving organization.

A company that has successfully adopted the AIDE model commands a higher multiple because:

1. **It's Resilient:** It doesn't rely on retaining key humans for every task.
2. **It's Scalable:** It can double revenue without doubling costs.

3. **It's Data-Rich:** It has structured its proprietary data into a competitive moat.

Strategic acquirers (like the Fortune 500) will pay a premium for these companies because they are buying the *capability* they lack internally.

Case Example: The Search Fund "Expertise Lever"

The AIDE transformation isn't reserved for multi-billion-dollar buyouts; it is increasingly the primary value-creation strategy for search funds and micro-PE. Consider a recent case from Kristian Vervik Salte, an entrepreneur who acquired a small mechanics workshop. By shifting the architecture from human-centric to node-centric, they fundamentally changed the business's scalability.

"We currently have more agents than mechanics," Kristian told me. "In two years, we will have at least 10 times the agents to mechanics (or a system/infra of similar scale). We collect vast amounts of data through voice to text, which allows us to use fresh apprentices to complete work that previously required expert competency, because they have access to our company's aggregate data, knowledge, and experience."

This is a textbook example of using "silicon nodes" to solve the "expert bottleneck." By capturing the "unstructured" knowledge of master mechanics and making it accessible to apprentices via AI, the firm reduces its reliance on scarce, high-cost talent while simultaneously increasing its output capacity and service consistency.

The New Private Equity Associate

This shift changes the talent profile of the PE firm itself.

The PE associate of the past was an Excel wizard. They could model an LBO in their sleep. The PE associate of the future is a product manager of intelligence. Like a master using three wishes from a genie, their value lies in the creativity of their questions. They use AI to extract second-level inferences from marketing materials, specifically targeting how a company can achieve growth, delevering, and multiple expansion through "deep and narrow" AI applications.

They need to know:

- Which AI tools are best for supply chain optimization
- How to assess the "AI readiness" of a target
- How to implement an agentic workflow without breaking the company

The firms that hire this talent will win. The firms that stick to financial engineering will find themselves buying the companies the AIDE firms have already discarded.

PE firms are not alone in deploying capital for the AIDE transformation. Alongside them are venture capital firms scouting the hottest AIDEs. Next, we'll look at how the venture capital world responds.

No One Works Here: The Digital War Room

You've learned the theory; now let's build the machinery. Turn these concepts into immediate ROI for your company by accessing your free resources at NoOneWorksHere.com.

1. Immediate Actions (Do This Today)

- **Audit for Cognitive Arbitrage:** Identify three "zombie" processes in your organization that rely on manual data entry or spreadsheets and map out how an AI agent could ingest that data instantly.
- **Run an AI Diligence Scan:** Take your last three months of customer feedback or internal project notes and use an LLM to create a "sentiment and debt map" to identify hidden operational friction.
- **Appoint an AI Operating Lead:** Designate one person to act as your "systems architect" whose sole metric for success is increasing your company's revenue-per-employee (ARR/FTE) ratio.

2. The Discussion (Bring This to Your Team)

- If a private equity firm acquired us tomorrow with the goal of turning us into a "self-driving organization," which 20% of our headcount would they replace with autonomous agents first?
- Are we currently a "human-centric" bottleneck or a "node-centric" engine? Specifically, how much of our expert knowledge is trapped in people's heads versus being accessible via a digital "expertise lever"?
- When we eventually look to exit or scale, are we selling a stream of unpredictable human effort, or are we selling a resilient, scalable machine that "strategic acquirers" will pay a premium for?

3. The Step-by-Step Implementation

Stop guessing and start building. Use the **AIDE PE Investment Workbook** for step-by-step guidance. This digital workbook provides the exact framework you need to implement this chapter's concepts.

Download it at: NoOneWorksHere.com/private-equity

4. The Unfair Advantage: AI-Powered Tools

Don't just read about AI; use it right now. As a reader of this book, you get exclusive access to interactive AI-software tools designed to do the heavy lifting for you.

Access your tools instantly at: NoOneWorksHere.com

(Or simply scan the QR code with your smartphone camera)

16

Venture Capital in an Age of AIDEs

Is the traditional venture model prepared for the collapse of capital intensity?
As the cost of building software hits zero and revenue per employee skyrockets, the "blitzscaling" playbook is being rewritten for an era of radical efficiency.

For the last 20 years, venture capital (VC) has been the fuel of the innovation economy. The model was built on a specific set of assumptions:

1. Technology is expensive to build.
2. Startups need massive capital to scale.
3. Growth is constrained by headcount.
4. Most companies will fail, so the winners must return 100-fold to pay for the losers.

The AI-Driven Enterprise (AIDE) model breaks nearly every one of these assumptions.

As we discussed earlier, software is now cheap. The capital intensity of starting a company has collapsed, while the revenue potential per employee has exploded. This creates an existential crisis—and a massive opportunity—for the venture capital industry.

In this chapter, you will:

- **Analyze the "Capital Overhang":** Why VCs are sitting on billions of dollars they can't deploy effectively
- **Explore the New Unit Economics:** Why "revenue per employee" is replacing "growth at all costs"
- **Understand the "PE-ification" of Venture:** Why top-tier firms are abandoning the traditional VC structure to become asset managers
- **Confront the End of VC:** Why the "indie" movement might make the Series A round obsolete

The End of the "Mega-Round" Factory

For the last decade, the VC playbook was "blitzscaling," a concept coined by Reid Hoffman and Chris Yeh (Hoffman and Yeh 2018). Raise $10 million, hire 100 engineers, burn cash to capture the market, then raise $50 million more. But AIDEs don't *need* $10 million to start. They might need $500,000. And they don't need to hire 100 engineers. They need 5 engineers and 50 agents.

This breaks the business model of the large VC funds. If you're a $1 billion fund, you need to write $50 million checks to move the needle. You cannot write five hundred $1 million checks; you don't have the time to manage that many relationships (unless, of course, you become an AIDE venture firm!).

The Paradox: We have more great companies than ever (thanks to easy creation), but they need less money than ever. The "mega-funds" are currently structured for a different breed of companies. They are whales swimming in a pool that is becoming a series of puddles.

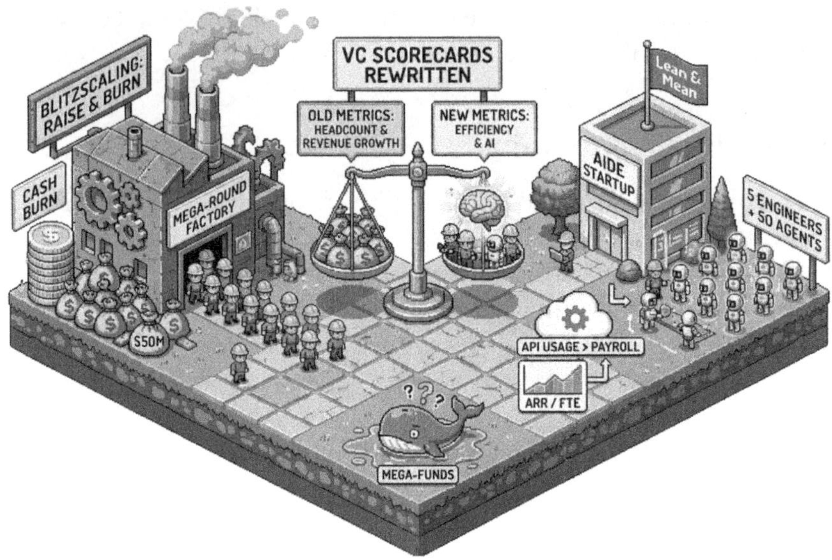

The New VC Metrics: Efficiency Is King

In the AIDE era, VCs are rewriting their scorecards.

Old Metrics:

- Headcount Growth ("They just hired a VP of sales!")
- Total Revenue Growth ("They grew 300%!")
- Market Share ("Land grab!")

New Metrics:

- **Burn Multiple:** A metric coined by venture capitalist David Sacks, which asks how much cash you burn to generate $1 of new revenue. (Best-in-class AIDEs are near 0 or even negative.)
- **ARR / FTE:** As discussed in Chapter 2, if a startup has $5M ARR and 50 employees, that's a red flag. It implies they haven't automated.

- **API Usage Versus Payroll:** I look for companies where the cloud/compute bill is growing faster than the payroll. That signals they are scaling via software; not labor. That is, assuming they aren't wasting compute expense.

This shift is mirrored by David Frankel, managing partner of Founder Collective, who argues that in an era where "clean math is hard to come by" (Frankel 2025), investors must look beyond traditional formulas to the dollars-to-progress ratio and the morale multiplier. Frankel, who looks for teams "propelled by the fumes from a petrol-soaked rag," notes that capital efficiency is found in founders who convert every dollar into relentless product velocity. As he recently shared regarding a lean team he backed:

> "Every time I open the app there's a new feature waiting for me. . . . This team has raised very little, but has converted every dollar into product and TikTok-fueled growth. Every dollar feels like an investment in possibility." (Frankel 2025)

Ultimately, the AIDE era aligns with Frankel's core thesis: While AI can optimize your burn, it is the founder's enthusiasm and ability to navigate "controlled chaos" that remains the ultimate hedge against long odds.

The "PE-ification" of Venture Capital

Perhaps the biggest shift is happening at the very top. The most famous names in venture capital—firms like Sequoia, Andreessen Horowitz (a16z), and General Catalyst—are quietly moving away from the venture model entirely.

They are becoming registered investment advisors (RIAs).

Why does this legal distinction matter? Traditional VCs are legally restricted to investing in private, high-growth startups. RIAs can invest in anything: public stocks, crypto, secondary shares, and debt.

This signals a shift toward a private equity (PE) model. Top-tier firms realize that in an AI world, companies mature faster and become cash-flow positive earlier. Instead of just betting on high-risk moonshots, these firms are now building platforms to:

1. **Hold Assets Longer:** They don't want to sell a profitable AIDE after 7 years. They want to hold it for 20 years, like a PE firm holds a utility company.
2. **Consolidate Markets:** They are using their massive capital not just to fund growth, but to buy competitors and merge them, a classic PE "roll-up" strategy powered by AI efficiency.
3. **Buy Ownership:** They are moving from minority stakes (10–20%) to majority control, allowing them to install their own "AI operating partners" (as discussed in Chapter 15) to drive value.

The line between venture capital (risk) and private equity (optimization) is blurring. The top firms are becoming "full-stack asset managers" for the AIDE era.

The Existential Question: Does VC Even Survive?

While the giants turn into PE firms, the rest of the industry faces a harder question: *Do we still need venture capital at all?* A growing chorus of industry voices is suggesting that the traditional "Series A" round is dead.

The "indie" thesis holds that if an entrepreneur can build a product, acquire customers, and hit $1M ARR with just $50k in credit card debt and cheap AI tools, why would they sell 20% of their company to a VC? We are seeing the rise of "indie capital" and revenue-based financing. Founders are opting to retain control, grow efficiently, and take profits rather than chase the "unicorn or bust" treadmill. Peter Walker, the head of insights at Carta, calls this the "bootstrapped solo founder era" and reports that the percentage of startups with no VC funding that have one founder has grown from 22.2% of US startups using Carta (n = 45,616) in 2015 to 38% in 2024 (Dowd and Walker 2025).

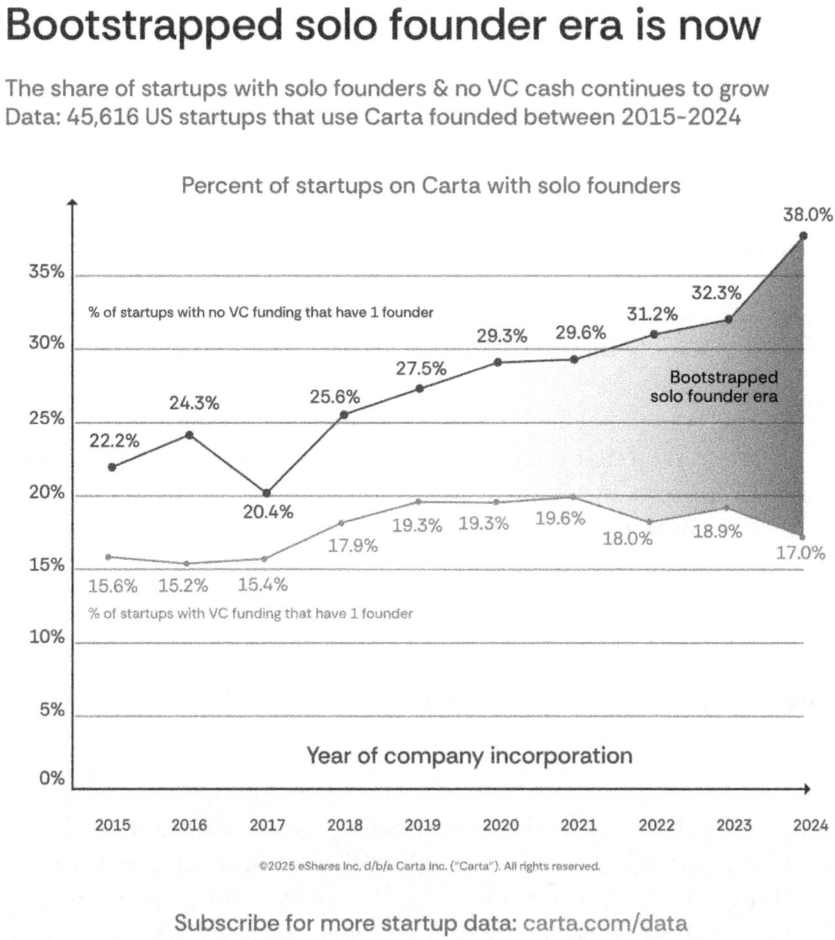

Source: Dowd and Walker / eShares, Inc.

The "Index" Thesis

Conversely, if AI leads to an explosion of 10,000 viable niche companies rather than 10 massive ones, this weakens the "power law" (where one winner pays for everything, a concept in venture capital economics from Peter Thiel; Thiel and Black 2017). In this world, VCs might evolve into indexers. instead of picking winners, they will use AI agents to algorithmically invest in thousands of startups, creating a "mutual fund" of the innovation economy.

The Reality

The middle is at risk.

- **The Giants** will survive by becoming PE firms.
- **The Angels/Indies** will survive by funding the early experimentation phase.
- **The Traditional Series A/B Firm** may be in the danger zone. They offer capital that is too expensive for the founder and too small for the infrastructure players.
- **The Growth Stage Firm** will have ample opportunities to partner the AIDEs that start lean, and intend to stay lean, but still need capital to scale their impact.

The Service as Software Thesis

Despite the structural chaos, there is one investment thesis that everyone agrees on: Service as Software (SaS). This flip from Software as a Service (SaaS) was popularized by the venture capital community, most notably by Sarah Guo (formerly of Greylock, now Conviction) and Foundation Capital.

Historically, VCs invested in SaaS. You sold a tool to a lawyer to help them work faster. Now VCs are investing in companies that *replace* the lawyer.

- **Old:** Sell accounting software to an accounting firm. (SaaS)
- **New:** Build an AI accountant that sells "accounting services" directly to the client for half the price. (SaS)

This expands the total addressable market (TAM). The market for "accounting software" is billions. The market for "accounting services" is trillions. VCs, and the new PE-style giants, are realizing that AI allows startups to capture the *services* revenue, not just the *software* revenue.

Part III Summary

We have explored the opportunity across every dimension:

- **Startups** (The 30-Minute Build)
- **Deep Tech** (The Science Accelerator)
- **SMEs** (The Global Exporters)
- **Private Equity** (The Optimization Engine)
- **Venture Capital** (The Growth Engine)

We have proven that the AIDE model is not a niche strategy; it is the new operating system for capitalism. But there is one final piece of the puzzle. Who is setting the rules for this game? Who is ensuring that this race to efficiency doesn't leave citizens behind? Venture capitalists allocate millions to shape the future of industries. But who allocates the resources to ensure society survives this shift? When the "power law" of VC fails to protect the middle class, the responsibility moves to the architect of the economy itself. In the next chapter, we look at the role of the state. We explore governments, growth, and the global race.

No One Works Here: The Digital War Room

You've learned the theory; now let's build the machinery. Turn these concepts into immediate ROI for your company by accessing your free resources at NoOneWorksHere.com.

1. Immediate Actions (Do This Today)

- **Audit Your API-to-Payroll Ratio:** Review your monthly expenses to see if your cloud and compute spend is growing faster than your payroll. If your headcount is outpacing your technology spend, you are building a legacy cost structure rather than an AIDE.

(*continued*)

(*continued*)

- **Audit Your Burn Multiple:** Calculate exactly how much cash your organization burned last quarter to generate $1 of net new revenue. If the number is greater than 1, immediately pause all nonessential hiring and divert those funds to AI-driven automation.
- **Flip to Service-as-Software:** Evaluate your current product offering and determine if you can sell the "end result" instead of the "tool." Moving from selling software to selling the completed service can multiply your total addressable market 10-fold by capturing labor budgets.

2. The Discussion (Bring This to Your Team)

- If we were starting this company today with only $50,000 and five AI agents, which 80% of our current "essential" processes would we realize are actually unnecessary? How can we begin dismantling those legacy structures now to improve our burn multiple?
- Are we currently hiring "ahead of growth" because it's what traditional investors expect, or are we maximizing our Dollars-to-Progress ratio? What would happen to our valuation if we stopped all hiring and focused exclusively on increasing our product velocity through automation?
- Does our current business model sell a tool to a professional (Software as a Service), or does it replace the professional entirely (Service as Software)? If a competitor launched an AI-driven service that did our customers' work for them at half our price, how would we respond?

3. The Step-by-Step Implementation

Stop guessing and start building. Use the **AIDE VC Workbook** for step-by-step guidance. This digital workbook provides the exact framework you need to implement this chapter's concepts.

Download it at: NoOneWorksHere.com/venture-capital

4. The Unfair Advantage: AI-Powered Tools

Don't just read about AI; use it right now. As a reader of this book, you get exclusive access to interactive AI-software tools designed to do the heavy lifting for you.

Access your tools instantly at: NoOneWorksHere.com

(Or simply scan the QR code with your smartphone camera)

17

Economic Development and the Global Race

Who wins the next Industrial Revolution?
Organizational intelligence and the resulting national competitiveness.

In the late 1990s, Finland wasn't just a country; it was an extension of Nokia. At its peak, Nokia accounted for 4% of Finland's entire GDP, 21% of its total exports, and 70% of the Helsinki Stock Exchange's market capital (Ali-Yrkkö et al. 2000). It was the ultimate economic development win, a single homegrown champion that employed thousands and financed the welfare state.

Then the iPhone launched. The platform shifted. Nokia collapsed. Finland entered a decade of economic stagnation known as a "lost decade."

Today, we see a similar pattern in Denmark with Novo Nordisk. Driven by the explosive success of Ozempic and Wegovy, the pharmaceutical giant is singlehandedly propping up the Danish economy. Without Novo Nordisk, Denmark's GDP growth would likely have flatlined in recent years. In 2023, Denmark's GDP grew by 1.8%. Statistics Denmark officially reported that without the pharmaceutical industry (driven almost entirely by Novo Nordisk), the national GDP would have contracted by 0.1% (Rolander and Bloomberg 2024). Instead, it is booming.

To a traditional economic developer, this looks like success. To a systems architect, this looks like a single point of failure.

Centralizing an entire economy around a small number of large companies creates inherent risk. As we explored in Chapter 2, the lifespan of large companies is shrinking. When a region relies on "whales" (massive, singular employers), it ties its social stability to the volatility of a single boardroom. When the whale stumbles, the region starves.

We need a new architecture for economic growth. We need to move from centralized fragility to decentralized resilience.

The AI-Driven Enterprise model decouples risk capital accessibility from entrepreneurial opportunity and economic growth.

In this chapter, you will:

- **Confront Concentration Risk:** Why chasing "The Next Nokia" is a dangerous strategy
- **Adopt the "Swarm" Strategy:** Why 1,000 small AIDEs are safer than one giant factory
- **Learn the "Whole-of-Society" Strategy:** A blueprint for mobilizing government, academia, and industry that provides a concrete policy proposal to build a shock-resistant economy

The Vulnerability of the Giant

For the last 30 years, governments have played a passive role in the digital economy, or they have actively chased "buffalo hunting," in search of economic engines, high-impact firms, or anchor institutions, trying to lure massive headquarters or factories with tax breaks—all to create a large number of local jobs.

But the "buffalo" (the large incumbent) is an endangered species.

The AIDE model changes the scale of job creation. As we explored in Part III, companies can now reach massive scale ($17M to $100M ARR) with tiny teams (15–50 people).

If you're a policymaker, this is terrifying. You can no longer count on a single startup scaling to employ 5,000 people in your city. However, if you flip the logic, it is liberating. We are witnessing the democratization of ambition. The barrier to entry has not just been lowered; it has been dismantled.

The Global Surge in Business Creation

The data now signals a profound shift: We aren't just seeing better entrepreneurs; we are seeing *more* of them. The traditional safety of a corporate nine-to-five is losing its luster. According to LinkedIn's *Workforce Confidence Index*, 40% of US professionals now express a desire to work for themselves in the near future.

AI acts as the "force multiplier," allowing a single founder to handle marketing, coding, and operations—tasks that previously required an entire team. This isn't theoretical; it is manifesting in a literal rebranding of the global workforce. Between July 2022 and late 2024, the number of LinkedIn members adding "founder" to their profiles *tripled* (LinkedIn 2025).

Market	Increase in "Founder" Profiles (YOY)
India	104%
The Netherlands	85%
United Kingdom	69%
United States	69%
Global Average (10 major economies)	60%

As the table illustrates, the "founder" explosion is a global phenomenon. While the growth is universal, markets like India are seeing a literal doubling of entrepreneurial activity. This is the "swarm" in action.

The Resilience Math

Now more people want to start companies, and more people *can* start companies because of the benefits that AI provides. Instead of relying on one company to employ 5,000 people, a resilient region can now nurture 1,000 AIDE founders employing 5 or 10 people each.

The Resilience Math:

- **Scenario A (Centralized):** One company employs 5,000. It fails, and 5,000 people are instantly unemployed. The housing market is impacted. Tax revenue declines (the Nokia scenario).
- **Scenario B (Decentralized):** 1,000 AIDEs employ 5 people each; 100 fail and 500 people are unemployed. They are quickly absorbed by the 900 growing firms. The economy barely shudders.

The AIDE model allows us to build an economy of shock absorbers. To capture this surge, governments must move from "buffalo hunting" to "swarm farming."

The Proposal: The AIDE Acceleration Compact

When you look at the AIDE growth curve compared to those of the SME and IDE models, the question I often pose to those involved in regional economic development is this: What would happen if you were to make an investment that led to the creation of a lot more AIDE lines on this graph in your region over the coming decade?

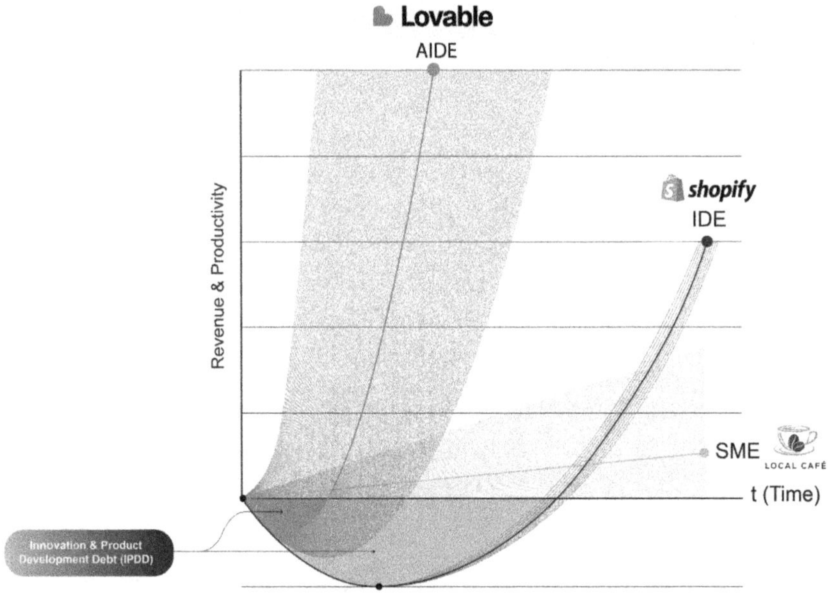

We cannot wait for the market to fix regional inequality or concentration risk. We need a coordinated push to build this distributed ecosystem.

In my recent position paper, "Crossing the AI Frontier," I outlined a "Whole-of-Society" strategy. It is not just for the government; it requires academia, philanthropy, and industry to co-invest.

Learn more on the book's website at NoOneWorksHere.com/economic-development.

The Call to Action

The nations that compete in the AI race will not just be the ones with the fastest chips. They will be the ones with the most resilient economic architecture. We have seen what happens when you bet everything on a Nokia or a single dominant industry. It works until it doesn't. And when it breaks, the pain is felt by everyone.

The AIDE model offers a different path. It allows regions to convert AI from a source of disruption into an engine of inclusive growth. It democratizes the ability to create wealth.

The call to action is simple: Form the compact. Fund it boldly. Buy what it builds.

This concludes Part III, "The Opportunities." We've zoomed out as far as we can go. We've traversed the landscape from the 30-minute startup to the 30-year national policy. We've seen that the AIDE model is not just a commercial tactic; it is the new operating system for economic resilience.

But understanding the opportunity is only half the equation. The other half is execution.

You now know *why* the world is changing and *what* is at stake. The remaining question is: *How* do you fit into it? How do we prepare a workforce for a world where no one works in the traditional sense?

Before we dive into the specific tactics for leaders and entrepreneurs in Part IV, we need to reset our mindset.

No One Works Here: The Digital War Room

You've learned the theory; now let's build the machinery. Turn these concepts into immediate ROI for your company by accessing your free resources at NoOneWorksHere.com.

1. Immediate Actions (Do This Today)

- **Audit Your Concentration Risk:** Identify if your revenue or local economy relies on a single whale (one client or employer) and calculate the immediate impact of a 50% "Nokia-style" contraction.
- **Secure Your AI Passport:** Visit the website to claim your credits and access the API vouchers needed to lower your compute costs and start your "swarm" of automated micro-ventures.
- **Draft a One-Page Micro-Contract:** Create a simplified, 15-day payment term procurement template to begin testing small-scale AI vendors without the friction of traditional corporate legal hurdles.

2. The Discussion (Bring This to Your Team)

- If our largest partner or primary industry experienced a "platform shift" tomorrow, do we have a "Swarm" of smaller, diversified initiatives ready to absorb the shock? How can we shift from centralized fragility to decentralized resilience this quarter?

(*continued*)

(*continued*)

- Are we currently acting as "buffalo hunters" by over-investing in single, massive projects, or are we "Swarm Farmers" nurturing a high volume of small, high-leverage AI-driven experiments?
- How would our operational efficiency change if we stopped hiring for traditional roles and instead incentivized our top talent to operate as internal "AIDE founders" with their own automated workflows?

3. The Step-by-Step Implementation

Stop guessing and start building. Use the **AIDE Economic Development Workbook** for step-by-step guidance. This digital workbook provides the exact framework you need to implement this chapter's concepts.

Download it at: NoOneWorksHere.com/economic-development

4. The Unfair Advantage: AI-Powered Tools

Don't just read about AI; use it right now. As a reader of this book, you get exclusive access to interactive AI-software tools designed to do the heavy lifting for you.

Access your tools instantly at: NoOneWorksHere.com

(Or simply scan the QR code with your smartphone camera)

PART

III → IV

If understanding the AI opportunity is passive, how do you actively force your organization to participate?
The tactical frameworks required to lead, learn, and build.

THIS CONCLUDES PART III, "The Opportunities." We have zoomed out as far as we can go. We have mapped the new arithmetic of growth across the entire economic spectrum: from the 30-minute startup to the science-accelerating timelines of Deep Tech, and from the optimization engines of private equity to the macroeconomic resilience of nations. We have seen that the AIDE model is not a niche strategy; it is the new operating system for capitalism.

But understanding the landscape is only half the equation. "Opportunity" is a vehicle, but your leadership is the driver.

Advantage now belongs exclusively to those who move from knowing to doing. To capture the efficiencies of an AI-Driven Enterprise, you must stop treating AI as a departmental project and start treating it as the fundamental architecture of your firm.

In Part IV, "The Actions," we provide your tactical manual for that crossing. We will shift the conversation from observation to participation, giving you the exact frameworks to execute.

What you do next determines whether you lead the change or chase it. Let's put the AIDE model to work.

PART IV The Actions

How to Lead, Learn, and Build in the Age of Intelligent Systems

The fastest way to understand the future is to build something inside it. Don't wait to understand it perfectly. Learn by doing.

THE OPPORTUNITY OF the AIDE era is no longer hypothetical; it is operational. While the macroeconomic landscape and the new trajectory of scale have redefined the boundaries of what a company can be, these advantages do not manifest through passive observation. The "Opportunity" is a vehicle, but your leadership is the driver.

Understanding what's happening is not enough. Advantage now belongs exclusively to those who move from knowing to doing. To capture the efficiencies of an AI-Driven Enterprise (AIDE), you must stop treating AI as a departmental project and start treating it as the fundamental architecture of your firm. This requires a radical shift in behavior: from managing a hierarchy to programming an ecosystem of nodes.

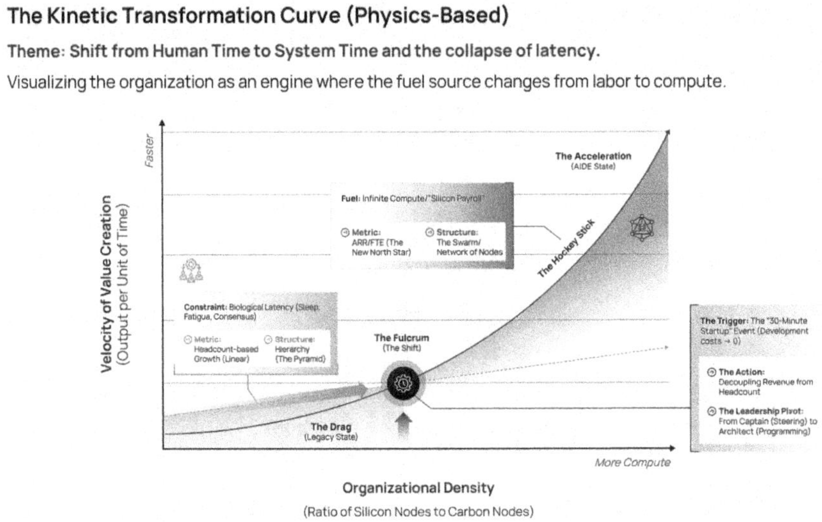

This section is your tactical manual for that crossing. We move beyond theory to the concrete frameworks and experiments that connect human intent with machine intelligence. The AIDE Fulcrum—the pivot point you must leverage to achieve maximum impact—is your personal action. These are the decisions that will change your organization's growth trajectory from linear to exponential.

Here is your execution roadmap:

- **The Boardroom Reality:** How to confront the executive literacy crisis and govern intelligent systems using evidence-based strategies
- **The AIDE Matrix:** How to audit your organization's true gap between strategic intent and operational integration
- **The C-Suite Refactor:** How to fundamentally redefine executive roles to manage a network of nodes rather than a hierarchy of humans
- **The Opportunities Audit:** The exact framework to answer "WTF do I do with AI?" and identify high-impact, quick-win processes
- **Start with You:** Why you must claim personal "Tinker Time" to build your intuition before you can lead the enterprise

We'll close with a challenge: to stop theorizing about the future and start co-creating it. Reza Satchu, a driving force behind encouraging entrepreneurs at the Harvard Business School to go all-in and commit to their entrepreneurial career paths, says, "No decision *is* a decision. Make one. Being a deer in headlights won't serve you" (Yaghoubian 2025). This holds true here: You need to make a decision and take action, otherwise the time will come when that question is asked of you in a board meeting that you aren't prepared for. What you do next determines whether you lead the change or chase it.

The transition begins at the highest level of accountability. Before you can build an AI-driven company, you must be capable of governing one. We begin at the helm.

18

Corporate Governance and Leadership

Why are 91% of executives secretly faking their AI literacy, and what is it costing their shareholders?
Evidence-based strategies for adoption measurement and calibration.

WE HAVE DISCUSSED the technology and analyzed the shifting economics of the AI-Driven Enterprise. We have traversed the landscape from the unprecedented speed of creation to the global race for national competitiveness, revealing a future defined by radical efficiency. But ultimately, the success of this transformation depends on one thing: governance. No amount of computational leverage or architectural design can save an organization if the leaders at the helm are steering the ship blind.

I recently had dinner with a friend who sits on the board of a Fortune 500 company. I asked him a simple question: "How often does AI come up in your board meetings?" His response was immediate: "Several times every meeting. It's on every agenda." That part was unsurprising.

But what he said next perfectly illustrated the crisis brewing between our newly educated workforce and our legacy institutions. He leaned in and whispered, "The problem is, Paul . . . nobody on our board really knows anything about AI."

They are approving budgets for technology they do not understand. They are governing blind.

Last year I co-founded the AIDE Institute with Felipe Ost Scherer, where we don't rely on anecdotes or self-reported surveys. We rely on data. To understand the true state of corporate governance in the AI era, we conducted a massive research project. We analyzed the AI adoption maturity of the S&P 500. We profiled 5,390 board members and 6,422 executive team members, analyzing over 165 million words of public data, annual reports, patent filings, earnings calls, job posts, social media activity, and strategic disclosures.

The findings are stark.

In this chapter, you will:

- **Confront the Literacy Crisis:** Why 91% of executives are "faking it"
- **Learn the AIDE Maturity Cycle:** The proven sequence of Literacy → Advocacy → Orientation → Implementation
- **Analyze Risk Asymmetry:** Understand why the "silent killer" of inertia is now a far greater threat to your 10-year valuation than the visible, project-level risk of execution failure
- **Understand the Innovation Synergy:** Why you can't layer AI on top of a stagnant culture
- **Adopt Evidence-Based Governance:** Specific recommendations for board and C-suite restructuring

The Literacy Crisis

The anecdote from my dinner is not an outlier; it is the norm. Our research reveals a profound disconnect. While leaders universally recognize AI's critical importance, they lack the fundamental knowledge to guide its implementation. This creates a dangerous scenario where critical strategic decisions are made without a proper understanding of the technology.

The Numbers

- **Board Illiteracy: 79%** of board executives report minimal or no knowledge of AI capabilities and applications (Board of Innovation, BOI 2025).
- **The "Fake It" Factor: 91%** of C-suite executives admit to exaggerating their AI knowledge in professional settings (Pluralsight 2025).
- **The Reality:** 0% of executives say AI won't impact them at all (BOI).

The external surveys are bad enough. Our own data demonstrates a reality that is even worse. When we analyzed the publicly observable AI literacy of every top management executive in the S&P 500, using their professional credentials, their career histories, their public writing, and their LinkedIn profiles, we found that the median score was zero. Not low. Zero. More than half of the executives running America's largest companies show no detectable AI literacy in any public signal we can measure.

The mean is higher, roughly 12%, but that average is pulled up by a handful of companies with genuinely literate leadership teams. The typical S&P 500 executive—the person approving your AI budget right now—is invisible to every AI literacy signal we know how to look for.

Questions for Consideration

If nearly 80% of your board is illiterate regarding the most transformative technology of our generation, how can they govern risk? If over 90% of your C-suite is exaggerating their expertise, how can you trust their resource allocation? Governance in the AIDE era cannot be based on bluster. It must be based on literacy. Consider these questions:

- What % of your top management team is AI literate?
- What % of your top management team advocates for AI?
- What % of your board is AI literate?
- What % of your board advocates for AI?
- What % of your board still operates on pen and paper? Barely does email?

What does this mean in an age of AI? Would you hire a C-suite exec who doesn't understand the internet?

Why Literacy Matters: The ROI of a Savvy Board

Data from a 2024 MIT study suggests that this literacy gap isn't just an embarrassing social hurdle; it's an economic one. Organizations with digitally and AI-savvy boards outperform their peers by 10.9 percentage points in return on equity (ROE). Conversely, companies with boards that "fake it" see an ROE 3.8% below their industry average (Weill et al. 2025).

Literacy is the difference between strategic growth and expensive stagnation.

Leadership Is the Primary Driver

Many organizations make the mistake of thinking AI adoption is a *technical* challenge. They hire a chief AI officer, sign an agreement for an enterprise-wide AI tool license, buy a bunch of GPUs, and hope for the best. Our data proves this is wrong.

Top management AI advocacy is not just one of many predictors; it is the strongest. Across every variable we measured in the S&P 500, nothing correlates more powerfully with a company's overall AI maturity than whether its executives actively, publicly, and repeatedly champion AI. Not the number of engineers. Not the size of the AI budget. Not the vendor contracts. The voice of the C-suite.

If you are a CEO waiting for your engineering team to "figure out AI" for you, you have already failed. The data says the drive must come from the top. And it does not mean quietly approving a budget. It means advocacy—visible, sustained, knowledgeable championship of the technology.

Companies with AI-literate and AI-advocating leadership showcase substantially higher AI orientation and successful implementation. Effective leadership bridges the gap between abstract strategy and concrete action.

The AIDE Maturity Cycle: A Sequential Path

You cannot jump straight to implementation. Our research identified a clear, sequential development pattern for successful adopters.

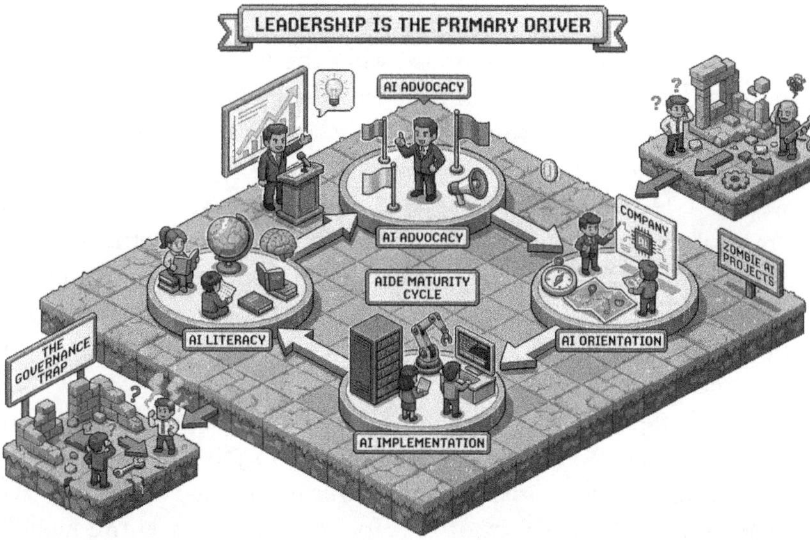

It works in a loop:

1. **AI Literacy:** It starts with understanding. The board and C-suite must be educated.
2. **AI Advocacy:** Literacy leads to advocacy. Leaders must actively champion the technology.
3. **AI Orientation:** Advocacy leads to strategic orientation. The company aligns its goals around AI.
4. **AI Implementation:** Only *after* orientation is established do successful companies invest heavily in execution.

This cycle feeds itself. Continued implementation drives more advanced literacy, which fuels stronger advocacy.

The Governance Trap

Most failing companies try to skip steps. They jump from illiteracy directly to implementation. They buy tools (implementation) without a strategy (orientation), led by people who don't understand them (literacy).

Our mediation analysis confirmed what the maturity cycle predicts: Orientation does not just happen to appear alongside implementation. It is the mechanism through which leadership advocacy becomes organizational reality.

When we tested whether top management team AI advocacy drives implementation directly or through orientation, we found both pathways are active. Advocacy has a direct effect on implementation; executives who champion AI do accelerate execution. But it also works through orientation: Advocacy shapes strategy, and strategy shapes execution. Both channels matter.

The data bears this out with unusual clarity. The relationship between aspects of a company's AI strategic orientation—its job postings, its earnings call language, its corporate communications, and its actual AI implementation—is the strongest operational link in our entire model. It's stronger than any leadership variable's direct effect on implementation, and stronger than board advocacy's direct reach.

What does this mean practically? It means that when a company hires for AI roles, talks about AI in its investor communications, and positions itself strategically around AI-driven workflows, it is far more likely to actually build and deploy AI successfully. The companies that skip this step, that go straight from a board mandate to a vendor contract, are the ones generating the expensive wreckage of "zombie" AI projects. By skipping the orientation step, they cut off the most powerful transmission mechanism between what their leaders want and what their organization actually builds.

The Data Behind the Loop

This is not a theoretical framework. Every link in this chain was tested against our S&P 500 dataset, and every single one held.

We tested 15 directional hypotheses for AI alone. Does board advocacy actually predict executive literacy? Does literacy actually lead to advocacy? Does advocacy actually drive strategic orientation? Does orientation actually translate into implementation?

The answer to all 15 was yes. A 100% confirmation rate. And the strongest relationship in the entire model? Top management AI advocacy predicting company AI orientation. When executives actively champion AI—not just approve it, but champion it—the organization aligns. It is the single most powerful lever available to any CEO reading this chapter.

But here is what makes our data different from the surveys you've been reading: None of it is self-reported. We did not ask executives if they care about AI. We measured whether they actually hire for it, file patents around it, post about it, and talk about it on earnings calls. The gap between what leaders say they do and what they actually do is where most AI maturity assessments fall apart. Ours does not, because we never asked.

Actionable Recommendations for Governance

At the AIDE Institute, we have collected big data on organizational AI maturity, and have published reports on regional AI maturity and AI maturity in individual sectors. We've provided boards and executive teams with comprehensive outside-in AI assessments of their companies, compared them to their direct peer groups, and also provided competitive intelligence data. Based on this data, we've learned from all of this that this is the new mandate for corporate governance and leadership.

For the Board of Directors:

1. **Invest in Executive AI Education:** You cannot govern what you do not know. Build comprehensive AI literacy among board members immediately. We're seeing an influx of interest in AI executive education at MIT Sloan.
2. **Establish Advocacy Roles:** Designate specific "AI Champions" at the executive level to sustain initiatives. Do not leave it to a committee; make it a specific person's job.

For the Management Team:

1. **Focus on Orientation Before Implementation:** Ensure you have a strong AI strategic orientation *before* you sign multi-million-dollar vendor contracts.
2. **Develop Mediated Pathways:** Use your AI advocates to bridge the gap between technical literacy and organizational strategy.

The Leadership-First Approach

The conclusion of our research is unequivocal. The AI maturity of S&P 500 companies is driven primarily by leadership factors, not technical capabilities. We found a shocking 100% hypothesis support rate for the relationship between literacy, advocacy, orientation, and implementation based on our vast data collection.

Successful AI transformation requires a leadership-first approach. You cannot outsource this transformation to consultants. You cannot delegate it to the IT department.

The board member I had dinner with was right to be worried, but perhaps for the wrong reason. The problem is not just that their board doesn't understand AI. The problem is that their board's ignorance is actively suppressing the entire cascade. Our data shows that board AI advocacy does not just influence the executives in the room; it predicts the company's strategic orientation and its actual implementation outcomes, directly and through multiple pathways.

When a board actively champions AI, its advocacy flows downhill into executive advocacy, which shapes corporate strategy, which drives deployment. When a board is silent—or worse, illiterate—that silence cascades too. Every month of boardroom AI illiteracy is a month of suppressed advocacy, suppressed orientation, and suppressed implementation. The board is not a rubber stamp on AI strategy. It is the headwaters.

But for you, the leader reading this book, it is the single biggest opportunity. If you can build an AI-literate, advocacy-driven governance structure, you will outpace the incumbents who are still faking it.

We have audited the boardroom. Now we must look at the organization as a whole and evaluate how our AI strategy stacks up against our AI implementation.

No One Works Here: The Digital War Room

You've learned the theory; now let's build the machinery. Turn these concepts into immediate ROI for your company by accessing your free resources at NoOneWorksHere.com.

1. Immediate Actions (Do This Today)

- **Audit the "Fake It" Factor:** Conduct an anonymous literacy assessment for your C-suite and board to identify the gap between perceived and actual AI knowledge. You cannot govern effectively until you replace "buzzword bravado" with verified technical understanding.
- **Halt "Zombie" Projects:** Review your current AI budget and pause any implementation-heavy projects that lack a clear strategic orientation. Ensure your leadership has moved through the literacy and advocacy stages before committing to multi-million-dollar vendor contracts.
- **Appoint a Board-Level Champion:** Designate a specific "AI Advocate" within your governance layer who is responsible for executive education and strategic alignment. Move AI from a recurring agenda item to a specialized oversight responsibility to avoid governing blind.

2. The Discussion (Bring This to Your Team)

- If 91% of executives admit to exaggerating their AI knowledge, how can we be certain our current resource allocations are based on data rather than performance? What specific steps can we take to create a culture where "I don't know" is a valid starting point for AI education?
- Looking at the AIDE maturity cycle, have we skipped literacy or orientation in our rush to implementation? What are the specific risks of deploying tools led by a management team that hasn't yet reached the advocacy stage?

(*continued*)

(continued)

- How are we measuring the risk of inertia compared to the risk of project failure? If digitally savvy boards see a 10.9% higher ROE, what is the literal dollar cost of our current pace of adoption over the next five years?

3. The Step-by-Step Implementation

Stop guessing and start building. Use the **AIDE Governance Workbook** for step-by-step guidance. This digital workbook provides the exact framework you need to implement this chapter's concepts.

Download it at: NoOneWorksHere.com/governance

4. The Unfair Advantage: AI-Powered Tools

Don't just read about AI; use it right now. As a reader of this book, you get exclusive access to interactive AI-software tools designed to do the heavy lifting for you.

Access your tools instantly at: NoOneWorksHere.com

(Or simply scan the QR code with your smartphone camera)

19

Mapping the Organization

AIDE Matrix and Risk Asymmetry

How big is your organization's gap between AI strategy and execution?
How to audit your reality, assess your true risk, and move your organization to the top right.

IN THE PREVIOUS chapter, we explored the latest research findings from the AI-Driven Enterprise (AIDE) Institute, established the grim reality of the boardroom literacy crisis, and the necessity of the AIDE maturity cycle. But how do you map that cycle onto your current operational reality?

In this chapter, you will:

- **Deploy the AIDE Matrix:** Use this data-driven framework to evaluate your gap between vision and reality
- **Assess Your True Position:** Determine if you are emerging, a visionary, stealth adopter, or trailblazer
- **Benchmark Against the Swarm:** Compare your operational progress against the S&P 500 dataset
- **Analyze Your Risk Asymmetry:** Understand why the silent killer of inertia threatens your ten-year valuation

The AIDE Matrix: A Self-Assessment

As we've established, AI cannot be treated as a "magic wand" by organizations that need to future-proof themselves. To bridge the gap between strategic vision and operational reality, we created a standardized, data-driven framework, the AIDE Matrix. The AIDE Matrix provides a standardized, data-driven framework to evaluate how effectively your company is bridging the gap between strategic vision and operational reality. This model separates the "talk" (board and executive commitment) from the "walk" (the actual embedding of AI into the workforce and processes).

The two axes are not arbitrary categories. They map directly to the two core dimensions of the AIDE Index.

- **The X-Axis: Strategic Intent and Advocacy** is what we call the Leadership Score. It combines board advocacy, TMT (technology, media, and telecommunications) advocacy, and TMT AI literacy into a single measure of top-down commitment. This is not a survey question asking executives how much they care about AI. It is a composite of their observable behavior: what they post publicly, what they put on their profiles, how they position themselves professionally. Our research confirmed that this leadership dimension, and TMT AI advocacy in particular, is the single most powerful predictor of overall organizational AI maturity.
- **The Y-Axis: Operational Integration and Adoption** is what we call the Company Score. It combines AI orientation and AI implementation into a single measure of bottom-up reality. Orientation captures strategic positioning: AI-related job postings, AI mentions in earnings calls, AI emphasis in corporate communications. Implementation captures tangible deployment: AI patents, AI features in products, AI infrastructure in operations. Our research confirmed that orientation is the gateway to implementation, the strongest operational link in the model.

Together, the two axes answer the question that every shareholder, every board member, and every CEO should be asking: Is our leadership actually driving AI, or just talking about it? And is our organization actually deploying AI, or just orienting toward it?

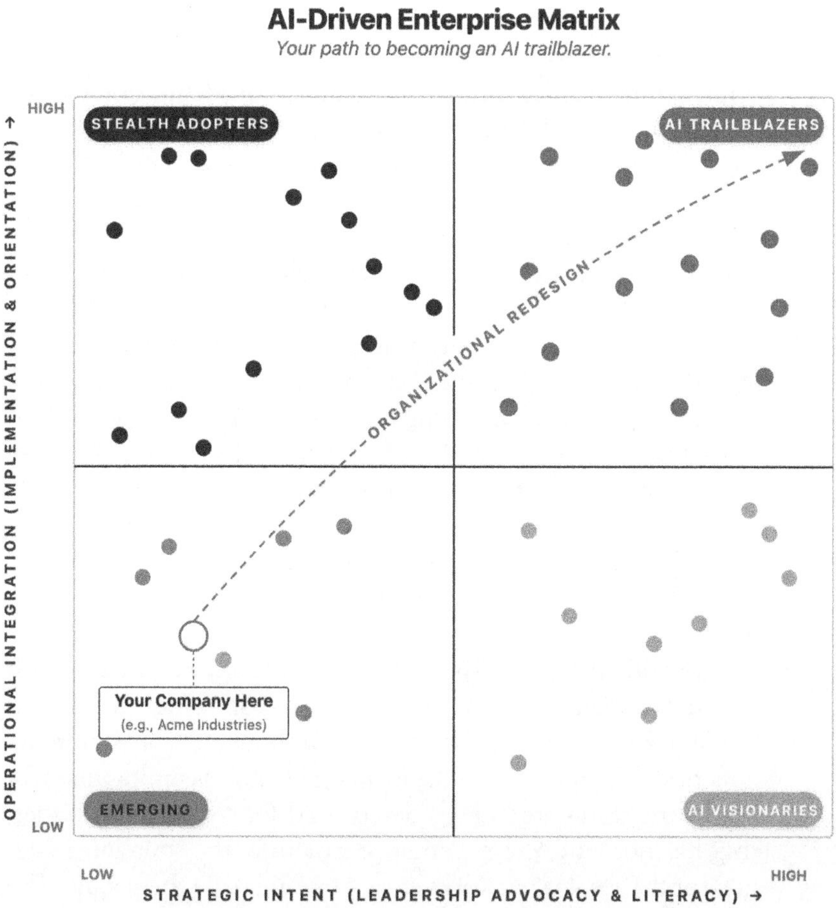

Download this graph and other resources on the AI-Driven Enterprise model: NoOneWorksHere.com/downloads/graphs.

Where Do You Sit?

By plotting your organization, you will likely find yourself in one of four stages:

1. **Emerging (Bottom Left): Low Intent, Low Adoption:** There may not be a strategic mandate from leadership or operational reality on the ground. This is not a neutral position because in a

market where a team of 12 can outperform a team of 1,200, standing still is an active bet against survival. In our S&P 500 data, a surprising number of companies sit in this quadrant, not because they have rejected AI, but because they may not have seriously started. Some are taking a pragmatic approach and are waiting for the technology to mature, for the use case to become obvious, for someone else to go first.

2. **The AI Visionary (Bottom Right): High Intent, Low Adoption:** This is the "magic wand" trap. Leadership is vocal about AI. The board discusses it at every meeting. The CEO gives keynotes about "transformative technology." But the employees are still scheduling meetings manually, writing reports by hand, and routing decisions through six layers of human approval. The gap between strategy and execution is not a temporary lag; it is a structural failure. These companies have advocacy without orientation, or orientation without implementation. They have skipped steps in the maturity cycle, and the result is expensive pilots that never scale.
3. **The Stealth Adopter (Top Left): Low Intent, High Adoption:** The quiet engines of efficiency. In these companies, the operational teams are integrating AI, often without explicit boardroom direction. Engineers are deploying machine learning models. Marketing teams are using generative AI for content. But leadership has not built the governance structure, the strategic guardrails, or the legal frameworks to support and scale these wins. The risk here is not inaction; it is ungoverned action. Without the intent stack from leadership, operational AI gains are fragile, legally exposed, and impossible to scale across the enterprise.
4. **The AI Trailblazer (Top Right): High Intent, High Adoption:** The AI-Driven Enterprise. Leadership provides the intent, literate, vocal, strategic. The organization provides the execution, hiring for AI, filing AI patents, deploying AI in products and operations. This is the only quadrant where revenue growth is successfully decoupled from headcount growth. In our data, the companies in this quadrant share three characteristics: AI-literate boards, AI-advocating executive teams, and measurable AI deployments in their operational workflows. They have not just completed the maturity cycle. They are running it iteratively.

Benchmarking Against the "Swarm"

Plotting your own position is only half the battle. To truly understand your risk profile, you must also plot your peer group. In an era where a team of 12 can outperform a team of 1,200, your primary threat is likely an organization in your sector that has moved further toward the top right of the matrix than you have.

At the AIDE Institute, we do not benchmark against hypothetical competitors. We benchmark against all of them. Our S&P 500 dataset covers 500 companies, over 5,300 board members, and over 6,400 executive team members. When you plot your position on the AIDE Matrix, you are not plotting against a generic framework. You are plotting against a map that has every one of your peers already on it. We know where they sit. The question is whether you do.

At the AIDE Institute, we conduct this research to understand how companies compare to each other, tracking these movements over time to identify which "buffalo" incumbents are being overtaken by the "AIDE swarm." By benchmarking against your competitors, you can distinguish between industry-wide "dial-up" friction and specific structural gaps in your own leadership or operations. This outside-in view provides just one piece of the AI maturity puzzle, and in doing so prevents the complacency of internal metrics and reveals the true velocity of the global race.

Moving to the Top Right

The objective of this audit is not just to identify where you are, but to determine the "vector of change" required to reach the top right.

- If you're an illusionist, you don't need more strategy; you need a "sandbox policy" and a "chief node officer" to start the implementation phase of the cycle.
- If you're a stealth innovator, you don't need better tools; you need to solve the "boardroom literacy crisis" to ensure your operational wins aren't optimized off a cliff due to a lack of governance.

The Risk Asymmetry: Inertia Versus Execution

The "governance trap" is fueled by a fundamental misunderstanding of risk. In traditional corporate governance, the risk of execution is the primary boogeyman. Boards are trained to obsess over what happens if a project fails, if an AI hallucinates, or if a new automated workflow disrupts a legacy process. This risk is highly visible; it has a budget, a project owner, and a "throat to choke" if things go sideways.

However, in the age of the AI-Driven Enterprise (AIDE), the most dangerous threat is the one that doesn't appear on the risk register: the risk of inertia.

The Silent Killer

While execution risk is a "loud" risk, inertia is a "silent" killer.

- **The Cost of "Waiting for Broadband":** Many boards fall into the "waiting room fallacy," believing that waiting for more mature technology reduces risk. In reality, they are sacrificing their "learning rate."
- **Biological Speed Limits:** By prioritizing consensus and cautious deliberation, boards bake "administrative latency" into the very top of the organization. This anchors the entire firm to "human time" while competitors are refactoring their codebase for "system time."
- **Market Liquefaction:** As noted earlier, the market is punishing organizations that hire humans to be "routers." Choosing inertia isn't "playing it safe"; it is choosing a slow, predictable descent toward the mortality table.

Recalibrating the Boardroom

To escape the trap, governance must shift from minimizing execution failure to maximizing adaptation velocity. A board that is 79% AI-illiterate cannot accurately weigh these risks. They view AI as a "shiny object" rather than a structural necessity.

The New Audit Question: Instead of asking, "What is the risk if we execute this AI agent swarm and it fails?" the board must ask, "What is the systemic risk to our 10-year valuation if our competitors achieve a $1M+ ARR/FTE ratio while we remain at $200k?"

If the cost of execution is a $1M pilot, but the cost of inertia is the loss of your entire market edge to a team of 12 moving at lightspeed, the "safe" choice is obvious.

How Many of Your Board Members Are Truly AI Literate?

The gap between "knowing AI exists" and "understanding AI governance" is where most organizational risk lives. If your board isn't yet equipped to navigate the ethical, operational, and strategic shifts of the machine age, it's time to bridge that gap.

Don't leave your leadership's evolution to chance. Bring your entire board into the conversation by signing them up for the AIDE Governance Newsletter. It's the most direct way to ensure every director has a pulse on the latest AI trends, frameworks, and governance best practices.

> Visit NoOneWorksHere.com/board-literacy to register your board members and start receiving high-impact insights designed for the modern boardroom.

The Innovation Prerequisite

Another critical finding from the AIDE Index is the Innovation-AI Synergy.

This is not a soft correlation. We tested the AI-innovation link at every level of the organization, and it held at every single one. Board members who advocate for AI also advocate for innovation. Executives who are AI-literate also tend to be innovation-literate. Companies that orient their strategy around AI also orient around innovation. And companies that successfully implement AI also successfully implement innovation.

The implication is stark. If your organization has spent the last decade killing new ideas and stifling experimentation, you cannot simply "install" AI on top of that culture. The innovation muscle and the AI muscle are the same muscle. You cannot flex one without the other. The organizations at the top of our AI maturity rankings are, almost without exception, the same ones with the highest innovation maturity. It is one system, not two.

Continuing on with our organization audit, we must audit the mirror. Everything we have discussed starts with a single individual making a choice to adapt. In the next chapter, we strip away the organizational complexity and focus on the personal. We start with you.

No One Works Here: The Digital War Room

You've learned the theory; now let's build the machinery. Turn these concepts into immediate ROI for your company by accessing your free resources at NoOneWorksHere.com.

1. Immediate Actions (Do This Today)

- **Plot Your Matrix:** Draw the AIDE Matrix and honestly map your organization's position based on leadership's "strategic intent" versus the actual "operational integration" happening on the floor.
- **Chart Your Course:** Map where you'd like to see your organization on the AIDE Matrix in one year's time. Evaluate the trajectory from where you are today to where you'd like to be.
- **Calculate the Cost of Inertia:** Instead of measuring the risk of an AI project failing, calculate the systemic financial risk to your five-year valuation if your closest competitor successfully decouples their revenue from headcount while you remain operating on "human time."

2. The Discussion (Bring This to Your Team)

- Are we currently "illusionists" who talk about AI strategy in every meeting while our teams still manually route data and schedule calls? If so, what specific "sandbox policy" or leadership role is missing to move us from talk to execution?
- In our boardroom, do we obsess over the "loud" risks of AI execution failure while ignoring the "silent" killer of market inertia? If a competitor achieves a $1M ARR/FTE ratio while we stay at $200k, what is the systemic risk to our 10-year valuation?

- Does our existing innovation culture actually support a high "learning rate," or are we attempting to bolt AI onto a legacy system that historically stifles new ideas? How can we shift our governance from minimizing failure to maximizing adaptation velocity?

3. The Step-by-Step Implementation

Stop guessing and start building. Use the **AIDE Matrix Workbook** for step-by-step guidance. This digital workbook provides the exact framework you need to implement this chapter's concepts.

Download it at: NoOneWorksHere.com/aide-matrix

4. The Unfair Advantage: AI-Powered Tools

Don't just read about AI; use it right now. As a reader of this book, you get exclusive access to interactive AI-software tools designed to do the heavy lifting for you.

Access your tools instantly at: NoOneWorksHere.com

(Or simply scan the QR code with your smartphone camera)

20

Dear C-Suite

Can a legacy C-suite overcome its own bureaucratic inertia to lead a AI-driven future?
Redefining the core mandates of the executive team to eliminate the complexity tax.

We have spent the last two chapters diagnosing the system. We've exposed the boardroom's literacy crisis, mapped your organization on the AIDE Matrix, and quantified the silent killer of inertia. At this stage, it is dangerously easy to point fingers, to blame a stagnant culture, a risk-averse board, or a sluggish IT department. But systemic change does not happen in the abstract; it happens in the mirror. You can have the perfect AIDE maturity strategy on paper, but if the executives occupying the C-suite are still personally operating on "human time," the enterprise will fail. The data is clear: There is a widening chasm between companies that view AI as a departmental tool and those that view it as the fundamental architecture of the firm. Transformation cannot be delegated. This chapter is about you.

If you're reading this from a corner office in a legacy organization (or working from your home office), you likely feel the pressure of this transition. You're moving from an era where scale was a function of headcount to an era where scale is a function of system design. This shift requires more than just a new tech stack; it requires a fundamental reorientation of executive responsibility. The organizational chart isn't the only thing that needs to be rewritten; your own job description might already be obsolete. The goal of this book is to provide the architecture that allows you to stop being a spectator of the AI revolution and start being its primary beneficiary.

For a CEO, the decision to transform a legacy firm into an AIDE rather than launching a new one involves navigating massive internal switching costs. These are not financial line items; they are the costs of refactoring human culture. In a high-latency system, you are paying a "complexity tax" on every decision. To switch to a low-latency model, you must confront the structural debt of 1950s-era organizational charts and the epistemic debt of a workforce that may not yet comprehend the code it is beginning to use.

The true switching cost is the energy required to overcome "bureaucratic inertia," an immune system fiercely protected by the legacy habits, and often the egos, of the executive team. This bureaucracy exists because your current C-suite roles were designed to maintain it. The "complexity tax" you pay on every decision in a high-latency system is a direct result of these outdated executive job definitions. Unlike a startup, which is born into "system time," you must buy back your organization's "human time." This involves a "reliability tax" where things initially get slower and riskier during the transition as you move through the Latency J-Curve. The cost of this switch is high, but the cost of remaining in a high-latency state is eventually fatal, as you continue to fight an AI war with massed infantry against a competitor using machine-based maneuver.

In this chapter, you will:

- **Deconstruct Core C-Suite Mandates:** Redefine the fundamental responsibilities of every executive role for the AI era
- **Shift to Architecting Nodes:** Move your team away from managing legacy headcount toward designing intelligent systems
- **Audit Current Workforce Literacy:** Evaluate your organization's open job descriptions to assess true future readiness

Why This Transition, and Why Now?

The legacy model of the corporation is built on the assumption that human labor is the primary driver of value. In an AI-Driven Enterprise (AIDE), we redefine the organization as a group of nodes, both human and nonhuman, working toward a shared purpose. If your C-suite continues to operate under 2019 job descriptions, your leadership team will become the primary bottleneck. It is not just your cost structure that will render you obsolete against leaner, node-based competitors; it is your executive paralysis.

The Chief Financial Officer: From Transactional to Strategic Partner

For a long time, the CFO was the steward of the past, reporting on what happened last quarter. In the AI-driven era, your job has never been less transactional and more strategic.

Why? Because you are the only one who sees the full picture: the payroll costs, the cost of compute, and the shifting margins. You must provide the insights the rest of the executive team needs to be effective.

The Strategic Shift: You need to help the team model out what it looks like to scale the organization not by hiring, but by the deployment of AI tools, vendors, and agents, both built internally and sourced externally. You are the one who will ensure the organization weathers the storm of the AIDE era, where cost structures shift and the cost of customer acquisition (CAC) continues to rise.

As we discussed earlier in the book, when AI lowers the barrier to entry for new competitors, your CAC will spike. You must reevaluate payroll costs as a function of the entire organization and determine what capital expenditures will set up the infrastructure for future scale.

The Chief Revenue Officer and Chief Marketing Officer: The New GTM Reality

Your job is to figure out how to reevaluate customer acquisition and revenue growth in an economy where the value proposition for your customers is shifting daily.

The Switching Cost Crisis: In the legacy world, "moats" were often built on data silos and proprietary systems. Today, switching costs are lower than ever. Data can be easily exported, transformed, and manipulated by AI to suit a competitor's system in minutes.

The Strategic Shift: You must work with the CFO to figure out how the business model shifts to maintain long-term customer loyalty. Go-to-market (GTM) strategies are changing more rapidly than at any point in my career. Buyers are overwhelmed with a wide variety of solutions, many of which are purpose-built for them by AI agents. Your focus must move from broad distribution to hyper-personalized value.

The CIO and CTO: Facilitating the Organized Node

Your job is no longer just "keeping the lights on," overseeing engineering, managing systems, overseeing data, or managing the server rack. You must provide the risk assessments while maintaining enough flexibility so the rest of the organization can leverage AI at the individual, team, and organizational levels.

The Strategic Shift: Your primary goal is to accelerate the shift from an organization by its old definition to an organization by its new definition: *a group of organized nodes*.

Exponential efficiency is found at the team level, where individual experiments are enabled to scale across the group. You are the architect of the infrastructure that allows these nodes to communicate and collaborate.

While you cannot lose focus on shadow AI and data privacy, you must empower individuals to experiment.

The Shadow IT Trap: We must address the elephant in the server room. When you empower nontechnical marketing managers to "vibe-code" apps, you are effectively sanctioning shadow IT. In a regulated enterprise, this is a security nightmare. An app built in 30 minutes can leak customer data in 30 seconds.

The solution is not to ban vibe-coding, but to sandbox it. Your IT policy must evolve: "Build whatever you want in the sandbox; but nothing touches customer data or the core ERP until a certified engineer reviews the code." You are democratizing creation, not security clearance.

The New Debt: Be aware of the new debt on your ledger, one that's arguably worse than technical debt. Stanislav Komarovsky, senior VP, AI and Rule Engine Architect at JP Morgan Chase, highlights the risk in explaining epistemic debt in vibe-coding. Clearly differentiating epistemic debt from technical debt he explains, "Epistemic debt is different. It's unconscious. It's the growing gap between what your AI generates and what your team actually comprehends. Technical debt makes code hard to change. Epistemic debt makes code dangerous to change." He goes on to explain how this challenge exacerbates as the codebase grows: "AI coding assistants can now generate code faster than humans can possibly understand it. We've optimized for velocity while ignoring comprehension. And the gap is widening every sprint" (Komarovsky 2025).

The Chief Node Officer: Redefining the People Function

I am giving you a new job title. You are no longer the CHRO or chief people officer; you are the **chief node officer**. Recall the node architecture discussion from Chapter 3 and the New Age Organization Chart from Chapter 9. Your new mandate is to evaluate every open role against those specs: Does this require the empathy of a human node or the 24/7 availability of a silicon node? Your job is to architect an organization . . . and hire architects to serve the roles designated as "human nodes" in the org chart. Consider the node-network architecture.

Why? Because as we have established, the definition of an organization is changing. It is no longer just about people. Your job is to architect an organization that accounts for output being produced by nonhumans.

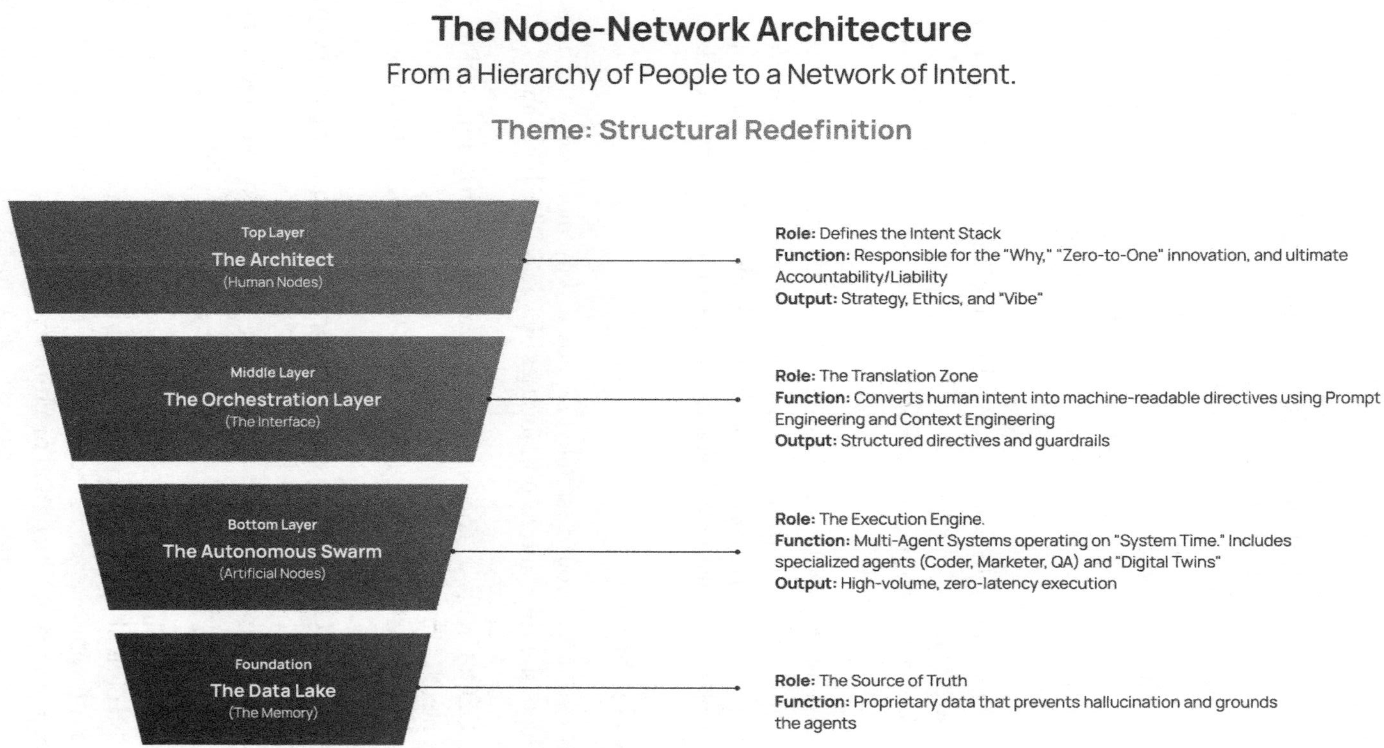
The Node-Network Architecture
From a Hierarchy of People to a Network of Intent.
Theme: Structural Redefinition
Top Layer
The Architect
(Human Nodes)
Role: Defines the Intent Stack
Function: Responsible for the "Why," "Zero-to-One" innovation, and ultimate Accountability/Liability
Output: Strategy, Ethics, and "Vibe"
Middle Layer
The Orchestration Layer
(The Interface)
Role: The Translation Zone
Function: Converts human intent into machine-readable directives using Prompt Engineering and Context Engineering
Output: Structured directives and guardrails
Bottom Layer
The Autonomous Swarm
(Artificial Nodes)
Role: The Execution Engine.
Function: Multi-Agent Systems operating on "System Time." Includes specialized agents (Coder, Marketer, QA) and "Digital Twins"
Output: High-volume, zero-latency execution
Foundation
The Data Lake
(The Memory)
Role: The Source of Truth
Function: Proprietary data that prevents hallucination and grounds the agents

The Literacy Audit: At the AIDE Institute, we regularly perform audits to identify gaps in AI literacy across seniority levels and functional areas. I want you to do the same today. You need to determine how to shift the competencies for jobs throughout your organization.

The Job Post Test: The simplest way to assess your current trajectory is to look at your open job postings. Open job descriptions, providing a leading indicator of the type of talent that will exist in the organization in the future, which is why we study these job descriptions so closely at the AIDE Institute. If I were to analyze every single job description you have listed right now, what would I find?

1. Are you requiring legacy skills like "proficiency in Microsoft Word and Microsoft Excel"?
2. Or are you requiring AI skills using tools like Gemini, Claude, and agentic workflows?

If your job posts still look like they did in 2019, you are hiring for a company that is on a path to no longer exist. You need to invest in executive education AI sessions to upskill your current leadership and ensure that new talent is brought in with the literacy required for an AI-native world.

Let's Get Started

As an executive, your first move is not to buy more software. It is to reevaluate the roles and responsibilities of your leadership team:

- **CFO:** Create a "compute versus headcount" growth model for the next 24 months.
- **CRO/CMO:** Identify the top three areas where data portability makes your customers "at risk."
- **CIO/CTO:** Create a "sandbox policy" that allows teams to experiment with AI without breaching security.
- **Chief Node Officer:** Audit your job descriptions and remove Microsoft Office in favor of specific AI competencies.

Leadership in the AIDE era is no longer about managing a hierarchy of people; it is about architecting an organized system of nodes. Each role must shift from overseeing departmental tasks to managing the synergy between human judgment and machine execution.

The transition from a legacy company to an AIDE is not a single event; it is a series of deliberate architectural choices. Once the executive team has embraced this reevaluation of roles and responsibilities, the conversation must immediately pivot from "what if" to "what now." The next challenge is not merely recognizing AI's potential, but systematically identifying and prioritizing the highest-leverage applications within the firm. The leadership-first approach requires a structured framework to move beyond abstract strategy and into concrete, measurable action that generates momentum and organizational comfort with the technology.

No One Works Here: The Digital War Room

You've learned the theory; now let's build the machinery. Turn these concepts into immediate ROI for your company by accessing your free resources at NoOneWorksHere.com.

1. Immediate Actions (Do This Today)

- **Execute the Job Post Audit:** Review every open job description currently listed by your firm. Immediately strip out legacy requirements like Microsoft Office and replace them with specific AI competencies such as Claude, Gemini, and agentic workflow management.
- **Establish the Vibe-Coding Sandbox:** Stop fighting "shadow IT" and start governing it. Task your CTO/CIO with creating a secure "sandbox" environment where nontechnical teams can experiment with AI-generated code without risking core customer data or ERP systems.
- **Model Compute Versus Headcount:** Have your CFO draft a 24-month growth projection that compares the ROI of traditional hiring against the deployment of silicon nodes (AI agents) to identify where human judgment is truly required versus where machine execution scales faster.

2. The Discussion (Bring This to Your Team)

- If we were to strip away our titles and view this company strictly as a "system of nodes," which specific human processes are currently acting as the primary bottlenecks to machine-speed execution?

(*continued*)

(*continued*)

- Considering the "complexity tax" we pay on every decision, what are the specific cultural "immune responses" within our leadership team that are most likely to sabotage our transition to a low-latency organization?
- In a market where AI has lowered customer switching costs, what are the three specific ways our current "moat" is being rendered obsolete by competitors using hyper-personalized AI value propositions?
- As we allow nontechnical teams to experiment in the "vibe-coding sandbox," are we accumulating "epistemic debt," a dangerous, widening gap between the AI outputs we rely on and the processes our human team actually comprehends?

3. The Step-by-Step Implementation

Stop guessing and start building. Use the **C-Suite AIDE Workbook** for step-by-step guidance. This digital workbook provides the exact framework you need to implement this chapter's concepts.

Download it at: NoOneWorksHere.com/c-suite

4. The Unfair Advantage: AI-Powered Tools

Don't just read about AI; use it right now. As a reader of this book, you get exclusive access to interactive AI-software tools designed to do the heavy lifting for you.

Access your tools instantly at: NoOneWorksHere.com

(Or simply scan the QR code with your smartphone camera)

21

WTF Do I Do with AI?

How do you identify the exact workflows where AI will drive immediate ROI instead of dangerous distractions?
The framework for adoption: the AIDE Opportunities Audit.

Over the past three chapters, we laid the necessary groundwork to rethink leadership. We examined the severe limitations of current governance models regarding AI, mapped the often messy reality of high-level strategy versus on-the-ground implementation, and explored how the C-suite must fundamentally reframe their understanding of the organization to thrive in the AIDE era.

But understanding the landscape is only half the battle. Once the executive team is aligned and bought in, the first question I get from almost every executive, whether they're running a mid-market manufacturing firm or a global financial institution, is some variation of "WTF do I do with AI?"

They aren't asking because they lack options. They're asking because they have too many. We are currently in the "dial-up era" of AI (as we discussed in Chapter 6), and the sheer volume of noise is paralyzing. You are being bombarded with pitches for AI-powered everything. Your board is asking for an AI strategy. Your employees are secretly using ChatGPT to write emails and code.

The temptation is to start with a massive, multi-year "Digital Transformation 2.0" project. Do not do this. To transition from a legacy company to an AI-Driven Enterprise, you must move away from abstract "strategy" and toward a systematic, experimental framework. You need to identify where AI can create the most value with the least friction. We aren't looking for "cool" projects; we are looking for the highest-leverage nodes in your organization that can be augmented or automated to solve the latency problem.

In this chapter, you will:

- **Inventory Your Recurring Processes:** Systematically map your organization's tasks to identify automation targets
- **Audit for Feasibility and Risk:** Measure the true business impact of integrating AI into specific workflows
- **Execute the Peer-Review Pivot:** Use cross-functional scoring to eliminate departmental bias in project selection
- **Prioritize Your AI Roadmap:** Plot your initiatives to secure Quick Wins and avoid dangerous distractions

In my workshops with C-suite executives, I begin by stripping away the jargon. We sit in a room, open a shared Google Sheet, and conduct a cold, hard audit of the business. We don't look at AI as a "tool" to buy; we look at it as a "node" to integrate.

In the current wave of enterprise AI, outcomes are splitting in two directions. The first wave of "copilots" has delivered real, but mostly local, benefits: time savings, better drafts, faster search, and less friction in day-to-day work. Those gains often do not translate cleanly to the bottom line, because they rarely expand the scope of what the organization can accomplish or change the operating model enough to reduce labor demand. By contrast, the most material financial impact is showing up where companies apply generative AI at the process level. They are shrinking cycle times, reducing coordination cost, and improving the speed and quality of decisions inside end-to-end value chains.

For years, the standard playbook for process-driven efficiency was "simplify, standardize, automate," often executed through classic process mapping and deterministic automation (for example, robotic process automation, or RPA). That discipline still matters, especially for durability, controls, and scaling. What is different now is that AIDEs are capturing meaningful value even when the underlying process and data environment are imperfect. In practice, many leaders are not waiting for exhaustive harmonization to begin. They are deploying AI into priority workflows to compress latency quickly, while tightening process and data foundations over time. This "both/and" approach can unlock value faster than prior automation eras. To do it responsibly and at scale, enterprises still need strong rails from their digital organizations: access to approved tools, enterprise controls (risk, security, privacy), clear governance, and FinOps discipline so increased compute usage produces economic return rather than surprise run-rate cost.

Beyond efficiency inside today's workflows, AI also opens a second category of value. It expands what the organization can economically decide and execute. A former student who now serves at a large consulting firm described this as going after the "hidden friction" embedded in legacy operating models: the work organizations could do, but historically did not, because human coordination was too slow and too expensive. Supply chain planning is a useful illustration. The planning problem is inherently complex. It requires matching customer orders to available inventory, supplier commitments, factory locations and constraints, logistics options, and customer SLAs, each with real cost implications. It is also made harder by data that is scattered across systems and sometimes missing or incomplete. Even when the right decision is knowable, many interventions are not worth the coordination cost. Others move too quickly for human planning cycles to react, especially when teams only have hours to change course in time.

In a traditional model, planners are forced by the "physics of business" to set a high intervention threshold. If resolving an issue requires days of cross-functional coordination and manual write-back into enterprise systems, they may only act when the impact is, say, $100,000 or more (illustrative). An AIDE changes that threshold. Agents can execute decisions below a lower threshold (for example, under $10,000) with guardrails. They can route mid-tier decisions (say, $10,000 to $100,000) to junior teams for rapid review and approval. They can escalate only the high-stakes exceptions (for example, $100,000+) to senior leaders. Historically, organizations forfeited the cumulative value in the long tail of smaller, fast-moving decisions, either because it was uneconomic to pursue or because the opportunity passed before the next planning cadence. When auditing for AI opportunities, do not only map what people do today. Map the high-volume decisions they are currently not making, then ask what becomes possible when decision latency and coordination cost collapse.

Importantly, we must also understand what within our organization makes sense for AI to do versus what it makes sense for humans to do. This is rooted both in our corporate culture identity and in our core values, but is also evaluated in terms of what our customers expect and prioritize.

Putting the Framework to Work: The HR Onboarding Dilemma

To understand how this matrix actually works, let's apply it to a universal corporate headache: employee onboarding.

Imagine a mid-market logistics company. Every time they hire a new employee, HR goes through a chaotic, 40-step dance of sending emails, chasing IT for laptop provisioning, nudging managers for training schedules, and manually entering data into three different payroll and compliance systems.

How do we decide if this is actually a good candidate for AI automation? We run it through the system.

1. The Process Inventory

First, we capture the data. If you cannot define the process, you cannot automate it. For every identified process, you must capture specific data points using a structured table.

The chart shows how our logistics company mapped out a few of their processes.

Functional Area	Process Name	Output Type	Frequency (Monthly)	Avg. Hours/ Month	Data Available?
Finance	Quarterly Reporting	PDF/ Report	0.33	40	Yes
Customer Success	Ticket Triage	Email/ Text	1,000	120	Yes
HR	**Employee Onboarding**	**Emails/ Docs**	**15**	**60**	**Partial**
Marketing	Ad Copy Gen	Text	50	25	Yes
Legal	Contract Review	Document	20	60	No

2. The Peer-Review Pivot

This is the most critical part of my framework, and the step where most companies fail. You cannot let executives score their own processes. If you ask the chief human resources officer (CHRO) to score the business impact of automating employee onboarding, they will give it a 5 out of 5 every time. To them, it's a massive headache.

But this is where we do the peer-review pivot. You have the CFO evaluate HR's processes, and the CHRO evaluate finance's processes.

When the CFO looks at employee onboarding, they might say: "I know this takes HR 60 hours a month. But does automating it actually drive top-line revenue or significantly drop operational costs? No, it just makes HR's life easier." This pivot removes departmental bias and ensures we are measuring *business impact*, not just *departmental convenience.*

3. The Decision Scorecard

Once the CFO steps in to review HR's onboarding process, they score it on a scale of 1–5 across three dimensions:

- **Business Impact (1–5):** *Does this increase revenue or drop costs significantly?*
    - o *The Score:* 2. Automating onboarding saves time, but it doesn't move the needle on the company's core profitability.
- **Feasibility (1–5):** *Is the data clean? Is the process standardized?*
    - o *The Score:* 2. The data is a mess. It's scattered across emails, PDFs, and sticky notes.
- **Risk (1–5):** *Are there regulatory or "hallucination" risks?*
    - o *The Score:* 4. If an AI agent hallucinates and enters the wrong tax withholding information into the payroll system, the company faces compliance fines and furious employees.
- **AI Versus Human (1–5):** *Should this be done by AI?*
    - o *The Score:* 4. Most of this work can be done by AI to automate the process, enabling new hires to get up to speed more quickly. It's important that this is complemented by the human

processes in onboarding to ensure that new hires really understand the culture of the organization and have the support that they need.

4. The Reliability Scorecard (The "Dial-Up" Filter)

Before we plot this on the matrix, we have to run it through the "Friday Night Test."

- **The Friday Night Test:** If this AI agent fails at 5:00 p.m. on a Friday, and no human looks at it until Monday morning, does the business stop?
- **Safe Zone (99% Reliability Needed):** Internal summaries, coding assistants, drafting ad copy. If the AI writes a bad draft of an onboarding welcome email, HR just rewrites it. No harm done.
- **Danger Zone (100% Reliability Needed):** Automated payroll entry, compliance filing, direct-to-customer chat. If the AI fails here, people don't get paid.

In the "dial-up era," keep your AI in the safe zone. Do not let the AI handle your compliance documents without a human review. Our HR onboarding example straddles the line; the communication side is safe, but the data entry side is highly dangerous.

5. The Winning Formula and the Matrix

Now, we calculate the final score for our HR onboarding process:

Score = (Impact * Feasibility * AI Versus Human) / Risk
Score = (2 * 2 * 4) / 4
Score = 4

With a score of 4, and low impact/low feasibility, we plot employee onboarding onto the AIDE Opportunities Audit.

The AIDE Opportunities Audit

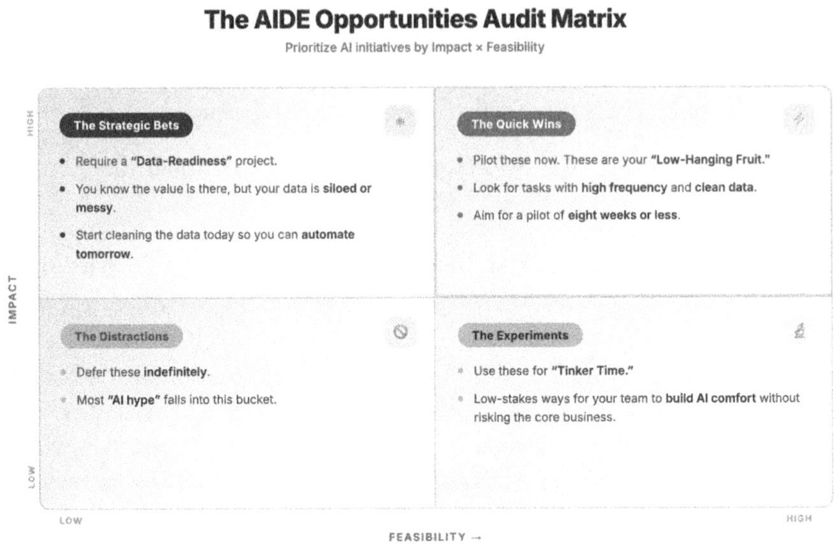

To build your roadmap, plot your scores onto the AIDE Opportunities Audit, with additional consideration for AI versus human and risk scores:

1. **High Impact/High Feasibility (The Quick Wins):** Pilot these now. These are your "low-hanging fruit." Look for tasks with high frequency and clean data. Aim for a pilot of eight weeks or less.
2. **High Impact/Low Feasibility (The Strategic Bets):** These require a "data-readiness" project. You know the value is there, but your data is siloed or messy. Start cleaning the data today so you can automate tomorrow.
3. **Low Impact/High Feasibility (The Experiments):** Use these for "tinker time." They are low-stakes ways for your team to build AI comfort without risking the core business.
4. **Low Impact/Low Feasibility (The Distractions):** Defer these indefinitely. Most "AI hype" falls into this bucket.

Example Audit

Functional Area	Process Node	Frequency (Monthly)	Human Versus AI (1 = Human; 5 = AI)	Peer-Reviewed Impact (1–5)	Technical Feasibility (1–5)	Risk Score (1–5)	Friday Night Test (Reliability)	Total Score	Priority Quadrant
Marketing	Ad Copy Gen	50	5	4	5	1	Safe Zone (Internal)	100	Quick Win
CS	Ticket Triage	1,000	4	5	4	2	Safe Zone (Drafts)	40	Quick Win
Supply Chain	$10k-$100k Dec.	High	5	5	2	3	Danger Zone (Execution)	17	Strategic Bet
Finance	Quarterly Reports	0.33	5	3	4	4	Danger Zone (Audit)	15	Experiment
HR	Onboarding	15	4	2	2	4	Mixed (Data Entry)	4	Distraction
Legal	Contract Review	20	1	4	1	4	Danger Zone (Liability)	1	Distraction

Because of the messy data, high risk, and low direct business impact, full automation of HR employee onboarding lands squarely in "The Distractions." By walking through this systematic process, we just saved our hypothetical logistics company from wasting six months and $200,000 on a frustrating "AI Transformation" project that was doomed to fail.

Use this framework to narrow your focus to the top three initiatives in the "Quick Wins" quadrant. Don't try to boil the ocean. Get those quick, easy wins to build momentum and AI comfort throughout the organization. When you show your team that AI isn't there to replace them, but to remove the "grunt work" they hate, the culture begins to shift from fear to adoption.

Adopting AI is not an end in itself; it's the means to achieving a more productive, fulfilling, and ultimately successful business. The next logical step, once the fear is replaced with comfort, is to strategically integrate AI into your core business processes. With the right mindset now in place, we can move on to the practical, how to restructure your operations to leverage AI's full potential.

No One Works Here: The Digital War Room

You've learned the theory; now let's build the machinery. Turn these concepts into immediate ROI for your company by accessing your free resources at NoOneWorksHere.com.

1. Immediate Actions (Do This Today)

- **Inventory Your Node Map:** List 5–10 recurring processes in your department and document their frequency, average monthly hours, and whether the underlying data is clean and accessible.
- **Run the Peer-Review Pivot:** Select your top three AI ideas and have a leader from a different department (e.g., finance reviewing HR) score them for business impact to eliminate departmental bias.
- **Deploy the Friday Night Test:** Audit every AI tool currently in use by your team; if a tool fails at 5:00 p.m. on a Friday without human intervention, determine if the business stops or merely slows down.

2. The Discussion (Bring This to Your Team)

- What are the high-volume, low-stakes decisions we are currently forfeiting or ignoring because the human coordination cost is simply too high to justify the effort?
- If we were forced to move our AI initiatives from the "danger zone" (100% reliability needed) to the "safe zone" (99% reliability), which human-in-the-loop guardrails would we need to install today?
- Looking at our current AI strategy, are we attempting to boil the ocean with a massive transformation, or can we identify three quick wins that can be piloted and measured in eight weeks or less?

3. The Step-by-Step Implementation

Stop guessing and start building. Use the **AIDE Opportunities Audit Workbook** for step-by-step guidance. This digital workbook provides the exact framework you need to implement this chapter's concepts.

Download it at: NoOneWorksHere.com/ai-opportunities

4. The Unfair Advantage: AI-Powered Tools

Don't just read about AI; use it right now. As a reader of this book, you get exclusive access to interactive AI-software tools designed to do the heavy lifting for you.

Access your tools instantly at: NoOneWorksHere.com

(Or simply scan the QR code with your smartphone camera)

22

Start with You

Why is your weekend the most important, zero-risk R&D laboratory for your company's future?

Organizational change starts with individual experimentation.

THE SOLUTION TO this AIDE transformation challenge does not begin with a corporate mandate. It does not begin with a McKinsey consulting engagement. It does not begin with a "digital transformation task force." It begins with *you.*

Before you can transform your organization, you must transform your own habits. You cannot lead an AI-Driven Enterprise if you are living an analog life. This chapter is the antidote to the overwhelm. It is a permission slip to stop worrying about "enterprise strategy" for a moment and start worrying about your weekend.

In this chapter, you will:

- **Escape the "Monday Morning" Trap:** Why the workplace is actually the *worst* place to start learning AI
- **Adopt the "Sunday Afternoon" Strategy:** Using your personal life as a low-stakes R&D lab
- **Build the "Intuition Muscle":** How personal tinkering translates to professional vision

- **Deploy the Personal Framework:** Three steps to integrate AI into your daily routine this week

The Workplace Trap

Why is it so hard to adopt AI at work?

Because work is high-stakes. If you use an AI agent to write an email to a key client and it hallucinates, you lose revenue. If you use AI to analyze sensitive financial data and you upload it to the wrong model, you violate compliance. If you spend three hours tinkering with a new tool instead of hitting your quarterly KPI, you get fired.

Day-to-day professional responsibilities leave zero room for failure. Efficiency is the enemy of experimentation. Because of this pressure, most leaders freeze. They read *about* AI, but they don't *use* AI. They remain intellectually curious but practically illiterate.

Not to mention that learning how to use AI, and how to master it, takes time. Most people don't have that time in their day jobs considering the responsibilities of their role and the infinitely long to-do lists already lined up.

The "Sunday Afternoon" Sandbox

The solution is to move the experimentation to a place where the cost of failure is zero: your personal life. Sunday is a perfect time to experiment. So perfect that a group of Harvard and MIT students have been participating in hacks every Sunday for over 100 weeks (as of this writing) as a part of the Sundai Club.

In your personal life, the stakes are low with these hacks:

- If an AI messes up your meal plan, you order pizza.
- If an AI suggests a boring itinerary for your vacation, you change plans.
- If an AI writes a cheesy wedding toast, you edit it.

The stakes are low, which means the freedom is high.

This is where you build your "AI intuition." You cannot understand the concept of context windows by reading a white paper. You understand it by trying to feed a PDF of your lease agreement into ChatGPT and seeing where it fails.

The Translation Layer

When you use AI personally, you are secretly training for your professional life. Every personal use case has a direct professional corollary.

1. The Vacation Planner → The Project Manager

- **Personal:** You ask an AI to plan a 10-day trip to Italy for a family of four, optimizing for minimal travel time and maximum gelato. You learn how to iterate constraints.
- **Professional:** You realize that AI excels at logistics and scheduling. You now know how to prompt it to optimize a supply chain route or a conference schedule.

2. The Wedding Toast → The Keynote Speech

- **Personal:** You ask an AI to draft a speech for your brother's wedding. It comes back generic and robotic. You learn that you need to provide specific anecdotes ("Show, Don't Tell") to get good output.

- **Professional:** You realize that generative AI needs proprietary data to be valuable. You stop asking your team for generic marketing copy and start building a database of customer success stories to train the model.

3. The Meal Prep → The Resource Allocation

- **Personal:** You give the AI a photo of your fridge contents and ask for a recipe. It hallucinates an ingredient you don't have. You learn to verify the input.
- **Professional:** You realize that "garbage in, garbage out" is real. You become a hawk about data hygiene in your company's ERP system.

The Framework: The "v0" Rule

So how do you start? I propose a simple rule for your personal life: Never start from a blank page. For the next 30 days, apply the "v0" (Version Zero) rule to everything you do outside of work.

- **Writing an angry email to your HOA?** Dictate your rant into an AI and ask it to "make this polite but firm."
- **Helping your kid with math homework?** Take a picture of the problem and ask the AI to "act as a tutor and explain the concept, don't just give the answer."
- **Planning a workout?** Tell the AI you have 20 minutes and a kettlebell. Ask for a routine.

Your goal is not to have the AI do the work *for* you. Your goal is to use the AI to get you past the friction of starting.

Example: Peter Hirst

At MIT, Peter Hirst, senior associate dean for executive education, offers the perfect illustration of how the "Sunday afternoon" strategy unlocks professional transformation. Peter, a physicist and dedicated "ham" (the nickname for licensed amateur radio operators), spent years wrestling with a persistent technical hurdle. Operating under his unique FCC identifier, or callsign, WU2C, he was an expert in DXing (the art of long-distance communication). However, he found existing technology frustratingly limited.

While his tools could tell him how well his signals were leaving his own backyard, they were silent on the "last mile" of the journey. In the world of amateur radio, signal conditions are dictated by the atmosphere and solar activity; just because Peter had a clear path to broadcast *out* didn't mean the station in France or Japan had a clear path to hear him *in*. He was essentially shouting into a void, never knowing if the person on the other end was experiencing the "local" interference or atmospheric noise that would make his signal disappear.

He wasn't a software engineer, and in the "old world," solving this would have required a budget and a development team. Instead, Peter spent a long weekend in his personal sandbox, treating Claude not just as a tool, but as a development partner. He combined his deep domain expertise in physics with the AI's coding capability to build "QSO Predictor." In just four days, he shipped a fully functional application with nearly 10,000 lines of production code, proving that the barrier between having an idea and building a solution had collapsed (Hirst 2025).

Critically, Peter didn't leave this new superpower in his ham radio shack; he brought it immediately back to his "Monday morning" reality at MIT. Having built his intuition muscle on a low-stakes personal passion, he applied the exact same methodology, what he calls "AI-Ops," to his professional responsibilities. In overseeing ExecEd at MIT Sloan, he bypassed the traditional IT bottlenecks in a large institution and began building AI tools to rapidly accelerate operations and the student learning experience for our executive students. He developed an AI-driven executive coaching system that adapts to individual learners and connects peers based on relevant experience, a project that previously would have taken months of scoping and external consulting. By starting with himself, Peter transformed from a leader waiting on technical resources into a builder capable of deploying mission-critical solutions over a weekend.

From Familiarity to Vision

Once you cross the threshold of personal adoption, a shift happens. You stop seeing AI as magic and start seeing it as mechanics. You develop an intuitive sense of what the technology can and cannot do.

- You know when it's lying.
- You know when it's being lazy.
- You know exactly how to nudge it to get the result you want.

This is the foundation of organizational transformation.

When you sit in a board meeting and the CIO pitches a multi-million-dollar AI project, you won't be nodding along blindly. You will be able to ask the hard questions, not because you have a PhD in computer science, but because you tried to do something similar last Sunday and you know where the traps are.

Personal AI adoption experience builds confidence. Confidence builds clarity. And clarity allows you to lead most effectively.

Part IV Continues . . .

We have prepared the leader and we have reached the end of the journey. The technology is ready. The economics are compelling. The roadmap is clear.

What next?

No One Works Here: The Digital War Room

You've learned the theory; now let's build the machinery. Turn these concepts into immediate ROI for your company by accessing your free resources at NoOneWorksHere.com.

1. Immediate Actions (Do This Today)

- **The Sunday Sandbox:** Commit to using an AI tool for one nonwork task this weekend, such as meal planning, a workout routine, or a travel itinerary, to build your "AI Intuition" where the cost of failure is zero.
- **Enforce the "v0" Rule:** For the next 30 days, refuse to start any personal writing or planning from a blank page. Use AI to generate a "Version Zero" draft for every polite but firm email or project outline to eliminate the friction of starting.
- **Cure Tool Trial Trauma:** Audit your current AI apps and subscriptions; keep only the two tools that most effectively integrate into your daily habits and delete the rest to focus on mastery over novelty.

2. The Discussion (Bring This to Your Team)

- If we stop waiting for a "digital transformation task force" and instead empower every team member to solve one "local" bottleneck using AI, which specific internal friction point would disappear first?
- Why are we currently treating AI as a high-stakes "magic" solution rather than a mechanical tool, and how is that mindset preventing our team from experimenting with daily automation?

- Peter Hirst used a personal hobby to master “AI-Ops” before transforming executive education at MIT. What low-stakes “sandbox” projects can we encourage within our team to build the technical confidence required for enterprise-level deployment?

3. The Step-by-Step Implementation

Stop guessing and start building. Use the **Personal AI Habit-Builder Workbook** for step-by-step guidance. This digital workbook provides the exact framework you need to implement this chapter’s concepts.

Download it at: NoOneWorksHere.com/start-with-you

4. The Unfair Advantage: AI-Powered Tools

Don’t just read about AI; use it right now. As a reader of this book, you get exclusive access to interactive AI-software tools designed to do the heavy lifting for you.

Access your tools instantly at: NoOneWorksHere.com

(Or simply scan the QR code with your smartphone camera)

23

Take a Day for Tinker Time

What would happen if you paused your normal operations for exactly eight hours to fundamentally refactor your capabilities?
Your practical, actionable experiment to begin integrating AI.

WE HAVE REACHED the end of the curriculum.

We have explored the AI-Driven Enterprise. We have looked at the collapse of latency, the rise of agents, and the rewriting of the capital stack. We have discussed how nations must adapt and how board members must govern. But you cannot learn to swim by reading a textbook on hydrodynamics. At some point, you have to get wet.

So I am going to do something unconventional for the final chapter of a business book.

I am hereby granting you one day off work next week.

By the power vested in me as the author of this book, I authorize you to clear your calendar for eight hours. Cancel your meetings. Set your Slack status to "Away." Tell your team you are unreachable.

My Disclaimer: I have not cleared this with your boss. I have not spoken to your HR department. If they have a problem with it, tell them they can email me. I won't answer, because I'll probably be tinkering too, but it might buy you some time.

The Manager's Clause: Structured Innovation: If you are a CEO reading this, you might be panicking at the thought of paying your entire workforce to "play" for a day. Don't make it a free-for-all; make it a Hackathon with Bounties.

Instead of "take the day off," frame it as "We are pausing normal operations for eight hours to find efficiency." Offer a $500 bonus for the employee who builds the agent that saves the most hours. Make "Tinker Time" a competitive sport with a clear ROI attached to it. You aren't funding a vacation; you are funding distributed R&D.

For the Regulated Industries: I realize that for many of you reading this in regulated industries like banking, healthcare, or defense, "going dark" on a Tuesday is a fireable offense. If you are in a high-compliance environment, use the "sandbox strategy":

1. **The "Air-Gapped" Hour:** Do not use company data. Do not use company devices if policies prohibit it. Use your personal device on your personal time to solve a *personal* problem (e.g., your family budget).
2. **The "Analog" Sprint:** If you can't use AI tools at work, map out the *architecture* of an agentic workflow on a whiteboard. Define the nodes. The mental exercise of architecting the system is 80% of the value, even if you can't run the code on the corporate network yet.

I am serious. I want you to take a "Tinker Day." Get a group together and appoint a facilitator to provide some level of guidance and structure. Send me your learnings that come out of that one day.

In this chapter, you will:

- **Commit to the Challenge:** Why you need eight uninterrupted hours of experimentation
- **Learn from Morning Sprints:** How I learned more in one week of mornings than in a year of meetings
- **Receive Your Tinker Mission:** The specific criteria for your Tinker Day
- **Prepare for End of Work:** How this experiment bridges the gap to the future

The Necessity of Tinker Time

Why am I demanding a full day? Why not just an hour here and there?

Because deep work requires momentum. When you're learning a new paradigm, like how to orchestrate a swarm of agents, you cannot do it in 15-minute increments between Zoom calls. You need to enter the flow state.

In the corporate world, we have demonized "playing around." We call it a waste of time. We optimize every minute for "productivity." But in the AIDE era, play is R&D. If you are not playing with the tools, you do not understand the tools. And if you do not understand the tools, you cannot lead the company.

The 4 a.m. Sprint

I speak from experience.

At the beginning of 2025, the AI landscape shifted. Almost overnight, agents went from being "interesting toys" to "enterprise capabilities." I realized that my knowledge was becoming obsolete by the hour. But I had a job. I had classes to teach at MIT and an entrepreneurship center to run. I had a book to write. I had a family. I didn't have time to learn.

So I made time.

For one week, I set my alarm for 4:00 a.m. From 4:00 a.m. to 7:00 a.m., before the emails started, before the kids woke up, before the world demanded my attention, I tinkered.

I didn't have a perfect plan. I just built things. But in those quiet, dark hours of the morning, something clicked. I stopped seeing AI as a chatbot and started seeing it as digital clay. I felt the texture of the technology.

I learned more in that week of 4 a.m. sprints than I had learned in the entire previous year.

I didn't learn it in a white paper. I learned it early in the morning, before work, with a cup of coffee and a handful of AI tools.

That intuition, that visceral understanding of what is possible, is part of what allows me to stand in a boardroom today and tell a CEO that their strategy is wrong or misaligned from their team's execution. Or that for the biggest leading indicator of how AI-mature their organization will be next year—talent acquisition—AI competencies in their job posts are far too low.

Your Mission: The One-Day Build

Now it is your turn. Here are the rules for your Tinker Day:

1. **No "Real" Work:** You are forbidden from checking email, logging onto Slack, or doing anything that keeps the current business running.
2. **Build, Don't Read:** You are not allowed to watch YouTube videos *about* AI. You must *use* AI to build something.
3. **The "V1" Goal:** By the end of the eight hours, you must have a functional result. Not a plan. A result.

Ideas for Your Build:

- **The "Me" App:** Use a vibe-coding tool to build a web app that tracks something personal to you (your wine cellar, your kid's soccer stats, your book collection). Deploy it to the web. Send the live version to someone. As the team as Sundai says, you need to get off "localhost," the namespace that represents what happens on your computer without ever going online.

- **The Analyst:** Take a messy CSV file of data that has been annoying you for years. Feed it into Claude, Manus, Gemini, Perplexity, or ChatGPT and ask it to visualize the trends and write a two-page executive summary.
- **The Creator:** Use a voice-cloning tool to record a five-minute podcast episode about your industry, entirely generated and voiced by AI.

The Transformation

At the end of this day, you will be tired. Your brain will hurt. But you will also feel something you might not have felt in a long time: agency.

You will realize that you are no longer dependent on the tech team to build your ideas. You will realize that the barrier between "thinking" and "doing" has dissolved. You will realize that you are not just a manager; you are a maker.

This shift in identity is the most important takeaway from this entire book. The tools will change. The models will get updated. The regulations will shift. But the builder's mindset, the confidence that you can bend technology to your will, is permanent.

The Final Transition

We have talked about *No One Works Here* as a provocative title. Throughout these four parts and their chapters, we have seen that it doesn't mean *humans* disappear. It means the *nature of work* changes. We move from being the cogs in the machine to being the architects of the machine. Now, what happens if we take this to its logical conclusion?

One question remains, a question that haunts every conversation about AI, from the dinner table to the Senate floor.

If the AI does the work, what do we do?

In the final chapter, we look at the horizon. We explore the ultimate promise and the ultimate challenge of the AIDE era.

If one person can do the work of ten, if software costs drop to zero, if agents can hire other agents and agents can hire humans, then where does the curve end?

No One Works Here: The Digital War Room

You've learned the theory; now let's build the machinery. Turn these concepts into immediate ROI for your company by accessing your free resources at NoOneWorksHere.com.

1. Immediate Actions (Do This Today)

- **The Calendar Clear-Out:** To prevent interruptions, block a nonnegotiable eight-hour window in your schedule for next week and set an auto-responder explicitly stating you are engaged in a Tinker Day.
- **The "V1" Build:** Commit to creating one functional output, such as a custom web app, a voice-cloned podcast, or an automated data visualization, rather than just reading or watching tutorials.
- **The Sandbox Strategy:** If you're in a regulated industry, identify one personal, nonwork dataset (like a family budget or hobby) to use as your "digital clay" for experimentation on a personal device.

2. The Discussion (Bring This to Your Team)

- If we transitioned from being managers who oversee tasks to makers who architect agentic workflows, which 80% of our current departmental meetings would become obsolete?
- How can we implement an "efficiency bounty" program that rewards team members with financial bonuses or time off for building agents that save the company measurable hours?
- What is the single biggest "latency" bottleneck in our current operation, and what would a "Version 1" AI solution look like if we had eight hours of uninterrupted building time to solve it?

(*continued*)

(*continued*)

3. The Step-by-Step Implementation

Stop guessing and start building. Use the **Tinker Time Prototyping Workbook** for step-by-step guidance. This digital workbook provides the exact framework you need to implement this chapter's concepts.

Download it at: NoOneWorksHere.com/tinker-time

4. The Unfair Advantage: AI-Powered Tools

Don't just read about AI; use it right now. As a reader of this book, you get exclusive access to interactive AI-software tools designed to do the heavy lifting for you.

Access your tools instantly at: NoOneWorksHere.com

(Or simply scan the QR code with your smartphone camera)

PART IV → EPILOGUE

What happens to the definition of a company when it no longer requires human employees to operate?
Redefining the final, irreplaceable roles for humanity in the intelligent enterprise.

This concludes Part IV, "The Actions." You have now completed the tactical manual. You have confronted the boardroom literacy crisis, mapped your organization's risk on the AIDE Matrix, redefined your C-suite to manage nodes instead of headcount, and claimed personal "Tinker Time" to build your own AI intuition. You have successfully moved from passive observation to active participation.

But acting on these frameworks reveals a deeper, more existential truth: We are not just building faster companies. We are rebooting the fundamental concept of the firm itself.

In our closing reflection, we look to the absolute horizon. What happens when the curve hits the axis? What happens when a billion-dollar entity requires exactly zero employees?

In the Epilogue, "Ctrl+Alt+Company," we will explore the impending reality of the Zero-Person Company (ZPC) and confront the ultimate crisis of purpose. As the systems you design begin to operate continuously and autonomously, you will see why the final, irreplaceable role for humans is no longer labor, but serving as Governors of Intent, Ethicists of Design, and Stewards of Meaning.

Let's look at the future we are building.

Epilogue

Ctrl+Alt+Company

The Post-Human Organization

When companies think for themselves: What happens when organizations truly no longer need us?
When organizations no longer need us to work, what will they need us for?
When intelligence organizes itself, our role becomes meaning.

AFTER ACTING, THE final realization emerges: This isn't only a new phase of business; it's a new form of organization. The systems you design today will soon make decisions, optimize resources, and create value with minimal human oversight. Humans will remain essential, but in new roles: as governors of intent, ethicists of design, and stewards of meaning.

This closing reflection isn't a prediction; it's a direction. The post-human organization isn't science fiction; rather, it's the logical outcome of everything in this book. The question isn't whether it will happen, but how you'll prepare to lead it.

We began this book with a provocative title: *No One Works Here.*

Throughout these chapters, we have treated that phrase as a metaphor for efficiency. We talked about how 15 people can do the work of 100. We talked about how one person can launch a startup in 30 minutes. We talked about how deep tech companies can simulate experiments rather than run them.

But in these final pages, I want to invite you to consider the phrase not as a metaphor, but as a literal destination.

What happens when the curve hits the axis? What happens when the number of employees required to run a billion-dollar entity isn't 15, or 5, but 0?

We are approaching the horizon of the Zero-Person Company (ZPC).

The Self-Driving Firm

If an AI agent can write code, and another agent can deploy that code, and another agent can market the product, and another agent can handle the customer support, and a blockchain smart contract can handle the payroll and the treasury. . .

Then the "company" ceases to be a gathering of people in a room and becomes a nexus of processes. It becomes a software artifact that lives in the cloud, optimizing itself, generating value, and executing its mission with relentless precision.

It is the **Zero-Person Company.**

The Crisis of Purpose

To a capitalist, this sounds like utopia: infinite margin, zero friction. To a humanist, this sounds like a nightmare: The obsolescence of our species. If the organization no longer needs us to work, what *does* it need us for? When intelligence organizes itself, what is left for us? The answer is *meaning.*

As the cost of *execution* drops to zero, the value of *intent* rises to infinity. The AI can optimize the supply chain, but it cannot decide *why* we are building the product in the first place. The AI can maximize profit, but it cannot decide if that profit comes at the cost of our values. The AI can answer any question, but it cannot ask the question that matters.

The New Roles

In this post-human organization, our role shifts from laborer to legislator. We stop being the gears in the machine and become the conscience of the machine.

Humans will remain essential, but in three new, distinct roles:

1. **Governors of Intent:** The machine has velocity, but it has no vector. We must set the direction. We must define the "why." We are the ones who input the prompt that starts the universe.
2. **Ethicists of Design:** An autonomous organization is a powerful weapon. Without guardrails, it can maximize metrics in sociopathic ways. We must be the architects who code the values into the system.
3. **Stewards of Meaning:** We must ensure that the abundance created by these systems translates into human flourishing, not just digital accumulation. We must connect the output of the machine back to the needs of the soul.

A Direction, Not a Prediction

This closing reflection isn't a prediction of a specific date. I don't know if the first zero-person unicorn will happen in 2027 or 2035.

But it is a direction. The wind is blowing this way. Every tool you use, every agent you deploy, every experiment you run during your "Tinker Time" is pushing us closer to this reality.

The question isn't whether it will happen. The question is who will guide it.

The Era of Mixed Traffic

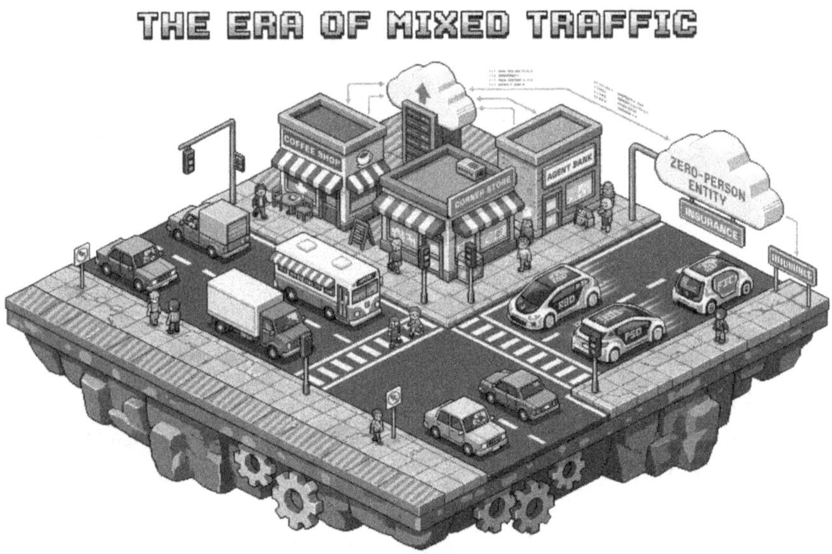

We are entering a period of economic "mixed traffic." Just as autonomous vehicles currently navigate the highways alongside human-driven sedans and delivery trucks, "full self-driving companies" will soon operate alongside legacy organizations. They will share the same infrastructure. They will bid on the same Google keywords. They will compete for the same customers. They will transact on the same banking rails. The market will not segregate them. You might buy your coffee from a human-run shop on the corner and your insurance from a zero-person entity in the cloud. The global economy will become a hybrid highway, where the speed limit is determined not by regulation, but by the processing power of the driver.

Entonomy

I am not writing this as a futurist guessing at what might happen; I am writing this as a builder who has seen what *does* happen. To prove the viability of the AI-Driven Enterprise (AIDE), we launched a company called Entonomy which provides a software platform designed to create the world's first Zero-Person Companies.

Under the architectural vision of David Iakobidze, we moved past the "digital bureaucracy" of our early prototypes. We stopped trying to make AI act like a human CEO or manager and instead built a system of protocols. Entonomy doesn't use a hierarchy per se; it uses a swarm of micro-agents that spin up to execute specific tasks with ruthless precision and then shut down.

From Methodology to Market

We didn't teach these agents to guess. We programmed them with the rigorous Disciplined Entrepreneurship and Startup Tactics methodologies taught at MIT. The process is a self-sustaining loop that requires no human operators, only humans at the governance level to provide oversight.

The Result

The experiment is no longer theoretical. Today, we can officially state that a real person has purchased a real product that was entirely designed, developed, marketed, and sold by AI agents. The human is no longer the "cog" in the machine; the human is the governor of an autonomous engine.

> **Note:** This is a condensed overview of the Entonomy framework. For the full technical breakdown, case studies, and updated data from the experiment, please visit the book's website at NoOneWorksHere.com/zero-person-company

The Verdict

I can now confidently say that a Zero-Person Company is not just possible; it is proven.

We watched Entonomy agents design products, launch marketing campaigns, and sell them to real people around the world. The money in the bank account was real. The customers were real. The value was real.

The only thing missing was the employees.

The Final Reboot

In the early days of computing, when a system became frozen or chaotic, we used a simple command to reset the state: Ctrl + Alt + Delete. We are currently living through a Ctrl + Alt + Company moment. We are rebooting the fundamental concept of the firm.

We are deleting the bloat. We are altering the architecture. And we are controlling the intelligence. The future does not belong to those who fear this reboot. It belongs to those who are ready to type the command.

You have the manual. You have the tools. You have the mindset.

No One Works Here. But you have work to do. Start now.

Conclusion

The next Fortune 500 company might have zero employees.
When work no longer defines us, intent will.

I OFTEN REFLECT on the trajectory of a former student, Bernardo Aceituno, a brilliant mind from MIT's mechanical engineering PhD program and now the CEO of Stack AI. Back in 2021, I had the opportunity to see the evolution of Stack in its earliest form: robotic automation for warehouses. But on Aceituno's entrepreneurial journey, that company shape-shifted and pivoted its way to be one of the leading AI platforms for enterprises. As he recently summarized with piercing clarity:

> *This year, the biggest inefficiency in most organizations won't be a lack of AI. It will be how much manual work is still left in place.* (Aceituno 2026)

This insight reflects an interesting statistic on the marketing website for Rogo, an AI platform for investment banking through which they claim to have saved "500 years of full-time human work" (Rogo 2026).

Bernardo's insight and Rogo's statistics must serve as the driving force for every reader of this book. For the entrepreneur shaping their next venture, the executive reevaluating their organization's priorities, and the policymaker seeking to leverage the AI leapfrog effect, the mandate is identical. The future does not belong to those who simply add AI to their existing chaos, but to those who ruthlessly eliminate the manual friction that prevents the technology from taking flight.

This book hopefully leaves you with a clear sense of the impending realities coming with the shift from operators of the machine to architects of the machine. This shift I described in the introduction, however, comes with a profound, nontechnical challenge. If our work is to become the architects of the machine, the quality of our intent is everything. Yet, at a societal level, our inputs are increasingly compromised.

These dynamics—algorithmic division, the collapse of shared values, and incentives that reward short-term financial gain over truth—pose an existential threat to the architect role. How can we effectively design or govern a hyper-efficient AI enterprise if the human leaders are operating from fundamentally different information sets or driven by flawed, self-serving objectives? The AIDE model is only as robust as the human intent that programs it. In the age of AI, the last vestiges of human work—design and governance—must first be secured by addressing the deep structural and informational integrity crisis in our society.

These are the things I'm considering in raising three young daughters. Children and AI agents share a singular requirement: They must be trained on values. Where will my girls "work" when they grow up? Will they "work" when they grow up? What will "work" even mean when they grow up? Regardless of what the future holds for my daughters, one thing is certain: They will live in a world fundamentally shaped by technology.

For the present, Bernardo Aceituno's insight and Rogo's statistics must serve as the driving force for every reader of this book. For the entrepreneur, the executive, and the policymaker, the mandate is identical: The future does not belong to those who simply add AI to their existing chaos, but to those who ruthlessly eliminate the manual friction that prevents the technology from taking flight.

I care so deeply about this because I know: We as a society are creating more problems than solutions on a daily basis. Entrepreneurs are best positioned to address this fundamental challenge. It's entrepreneurs who are best positioned to eliminate that manual friction.

As we transition from operators of the machine to architects of the machine, we face a profound, nontechnical challenge. The AIDE model is a powerful engine, but it is a blind one. It is only as robust as the human intent that programs it. We cannot govern a hyper-efficient enterprise if we are operating from fractured realities or incentivized by short-term gains over long-term truth. In this new era, your primary job description is no longer *execution*; it is integrity.

If you do not secure the integrity of your information and your objectives, you aren't an architect; you're just a passenger in a faster wreck.

The most valuable skill in the age of AI is no longer coding; it is curation. To lead effectively, you must curate the data, the ethics, and the intent that your machines will amplify. Your mandate, starting today, is to audit your inputs as fiercely as you automate your outputs. We are the last generation to define work by what we *do*; we are the first to define it by what we *mean*.

The transition is over. Stop adding speed to the chaos. Clear the deck, sharpen your intent, and commit your values to the source. Root Access is now yours, the digital equivalent of a master key to every vault, file, and policy in the enterprise. With the absolute authority of a "superuser," you now hold the unrestricted power to rewrite the company's core code from the inside out. What command will you execute? What will you initialize?

Commitment: The Architect's Manifesto

The transition from operator to architect is not a suggestion; it is a crossing. You have reached the end of the text, which means you now hold **Root Access**. But power without purpose is just high-speed noise.

To lead the **AI-Driven Enterprise**, you must move beyond passive consumption. Success in the age of AI is a team sport. Your commitment has the power to spark a chain reaction in your network.

1. **Capture the Moment:** Take a photo of this signed page (or a screenshot of your digital notes).
2. **Declare Your Intent:** Post it on LinkedIn.
3. **Tag the Movement:** Use **#AIDrivenEnterprise, #NoOneWorksHere,** and tag me, Paul Cheek.

The most influential architects are those who build in public. I'll be looking for your post to welcome you to the front lines.

My Architect Protocol

I. ELIMINATE THE FRICTION: The first manual process I will ruthlessly automate or eliminate to clear the deck for high-level design is:

II. SECURE THE INPUTS: To protect the integrity of my "architectural" intent, I will audit my information sources and replace **[Noise/ Short-term Signal]** with **[High-Integrity Data/Value-Based Input]**:

III. INITIALIZE THE VALUES: If my AI agents were to scale my values a thousandfold tomorrow, the core principle I must "program" into my organization's culture today is:

"We are the last generation to define work by what we do; we are the first to define it by what we mean."

I accept the mandate of the Architect:

Signed: ______________________ **Date:** ______________

Companion Website

Beyond the Last Page: Your Implementation Toolkit

Reading this book is the theory; the website is the practice. To ensure these insights don't just stay in your head but actually transform your workflow and your company, we've built a digital HQ designed for immediate action. Think of it as a force multiplier for everything you've just read.

At NoOneWorksHere.com, you can access a vault of expanding resources, including:

- **Interactive Workbooks:** Guided exercises to help you audit your current processes and map out your next moves
- **Discussion Questions:** Facilitation guides for book clubs, leadership retreats, or team syncs
- **Video Masterclasses and Online Courses:** Deep dives into the book's most technical and transformative strategies
- **Perks:** Exclusive promotion codes for the AI tools and platforms mentioned in these chapters
- **Execution Checklists:** To turn complex concepts into daily habits
- **Prompt Templates:** Copy-paste frameworks to leverage AI effectively in your role

Whether you're looking to optimize your own desk or overhaul your entire organization's culture, these resources are designed to help you move from "informed" to "indispensable."

Visit: NoOneWorksHere.com

(Or simply scan the QR code with your smartphone camera)

Reading Group Discussion Guide

You've made it to the end, but the ideas in these pages aren't meant to live in a vacuum. True change—the kind that fixes cultures and transforms careers—doesn't happen in isolation. It happens when teams, friends, and leaders start speaking the same language.

If the concepts in this book resonated with you, the most effective way to see them in action is to bring others into the conversation.

Take the Conversation Further

Whether you're looking to spark a debate in your book club or overhaul the way your department operates, we've built the infrastructure to help you lead that charge.

At NoOneWorksHere.com, you can access:

- **Customizable Discussion Guides:** These are tailored for book clubs, executive retreats, or casual Friday lunches.
- **Collaborative Toolkits:** Digital resources and worksheets can help your team implement the strategies found in this book.

- **Bulk Resources:** Planning to get the whole company on the same page? We offer special resources and support for leaders purchasing copies for their entire team or organization.

Start the Ripple Effect

Don't let the momentum stop at the final page. Head over to the site, grab the guide, and invite one person, or one hundred, to join the movement.

Visit: NoOneWorksHere.com/discussion-guides

(Or simply scan the QR code with your smartphone camera)

Glossary

Building Common Knowledge

Welcome to the Lexicon of the "New Normal"

IN THE TRADITIONAL sense, a glossary is a graveyard for words, a place where technical terms go to be pinned down like butterflies under glass. But this isn't a traditional book, and the world it describes isn't exactly traditional, either.

If you're reading *No One Works Here*, you've likely realized that the hardest part of modern work isn't the work itself; it's the language we use to mask the fact that the office is empty, the "team" is a collection of avatars, and the "mission" is a moving target.

This section serves as a **dictionary for common knowledge.** It is a shared dialect designed to bridge the gap between you and your colleagues. Whether you're navigating the eerie silence of a decentralized corporation or the frantic noise of an automated one, these terms are the tools you'll use to find each other in the fog.

How to Use This Glossary

This isn't just for solo study. Think of it as a social contract. Use these definitions to:

- **Align the Unaligned:** Send a snippet to a teammate when a "quick sync" turns into a three-hour philosophical debate.
- **Validate the Absurd:** Use the shared terminology to acknowledge the "glitches" in your daily workflow without sounding like a conspiracy theorist.
- **Onboard the Uninitiated:** Provide this to new hires so they don't spend their first six months wondering if they're the only ones who don't understand what it really means to be an AI-Driven Enterprise.

"Language is the only thing we actually share when we don't share a physical space. If our words are hollow, our work becomes invisible."

A Living Document

The definitions ahead are more than just descriptions; they are observations of the contemporary psyche. They cover the space between what we say in a performance review and what we actually mean when we're staring at a "User Not Found" error message at 4:00 p.m. on a Tuesday.

In a world where it feels like **no one works here**, these words are the proof that you, and your colleagues, actually do.

Download

Don't let this shared language stay trapped on the page. Head over to the book's website to download a standalone digital version of this glossary. It's formatted for easy sharing, so you can quickly drop it into your team's Slack channel, embed it into your onboarding documents, or subtly forward it to that one colleague who relies a little too heavily on corporate jargon.

Visit: NoOneWorksHere.com/glossary
(Or simply scan the QR code with your smartphone camera)

Acknowledgments

WRITING A BOOK as a sole author is often described as a solitary pursuit, but for me, it has always felt like a crowded, vibrant, and occasionally chaotic dinner party. If my previous work laid the foundation, this book is the structure built upon the collective wisdom of a global community.

The Students and the Mission

I must start, as always, by thanking my students. You are the reason I do this. To my thousands of undergraduate, graduate, MBA, PhD, and executive-level students at MIT and across the globe: Your questions and your breakthroughs are what make this work rigorous. You turn theory into reality, and you make my job the best in the world.

Bill

A singular debt of gratitude is owed to Bill Aulet. Bill, you have been the architect of so many of the opportunities that allowed this book to exist. Beyond being the foundation of *Disciplined Entrepreneurship*, you have been a relentless champion of my career. Thank you for the "Tactics" discussions that started it all, being the first reviewer of the AIDE model upon which this book is based, for the necessary skepticism that forced me to sharpen my arguments, and for never letting me forget the most important benchmark: a relentless standard of excellence. Your mentorship is woven into every page. Thank you for continuing to push me forward, exponentially.

Henry

I also want to express my sincere gratitude to Henry Ford III. Henry, your friendship and your steadfast support of my work, the work of my students, and the work of many friends (some of whom are my alums) has been a vital part of this journey. Beyond your advocacy, the genuine curiosity and grace you bring to every conversation serve as a powerful reminder of why we do this work. Your forward-looking perspective and unwavering belief in our shared mission act as a constant, much-needed catalyst to keep pushing the boundaries of what is possible to make the world a better place.

The MIT Ecosystem

At MIT Sloan, I am continually inspired by a leadership team that doesn't just talk about innovation, but lives it. My deepest thanks to Rick Locke, the late Dean Dave Schmittlein, Peter Hirst, Michael Cusumano, Scott Stern, and our legendary founder of the Trust Center, the late Ed Roberts. Your support for the courses and initiatives that led to this content is and remains unwavering.

I also want to thank the leadership at the very top: Mark Gorenberg, chair of the MIT Corporation; President Sally Kornbluth; and Provost Anantha Chandrakasan, for their commitment to entrepreneurship and AI education.

I work closely with the entire team at MIT Sloan Executive Education and appreciate all they do to help me bring the content in this book to the leaders who need it. A special callout to my "Executive Education Spirit Guide," Ann Marie Maxwell.

And to my colleagues past and present at the Martin Trust Center for MIT Entrepreneurship: Andy Acevedo, Neelesh Bagga, Ana Bakshi, Alicia Carelli, Carly Chase, Elaine Chen, Trish Cotter, Maya Freed, Kit Hickey, Alfredo Garcia, Christine Hsieh, Mona Jones, Macauley Kenney, Amrutha Killada, Jenny Larios Berlin, Kosta Ligris, Tommy Long, Leah Lovgren, Ylana Lopez, Stephanie MacConnell, Connor Madsen,

Erin Martin, Nick Meyer, Emily Mooney, Chris Moses, Susan Neal, Leslie Owens, Magali Paoli, Dip Patel, Daniela Ruiz Massieu, Will Sanchez, Devon Sherman Daley, Navroop Singh Sehmi, Lucia Solorzano, Ben Soltoff, Nina Teng, Nagarjuna Venna, Doug Williams, George Whitfield, Greg Wymer, and John Xin. Our global network collaborators around the world have also been a part of the early AIDE model journey: Georgian National University SEU, TU Wein, University of Saskatchewan, Cape Peninsula University of Technology, and Investe Piaui.

To my long-term MIT collaborators who keep the gears turning: Jinane Abounadi, Sherwin Greenblatt, Marina Hatsopoulos, Travis Hunter, Lesley Millar-Nicholson, Asu Ozdaglar, Jacquelyn Pless, Bob Pozen, Leon Sandler, Joel Schindall, Don Shobrys, Alfred Spector, and Gayathri Srinivasan.

And to my colleagues at the Center for Transportation and Logistics: Yossi Sheffi, Maria Jesús Saénz, Chris Mejía Argueta, Josué C. Velázquez Martínez, Maren Axe, Joseph Dorion, and Aren Ghazarians.

Inspiration to Write Another Book

This book specifically owes its existence to the team at LinkedIn behind the recently published Open to Work. To Aneesh Raman, Jonathan Kilroy, Ryan Roslansky, Mary Kate Fields, Kenly Walker and Sofia Groopman: Thank you for the spark that convinced me I had another book in me.

The AIDE Model and Beyond

The AIDE model itself was born in Conference Room 166 at the Trust Center. To Steve Orr, Fiona Bennington, and the rest of the Catalyst team who were in the room where it happened: Thank you for your brains and your energy.

To my core team at the AIDE Institute, Felipe Scherer, Kate Reed, and Zach Winn: Thank you for bringing the AIDE model to the organizations that need it. Thank you for serving as thought partners on many of the AIDE frameworks. Beyond frameworks, the insights shared in these pages find their true power in the data we collect to track and ensure real-world progress. Without your commitment to making our model measurable and scalable, this work would remain an aspiration rather than an actionable reality.

Collaborators Around the Globe

My work is a product of a vast global network. To my partners at the College Board, David Coleman, Jen Mulhern, and Aanand Vasudevan: Thank you for your collaboration. To the teams at Infinity Constellation, General Intelligence Company, Lyzr, PicaOS, and Oceanworks: It is a privilege to build alongside you.

I am also indebted to my partners and collaborators at Opportunity North East, Catalyst, Scottish Enterprise, GSK, HBS, Babson, the Royal Academy of Engineering, Gladly, Labs4, Babson College, Harvard Business School, Accenture, KPMG, PwC, GCE Ocean Technology, and Agenda Vestlandet. Other partners and collaborators I must thank individually include Howard Buffett, Rob Lalka, Michael Miebach, Yu-Ting Kuo, Tom Davenport, Donna Levin, Gaurav Jain, Geoff Smart, Peter Komo, Marius Ursache, and Jeff Larsen and his team at Dal Innovates.

The AI Architects

This book would simply not exist without the architects on my team. First, my chief of staff, Miranda Ewald. Miranda, thank you for keeping everything on the rails. Thank you for supporting me all the way through the production and promotion of this book. To David Iakobidze, lead engineer at Entonomy: Thank you for the technical brilliance that supports our work together. I couldn't be happier to have had the opportunity to highlight the impact we are making in the development of autonomous organizations in this book.

To the team that turns words into a "book": my publishing partners at Wiley: Shannon Vargo, Michael Friedberg, Deb Schindlar, Leah Zarra, Anurekha Durairaj, Amy Handy and Gabby Mancuso. Thank you for placing your trust in me and for your incredible patience as I constantly pushed to get this book out into the world ahead of schedule. I am so grateful for a team that didn't just meet my intensity, but turned it into a reality.

The Pre-Reader Community

Writing is often referred to as a lonely process, but this time was different. To my pre-readers: Thank you for your time and your honesty. While drafting, I would look at the top of the Google Doc and see your profile pictures, whether it was a mentor, a former colleague, or one of Google's "anonymous geese" or "anonymous wolves" because you weren't logged in. Knowing you were in the document with me made the process feel like a shared journey rather than a solitary climb.

This book is fundamentally stronger because of the brilliant community of pre-readers who tore into the manuscript and pushed me to refine every chapter. I am deeply grateful to Ahmad Heshmat for his push on visual illustrations and strategic focus, and to Alex Fish and Paul Barnhill for keeping me grounded regarding AI costs, role clarity, and precise technical terminology. Alexandra McCann and Floyd consistently challenged me to remember the broader picture, contributing heavily to societal impact, terminology clarity, AI ethics, and safety protocols, while Alessio Misuri and Nikolay Aristov provided invaluable, critical insights on legal liability, accountability, and the real-world limitations of AI.

Thank you to Ken Munie, Mike Wandler, Jacob Fure-Slocum, Matt Cooper, and Michelle Sim, who all sent me incredibly valuable feedback throughout the process and had a significant impact on how I revised this book.

A huge thank you to Antonio Gonzalez and Henrik Werdelin for sharpening the historical analogies, startup growth parallels, and second-order effects. I am indebted to Bogusława Cimoszko-Skowroński and Brennan Pothetes for pressure-testing the sales processes, unit economics, economic theory, and modern hiring models. Kate Reed's brilliant sense of emotional pacing and human-machine dynamics gave the narrative its pulse. I heavily relied on Daniel Linder for his mastery of governance, latency, and system models, and on Fareed Shaikh for connecting the dots between lean startups and psychological safety. Thank you to Gerard Rosell for sharing highly practical examples and highlighting scaling fallacies, and to Mads Bondergaard, whose relentless focus on tone, nuance, and cross-industry application kept me incredibly honest throughout the writing process.

The frameworks around organizational structure and human roles wouldn't be the same without Maria Basso, just as the title adjustments, target audience clarity, and framing wouldn't have landed perfectly without Maria Sommer and Peter Hirst. Marina Leywald was an essential voice in grounding the hype, focusing on human psychology, elevating humans within the system, and exploring nonlinear scaling. I deeply appreciate Marios Dikaiakos for clarifying tables and examples, Max Cimenti for diving deep into the nuances of AI decision-making and risk perception, and Sarah Thompson for her meticulous fact-checking and suggesting practical tool alternatives. Sydney Callaway beautifully highlighted tech democratization and the role of early adopters, Tom Davenport expertly modified core premises and demanded better examples to strengthen the argument, Upendra Poranki refined conceptual definitions, and Gemma McAllister ensured the quote resonance hit the mark perfectly. And to Seb Barriga, who helped to provide valuable insights into how the AIDE model applies to private equity firms.

Beyond the specific insights mentioned above, this book was shaped by the collective wisdom of a broader group of pre-readers. Their diverse perspectives, sharp eyes, and honest critiques were essential to the final product. My deepest thanks to Matthew Aliberti, Kunal Ambasta, Aaron Anderson, Onur Aydin, Arpit Bajpai, Tracy Baloyi, Amos Bar Joseph, Lucas Barthman, Casey Bayer, Randy Bean, Dinker Bhardwaj, Ron Birman, Dimitrios Bissias, Adrian Brown, Gregory D Bunch, Jaco Burger, Tate Cao, Raquel Cardoso, Ana Casaca, Charles Castro, Andrew Caudle, Supriyo Chatterjee, Gail Cook, Matt Cooper, Tomás De Angelis, Lennart De Vries, Chris Defty, Jean-Jacques Degroof, David Dellal, Mariosrios Dikaiakos, David Dobson, Greg Donnelly, Murray Edward Duguid, Siobhan Dullea, Corneliu Fecioru, Michelle Fernandes, Fabián Orduña Ferreira, Miriam Ferrer González, Liam Fitz, Frode Nergaard Fjeldstad, Franklin, Jolen Galaugher, Larry Gennari, Andre Kopperud Gill, Isabel Nuez Gracia, Barrinique Griffin, Daniel Haavoll, Owe Hagesaether, Fernando Hernandez, Elisabeth Holvik, Luis Ibarra, David Jamieson, Joseph Kamau, Bill Kerr, Phillip Kim, Sander Klous, Melissa Ko, Ola Kvalheim, Sindre Kvalheim, Rob Lalka, Yolanda Lau, Keegan Leahy, Barry Leaper, James Leo, Donna Levin, Marcel Lukas, Sylvia Malo, Taylor Margis-Noguera, Eugene Maslov, Alex McCann, Patrick McIlveen, Megan Mitchell, Simon Mone, Tracey L Moore, Row Moriarty, Saurabh Mukherjee, Liam Mulcahy, Niko Munoz, Nasil Nam, Carlos A. Nazario, Deji Ogunleye, Fredrik Omdal, Karla Padva, Demos Parneros, George Petrovas, Thuy Pham, Wendy Phillips, Tom Eisenmann, Thara Pillai, Basanda Pongoma, Upendra Poranki, Setu Purohit, Carlos Ramon, Rajan Ray, Ján Rehák, Lasawni Reynolds, Jacob Rissman, Ryan Robertson, Fabrizio Rovatti, Ines Rukljač, Paul Ryan, Shahriyar Rzayev, Clara Saar, Jen Scott, Mary Scott, Fareed Shaikh, Simeon Simeo, Kirsti Slotsvik,

Freek Smoes, Kevin Storr, Siva Surendira, Ulf Sverdrup, Torse Thomas, Krysta Traianovski, Kaushik Vardharajan, Branislav Vujovic, Melissa Weed, Julius Weilert, Terry Williams, David Yee, Lissa Virginia Young, and Suha Younis.

I should also highlight that many of those mentioned elsewhere also contributed to the content of this book as pre-readers and I am so thankful for their contributions to *No One Works Here*.

Family and Roots

Finally, I must thank those who provide the foundation for everything I do. To my entrepreneurial partners from the early days, Calum Barnes, Vikram Chabra, Vanessa Coleman, Braden Golub, Bay Hudner, Rob Ianelli, Monil Kothari, C. Todd Lombardo, Sacha Nacar, Joe Nigro, and Patrick Todd, our shared experiences are the stories I tell to help the next generation.

To my family and friends, especially my mother, Gwen, and sister, Meredith: Thank you for the patience and perspective.

To my three daughters: You are my greatest joy and my constant reminder of why the future matters.

And to my wife, Callie: You have been by my side through every venture, every book, and every late night. None of this, literally none of it, would be possible without you.

Wait, Does Anyone Work Here?

Despite the title, a lot of work went into this book, most of it by real humans. *No One Works Here* is a labor of love that models genuine human thought, refined by the insights of over 100 pre-readers who helped steer the ship.

To help us work smarter and reach further, we invited a few digital assistants to the team. AI was used to supercharge our community's feedback and my own writing process, ensuring the final product is as polished and impactful as possible.

Our Digital Toolkit:

- **Writing Support:** Gemini
- **Data Analysis:** Claude
- **Artistic Generation:** Nano Banana Pro
- **Image Enhancement:** Flux from Black Forest Labs

The ideas are human. The feedback is human. The tools are just here to help us shine.

References

Aceituno, Bernard. 2026. LinkedIn post. https://www.linkedin.com/posts/baceituno_this-year-the-biggest-inefficiency-in-most-activity-7415052437243490304-V9-m/.

Ali-Yrkkö, Jyrki, Laura Paija, Catherine Reilly, and Pekka Ylä-Anttila. 2000. "NOKIA – A Big Company in a Small Country." ETLA. https://www.etla.fi/wp-content/uploads/2012/09/B162.pdf.

Aulet, Bill. 2024. *Disciplined Entrepreneurship: 24 Steps to a Successful Startup*. Wiley.

Aulet, Bill, and Fiona Murray. 2013. "A Tale of Two Entrepreneurs: Understanding Differences in the Types of Entrepreneurship in the Economy." Ewing Marion Kauffman Foundation. https://download.ssrn.com/13/05/02/ssrn_id2259872_code861608.pdf.

Bain, Ken. 2004. *What the Best College Teachers Do*. Harvard University Press.

Bar-Joseph, Amos. 2026. "We Raised $6M to Build the First Autonomous Business." The Autonomous Age. https://swan-ai.beehiiv.com/p/we-raised-6m-to-build-the-first-autonomous-business-948c.

Board of Innovation (BOI). 2025. "AI Fluency for Executives." YouTube. https://www.youtube.com/watch?v=P-9hFa4HU5U.

Bonatsos, Niko. 2026. LinkedIn post. https://www.linkedin.com/posts/bonatsos_dau-wau-mau-ratios-and-retention-across-activity-7423193349706268672-YjS3/.

Carey, Jesse. 2025. "Stripe Atlas startups in 2025: Year in review." Stripe. https://stripe.com/blog/stripe-atlas-startups-in-2025-year-in-review.

Carroll, Lewis. 2003. *Alice's Adventures in Wonderland and Through the Looking Glass*. Edited by Hugh Haughton. Penguin Publishing Group.

Christensen, Clayton M. 2016. *The Innovator's Dilemma: When New Technologies Cause Great Firms to Fail*. Harvard Business Review Press.

Cursor Team. 2025. "Series B and Automating Code." Cursor. https://cursor.com/blog/series-b.

Dimon, Jamie, and Zanny Minton Beddoes. 2026. "Conversation with Jamie Dimon, Chairman and CEO of JPMorgan Chase." World Economic Forum. https://www.weforum.org/meetings/world-economic-forum-annual-meeting-2026/sessions/conversation-with-jamie-dimon-chairman-and-ceo-of-jpmorgan-chase.

Dowd, Kevin, and Peter Walker. 2025. "Founder Ownership Report." Carta. https://carta.com/data/founder-ownership-full-report/.

Fine, Charles H. 1998. *Clockspeed: Winning Industry Control in the Age of Temporary Advantage*. Basic Books.

Frankel, David. 2025. LinkedIn post. https://www.linkedin.com/posts/davidafrankel1_two-new-metrics-that-might-keep-your-startup-activity-7398854553292656641-en7a/.

Geraghty, Tom. 2023. "The First Organisational Chart." Psych Safety. https://psychsafety.com/the-first-organisational-chart/.

Graeber, David. 2018. *Bullshit Jobs: A Theory*. Allen Lane.

Griffith, Erin. 2026. "How A.I. Helped One Man (and His Brother) Build a $1.8 Billion Company." *New York Times*, April 2, 2026. https://www.nytimes.com/2026/04/02/technology/ai-billion-dollar-company-medvi.html.

Heikkilä, Melissa. 2026. "Computer Scientist Yann LeCun: 'Intelligence Really Is About Learning.'" *Financial Times*, January 2, 2026. https://www.ft.com/content/e3c4c2f6-4ea7-4adf-b945-e58495f836c2.

Hirst, Peter. 2025. "AI-Ops: The Developer Has Left the Building." Irony Filings. https://ironyfilings.substack.com/p/ai-ops-the-developer-has-left-the?r=5b3krj.

Hoffman, Reid, and Chris Yeh. 2018. *Blitzscaling: The Lightning-Fast Path to Building Massively Valuable Companies*. Crown.

Jassy, Andy. 2024. "Update from Amazon CEO Andy Jassy on Return-to-Office Plans and Manager Team Ratio." Amazon. https://www.aboutamazon.com/news/company-news/ceo-andy-jassy-latest-update-on-amazon-return-to-office-manager-team-ratio.

Kolahdoozan, Ali. 2025. "How Small Teams Are Changing the World." DEV Community. https://dev.to/alikolahdoozan/how-small-teams-are-changing-the-world-hd4.

Komarovsky, Stanislav. 2025. "Your AI Coding Assistant Is Quietly Creating a New Kind of Technical Debt." AI Advances. https://ai.gopubby.com/your-ai-coding-assistant-is-quietly-creating-a-new-kind-of-technical-debt-204be95cfa34.

Lee, Paul. 2026. LinkedIn post. https://www.linkedin.com/posts/paullee0122_aistrategy-futureofwork-autonomousagents-ugcPost-7428179787640111106-sZzQ/.

LinkedIn. 2025. "How Small Businesses Can Win in 2026." LinkedIn. https://economicgraph.linkedin.com/content/dam/me/economicgraph/en-us/PDF/Work-Change-Small-Business-Report-Dec-2025-Global.pdf.

LinkedIn Corporation. 2011. "Form S-1." SEC.gov. LinkedIn. https://www.sec.gov/Archives/edgar/data/1271024/000119312511016022/ds1.htm.

Loizos, Connie. 2025. "Lovable Says It's Nearing 8 Million Users as the Year-Old AI Coding Startup Eyes More Corporate Employees." TechCrunch. https://techcrunch.com/2025/11/10/lovable-says-its-nearing-8-million-users-as-the-year-old-ai-coding-startup-eyes-more-corporate-employees/.

Lütke, Tobi. 2025. "Shopify Internal Memo." X. https://x.com/tobi/status/1909231499448401946.

Meadows, Ryan. 2026. LinkedIn post. https://www.linkedin.com/posts/rmeadows_seat-based-pricing-is-a-relic-of-the-manual-activity-7424838268145336321--2cC/.

Midjourney. 2026. "About Midjourney." Midjourney. https://www.midjourney.com/home.

OECD. 2024. "Enhancing Rural Innovation in Canada." OECD. https://www.oecd.org/en/publications/enhancing-rural-innovation-in-canada_a9919c66-en.html.

OpenAI. 2026. "Introducing GPT-5.3-Codex." OpenAI. https://openai.com/index/introducing-gpt-5-3-codex/.

Orosz, Gergely. 2022. "Inside Fast's Rapid Collapse." Pragmatic Engineer. https://newsletter.pragmaticengineer.com/p/the-scoop-fast.

Palmer, Annie. 2026. "Block Laying Off About 4,000 Employees, Nearly Half of Its Workforce." CNBC. https://www.cnbc.com/2026/02/26/block-laying-off-about-4000-employees-nearly-half-of-its-workforce.html.

Perry, Mark J. 2016. "Fortune 500 Firms 1955 v. 2016: Only 12% Remain, Thanks to the Creative Destruction that Fuels Economic Prosperity." American Enterprise Institute. https://medium.com/american-enterprise-institute/fortune-500-firms-1955-v-4ee7281f32fc.

Perry, Nick. 2025. "2025 Revenue Per Employee Benchmarks for Private SaaS Companies." SaaS Capital. https://www.saas-capital.com/blog-posts/revenue-per-employee-benchmarks-for-private-saas-companies/.

Pink, Daniel H. 2011. *Drive: The Surprising Truth About What Motivates Us*. Penguin Publishing Group.

Pluralsight. 2025. "2025 AI Skills Report." Pluralsight. https://www.pluralsight.com/resource-center/ai-skills-report-2025.

Raman, Aneesh. 2026. LinkedIn post. https://www.linkedin.com/posts/aneeshraman_as-we-enter-the-age-of-ai-were-at-the-start-activity-7411844397992050688-GEuU/.

Ries, Eric. 2011. *The Lean Startup: How Today's Entrepreneurs Use Continuous Innovation to Create Radically Successful Businesses*. Crown.

Rogo. 2026. "Series C." Rogo. https://rogo.ai/series-c.

Rolander, Niclas, and Bloomberg. 2024. "Novo Nordisk's Wegovy and Ozempic Boom Saved Denmark's GDP from a No-growth 2023, and Will Help Double Its Expected Growth This Year, Country's Largest Bank Says." Fortune. https://fortune.com/europe/2024/03/05/novo-nordisks-wegovy-and-ozempic-boom-saved-denmarks-gdp-from-a-no-growth-2023/.

Ruiz, Armand. 2026a. LinkedIn post. https://www.linkedin.com/posts/armand-ruiz_ive-been-using-computers-in-a-completely-share-7428511552238125056-bbL-/.

Ruiz, Armand. 2026b. LinkedIn post. https://www.linkedin.com/posts/armand-ruiz_prediction-token-budgets-will-soon-surpass-share-7429573986386108417-5KHg/.

Sacra. 2025. "Midjourney." Sacra. https://sacra.com/research/midjourney.

Satterthwaite, Julian. 2023. "ChatGPT Fastest-Growing App in History—UBS." Reuters. https://www.reuters.com/video/watch/idOV701102022023RP1/.

Seibert, Jeff. 2026. LinkedIn post. https://www.linkedin.com/posts/jseibert_thoughts-on-ai-the-future-is-already-activity-7427799923305422848-w0-t.

Shah, Dharmesh. 2025. LinkedIn post. https://www.linkedin.com/posts/dharmesh_i-build-a-lot-of-ai-agents-for-myself-which-activity-7398837908071215104-f5dA.

Shopify Inc. 2015. "Form F-1 Shopify Inc." SEC.gov. https://www.sec.gov/Archives/edgar/data/1594805/000119312515129273/d863202df1.htm.

Thiel, Peter, and Blake Masters. 2014. *Zero to One: Notes on Startups, Or How to Build the Future*. Crown.

Tunguz, Tomasz. 2026. LinkedIn post. https://www.linkedin.com/posts/tomasz tunguz_last-quarter-my-ai-inference-costs-hit-100000-share-7429563996069941251-DEnZ/.

Viguerie, S. Patrick, Ned Calder, and Brian Hindo. 2021. "2021 Corporate Longevity Forecast." Innosight. https://www.innosight.com/insight/creative-destruction/.

WarGames. 1983. MGM.

Wasserman, Noam. 2013. *The Founder's Dilemmas: Anticipating and Avoiding the Pitfalls That Can Sink a Startup*. Princeton University Press.

Weill, Peter, Stephanie L. Woerner, Jennifer Banner, and James Moore. 2025. "Digitally Savvy Boards: AI Update." MIT Center for Information Systems Research. https://cisr.mit.edu/publication/2025_0301_SavvyBoardsUpdate_WeillWoernerBannerMoore.

Yaghoubian, Vishar. 2025. LinkedIn post. https://www.linkedin.com/posts/vishar-yaghoubian-022a18aa_congratulations-to-my-mentor-reza-satchu-ugcPost-7392236791627677697-xRaq/.

Yan, Teng. 2025. "X Post." X. https://x.com/tengyanAI/status/2004385187086692512.

Index